Fields of Power, Forests of Discontent

Fields of Power,
Forests of Discontent

Culture, Conservation, and the State in Mexico

Nora Haenn

The University of Arizona Press   Tucson

The University of Arizona Press
© 2005 The Arizona Board of Regents
♾ This book is printed on acid-free, archival-quality paper.
Manufactured in the United States of America

10   09   08   07   06   05   6   5   4   3   2   1

Library of Congress Cataloging-in-Publication Data
Haenn, Nora, 1967–
Fields of power, forests of discontent : culture, conservation, and the state in Mexico /
Nora Haenn. — 1st ed.
p. cm.
Includes bibliographical references and index.
ISBN 0-8165-2399-1 (cloth : alk. paper)
1. Nature conservation—Political aspects—Mexico—Reserva de la Biosfera Calakmul Region.
2. Nature conservation—Economic aspects—Mexico—Reserva de la Biosfera Calakmul Region.
3. Sustainable development—Mexico—Reserva de la Biosfera Calakmul Region. I. Title.
QH77.M6H34 2005
333.95′16′0972—dc22
2004018005

Publication of this book is made possible in part by the proceeds
of a permanent endowment created with the assistance of a
Challenge Grant from the National Endowment for the
Humanities, a federal agency.

Contents

Illustrations

Photographs
following page 109
El Señor de Calakmul, reproduction of a mask
A resident of Orozco
A pond in Calakmul
A man with a jaguar cub
The home of a wealthy individual
A boy with a homemade toy
Clearing a cornfield
Families receive food aid
Aid program staffers
Doña Belén and Don Antonio

Tables

Acknowledgments

Academic careers are often itinerant, and more so when fieldwork and virtual communities add to the travels. Some of the people I thank here were patient sounding boards, read drafts, commented, provided audiences with whom I could test ideas, and pushed me to revisit literature and field data. They formed the collegial academic community that nurtures ideas. Other people helped out with the hidden aspects of academic work, work that made my life possible and so was crucial in bringing this volume to print. These folks provided comfort during the rocky early days of an academic career. They collected me from airports, cared for Roosevelt, bailed me out of job crises, cleaned house, cooked dinner, and, overall, were steadfast friends. "Coming home is just like going to the field," said Lisa Cliggett, and she was right. Returning from fieldwork, I approached people differently. Many of the people I mention below have been important to both the ideas and quotidian cares behind this book. But, they also helped me by sharing themselves and expanding my understanding of ways to-be-in-the-world. I still have much to learn in this regard, but I want to acknowledge them for their contributions thus far. The travels have all been worthwhile.

I have ordered the thanks according to place (some people have since moved on), and I start with the most important place of all.

Calakmul, Campeche

The people of Orozco and San Lorenzo and other ejidos. So much comes up in writing those words, I can only hope I do them justice in these pages. I also must include in these first lines Mauro Sanvicente and Sophie Calmè, because they both have made so much of my life in Calakmul possible. A todos muchas, muchísimas gracias.

At the Biosphere Reserve offices, Don Deocundo Acopa and Esteban Martínez were my crucial early teachers, providing orientation in forests where wood spirits would have mischievously led me astray. At the Regional Council, Santiago Perez Oy, Wilfrido Díaz, Manuel Velázquez, and Sandra and Manuela Caamas Tun more than tolerated periodic questioning. Miguel Sosa, Hugo Medrano, Miguel Acopa, Gloria Tavera, Carlos

Uk, Don Chato, Paquito Novel, and Jenny Ericson, Calakmul's ingeneiro and research community, were both informative and great company. Alberto Villaseñor, Neli Pérez, and Guillermo Mex continue to act as guides to Calakmul's complexities and treasured friends.

Staff of PRONATURA, Península de Yucatán, A.C., introduced me to southeast Campeche and continued to support my research in the subsequent months. Roberto Delgadillo, Norma Poot, and Eckart Boege in Zoh Laguna, and Joann Andrews, Susana Rojas, Pepe de la Gala, and Armando and Fernando Sastre in Mérida were all helpful at different times and provided an important counterbalance to my work with the Biosphere Reserve. Anne McEnany, Dave Younkman, Brian Houseal, and Joe Keenan supported me at The Nature Conservancy. Brian deserves special thanks for first suggesting Calakmul as a research site, and Anne and Dave deserve kudos because, well, they're Anne and Dave.

Also, in Mérida, Gabriela Vargas Cetina, Francisco Fernandez, Igor Stefan, Allan Burns, and Betty Faust, provided an anthropological community, good food, and rest from the field. Allan helped me when I was just getting to know the peninsula, and he taught me to be kind to beginners. Francisco taught me that the moment I think I can't possibly take a break from fieldwork is probably the moment I need to get some distance. Gabriela and Igor offer such original perspectives; they have taught me to look at Calakmul differently.

I count among the most innovative thinkers about people and environment in Calakmul, Kristin Cahn van Seelen; faculty at ECOSUR, Chetumal; Julia Murphy; and Reyna Sayira Maas Rodríguez. Their various influences can be found throughout the text. Aureliano Gómez Gómez, Rebeca Álvaro López, Bentura Trejo Cruz, Charles Wright, and María Erisilia Ku formed the hardworking team that made the 2001 survey possible.

The Virtual Community

Detailed commentary on earlier drafts came from Norman Schwartz, Billie Lee Turner, Paige West, Peter Wilshusen, Michael Dove and students in his "Society and Environment" seminar, as well as an anonymous reviewer. They made the manuscript significantly better. Neil Harvey, Kim Batchelder, and Cristina Lasch also provided key support. Matthew Restall reviewed an earlier version of chapter 3. Melissa Johnson, Kate Christen, and Uehli Hostettler, companions in social ecology, I thank for their varied insights.

Research for this book was carried out with support from a variety of funding agencies: the Wenner-Gren Foundation for Anthropological

Research, the Fulbright program's U.S.–Mexico Commission for Educational and Cultural Exchange, and NSF Grant BCS1193739. Write-up took place with a grant from Indiana University's College of Arts and Sciences and a fellowship in Anthropology and Demography from the Mellon Foundation via the Carolina Population Center. Thanks to the journal *Ethnology* for permission to reprint the article "Nature Regimes in Southern Mexico: A History of Power and Environment," published in 2002, vol. 41, no. 1.

Bloomington, Indiana

Parts of this book look different from its earlier versions, but parts do not, and people instrumental at the early stages will still see their contributions. Richard Wilk, Carol Greenhouse, Emilio Moran, and George Alter guided this project from its first days. My deepest gratitude goes out to all of them. My writing group, Lisa Cliggett, David Abramson, Bridget Edwards, and Liz Faier plodded through the earliest drafts of chapters, when I was just getting my grammatical, let alone theoretical and ethnographic, bearings. Bradley Levinson, Hillary Kahn, and Phil Parnell pointed out useful literature that reshaped my thinking on some central issues. Finally, my work in Bloomington could not have been completed without the friendship of Eric Haag, Liahna Gordon, Debra Unger, Kip Andres, Ilana Gershon, Caroline Carlson, and, again, Lisa Cliggett.

North Carolina (Twice Over)

First, in Cullowhee, thanks to Eunice and Sterling Hensley, Beth Johnson, Gary and Mary Smith, Nyaga Mwaniki, Julie Barnes, and Tristan Fuierer, for the dinners, drives, hikes, and southern warmth. Cullowhee taught me how much the rural United States has in common with rural Mexico and to value rural lives all the more in this urbanizing world.

Second, in Chapel Hill, thanks to Dick Bilsborrow for getting me there. The bulk of the book's rewrites took place in Chapel Hill while I was on a Mellon Foundation fellowship, which Dick made possible. The staff at the Carolina Population Center were superb. Tom Heath and Cara Crisler created a seamless atmosphere for research. Laurie Leadbetter and Judy Dye gave bibliographic materials and editing help, respectively. Graphics savant Tom Swasey made me graphics literate. In Chapel Hill, I met David Carr, whose work served as an important model for the 2001 survey; Arturo Escobar, who rightly insisted on close attention to the state; and Carole Crumley and Julie Flowerday, who shared their beautiful house. Funds from the Mellon Foundation provided seed money for a grant from the National Science Foundation, and I thank Stu Plattner for seeing this possibility and facilitating the 2001 survey.

Tempe, Arizona

It's a long way from tropical forests to desert terrain. Madelaine Adelman, Sokai Barett, and Marie Navarre have helped the transition most, alternately covering the home front and pushing my mind in new directions. Eric Keys explains geography to me and keeps me connected to the Clark University crowd. Ellen Rees, along with Madelaine Adelman and Muna Ali, read chapter drafts and carried out quality control.

The department of anthropology at Arizona State University gave me more leave time than any junior professor I know. John Chance and Sander van der Leeuw made that time possible. Research at ASU has made me think about Calakmul in light of everyday expectations of environment and development in the United States, while ASU's undergraduates have shown me ways to communicate the differences between the two places. For their moral and intellectual support in these endeavors, I thank Robert Alvarez, Mena Bell, Marilynn Bubb, James Eder, Michelle Hegmon, Keith Kintigh, Leif Jonsson, Ben and Peggy Nelson, Chuck Redman, Marsha Schweitzer, Kate Spielmann, and Barbara Stark. Tod Swanson creates a vibrant setting at ASU for Latin American issues. Tod brought Florencia Mallon to campus, who helped me revisit the identities of underdevelopment outlined in chapter 5.

Philadelphia

This is where it all started. Given the size of my family (ten siblings and more than sixty cousins), is it any surprise I would study cultural communities? Since the dedication is theirs, I'll be brief. In addition to Mom, Joe, and all the sisters, some people deserve special mention for their support during the delicate years: Mert Corr, Anne Corr Potterton, Cathy Haenn Shannon, Joe and Janet Corr, Jean Corr O'Neill, Paul Corr, Gerald Corr, and Alan and Diana Sigler. And, finally, thanks to my new family, Luis, Tatiana, and José, who have changed me for the better. I hope it shows.

Fields of Power, Forests of Discontent

To my first teachers,

Mom,

Dad,

MaryGrace,

Nancy,

Meg,

Christine,

Ginny,

Trisha,

Teresa,

Cecilia,

Rosemary,

and Joe

1

Conservation-Development at Calakmul

During the 1990s, tropical forest preservation took a new turn as environmental groups across the globe enlisted people living in and around protected areas to conservation efforts. Scores of community-based conservation and sustainable development programs, administered by international and national organizations, went into effect (Agrawal and Gibson 2001; Western and Wright 1994). Established on the belief that local people posed the most significant threat to protected areas, these programs encouraged local responsibility for conservation.

In this book, I consider these events as they affected people living near the Calakmul Biosphere Reserve, located in southern Mexico close to Guatemala and Belize (see fig. 1.1). Calakmul's Biosphere Reserve is Mexico's largest protected area for tropical ecosystems. Housing numerous threatened species—such as jaguar, ocelot, and tapir—the Reserve sits in tension with the practices of slash-and-burn farmers who live on its borders. Such conflicts are common in relation to protected areas, but the situation at Calakmul was different in an important way. In the mid-1990s, government agents and local people at Calakmul undertook an expansive and dynamic program aimed at alleviating those tensions. Together, the Reserve offices and the Xpujil (pronounced sh-poo-heel) Regional Council, a peasant, or *campesino*, group, sponsored a conservation-development agenda that aimed to improve local people's standard of living while preserving natural resources. The Reserve-Council alliance offered Calakmul's people a series of environmental programs: environmental education, wildlife management, organic agriculture, reforestation, agroforestry, sustainable timber harvesting, ecotourism, and the establishment of village protected areas. Thousands of Calakmul's residents participated in this agenda and its apparently democratic governing process. The Council held monthly meetings in which hundreds of village representatives oversaw administration by their elected board of campesino managers, requested additional development programs, and commented on the work of the university-trained staff, known as *ingenieros*, or engineers, hired to provide technical know-how. This combination of energetic programming and campesino activism held great allure.

The alliance counted on the help of numerous actors. Foreign researchers; state agencies; the Mexican offices of the World Wildlife Fund;

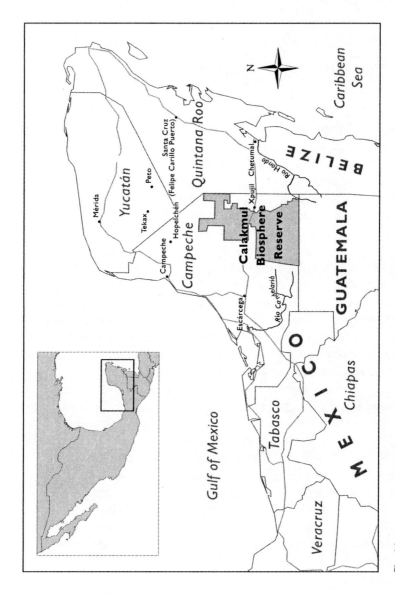

Fig. 1.1. The Calakmul Biosphere Reserve and neighboring political entities.

PRONATURA, Península de Yucatán; and the Calakmul Model Forest all collaborated with Reserve-Council efforts. Ingenieros for these groups might find attendance at Council assemblies necessary to maintain good public relations, especially as the Council's advisor, the Reserve director, was known as the most powerful governing official in the area. Not only Mexican environmentalists respected the director's authority; international environmentalists were sure to court his opinion. PRONATURA and Calakmul Model Forest—two nongovernmental organizations (NGOs)— were staffed by Mexican nationals, but the groups depended on international funding (by the United States and Canada, respectively) for their survival. U.S. and Canadian sponsorship meant that a stream of international environmentalists, development agents, private donors, researchers, and students flowed through Calakmul. These observers were especially attracted to the Reserve-Council alliance and its promise of a grassroots environmental movement capable of reconciling conflicts between conservation and development (see Kingsolver 2002).

As I describe below, this particular conservation-development agenda quickly passed away, and while many assessments of such programs focus on why they are or are not successful, in this book I want to pose different questions. How do people live conservation in an everyday way? How might those everyday experiences affect environmental management strategies more generally and the way people relate to one another? In my thinking, human-environment relations have two parts, simultaneously related and distinct. The first part is a direct physical connection between a person and the environment, for example, when someone fells or plants a tree. The second part is an indirect connection, for example, when lawmakers decree that someone else, either farmers or other state agents, encourage forest preservation. Indirect connections take place when social relations encourage certain kinds of environmental practices over others. Over the course of this text, I think through conservation in light of both direct and indirect environmental relations, because, in the context of protected areas, the entangling of these two points makes for an especially complicated environmental setting. Furthermore, as pressing as these issues were for Calakmul, this tension was also playing out in Guatemala, Belize, and elsewhere in Mexico, where environmentalists viewed contiguous forests as forming a unitary Selva Maya, or Maya Forest (see chap. 7). Across these locales, state agents, private sector environmentalists, and academics questioned the key to finding sustainable environmental management strategies. For instance, do farm practices hold the solution to the forests' future, or do the cultural and regulatory environment surrounding those practices? Are farmers themselves responsible for forest management, or is the larger society through mechanisms such as policies, laws, and popular opinion?

Biosphere Reserves and Sustainable Development

Biosphere reserves, such as Calakmul, are supposed to act as testing grounds for just such questions. As described by the United Nations Educational, Scientific, and Cultural Organization (UNESCO), whose Man and Biosphere Programme collaborates with national governments in reserve designations, the characteristics of a biosphere reserve include the following:

— zoning for both conservation and development
— involving local communities and local knowledge in reserve management
— acting as sites for working through conflict over natural resource management
— building policy out of research and subsequent monitoring.[1]

Originally, however, the protected area that is now Calakmul was not intended to be an ecological park. Instead, the area was supposed to encompass the Calakmul archaeological site housing an ancient Mayan city, the city that now sits within the heart of the Reserve's southern portion.

An early protagonist of the Reserve, William Folan, describes how he and a group of colleagues first planted the idea of an archaeological park in the late 1970s and early 1980s (Folan and García Ortega 2003). Excavations had demonstrated the site's impressive size. Calakmul is the largest pre-Columbian Mayan city ever documented. Folan and his colleagues were first interested in protecting this archaeological heritage. By 1983, however, when promotion of a protected area became official policy at Mexico's Secretary for Urban Development and Ecology (SEDUE), the plans had changed to include the expanse of surrounding forest. In all, the Calakmul Biosphere Reserve would encompass 723,300 hectares or 1,787,000 acres.

Many players would have a role to play in the Reserve's official, 1989 declaration. O'Neill writes that, in the 1980s, countries throughout the world responded to international conservation pressure by creating minimal park systems (O'Neill 1996). At Calakmul, this pressure came in the form of reconnaissance visits from such groups as World Wildlife Fund and The Nature Conservancy (through its local partner, PRONATURA, Península de Yucatán). During the mid-1980s, these groups compiled information on area vegetation and fauna that would be used to justify the Reserve's creation. The U.S.-based MacArthur Foundation and Conservation International would fund Folan's efforts, including research into climatology and hydrology (Folan and García Ortega 2003). *National Geographic* magazine featured Calakmul in its landmark issue advocating a "Ruta Maya," a multinational corridor of protected areas catering to both biodiversity conservation and ecotourism (Garrett 1989). These international agents found willing counterparts in Mexico's growing environmental bureaucracy (Simonian 1996). During the early 1980s, Mexico created its National System of Protected Natural Areas, and federal officials at SEDUE, in advocating the Reserve, argued for its inclusion in this new government entity. Meanwhile, back in Campeche state, where the Reserve would be located, a local group headed by the governor's wife took up the cause.

This political pressure would outweigh any scientific rationale for the Reserve's creation. As we will see, not only was scientific information on the area lacking, but William Folan calls the Reserve's boundaries an "improvisation," noting that state agents used few ecological considerations in drawing up Reserve borders (personal communication 2000). Instead, authorities focused on extensions of unoccupied lands, even though much of this territory was claimed by campesinos living at some distance from Calakmul (see chap. 3)

This focus on unoccupied lands suggests the ideals of a biosphere reserve were not forefront in Calakmul's creation. Instead, at its birth, Calakmul was more akin to a traditional park, one whose borders draw a sharp line between protected area and surrounding communities. Below, I describe early Reserve policies that similarly point in this direction. Because of an antagonism toward local communities, following the Reserve's declaration, government officials soon had serious social problems on their hands. State authorities would need the Biosphere Reserve's development component to calm this rebellion.

The Birth of a Conservation-Development Agenda

When I first arrived at Calakmul, the Reserve's director, Deocundo Acopa, described conservation to me with a wave of his hand, saying, "It's all politics." This certainly seemed the case given how the alliance between the Reserve and the Regional Council came about. Acopa and the Council's peasant leaders described its origin, proffering a political mythology, a story that looks quite different from that told above. They described how, prior to the advent of the Reserve in 1989, government agents had little authority in Calakmul (see chap. 2 for a reconsideration of this point). The area had few schools, health care clinics, paved roads, or other services. Neglected by government authorities, Calakmul's farmers joined the Revolutionary Democratic Party (PRD). During most of the twentieth century, the ruling Institutional Revolutionary Party (PRI) held a near monopoly on government offices throughout Mexico. People in Calakmul often described "the PRI" as synonymous with "the government." Because of this, people's allegiance with the PRD implied rejection of state authority. As PRD supporters, Calakmul's residents were viewed as seditious by governing authorities in PRI-dominated Campeche.

These tensions converged on the Biosphere Reserve, whose declaration, campesinos asserted, came as a surprise.[2] In my conclusions, I discuss further the biosphere reserve as a model of environmental protection. Here, I present events as campesinos experienced them, with little understanding of the Reserve's objectives. Instead, the Reserve became a rallying point for social and economic frustrations. People argued they had moved to Calakmul in search of a better life. Upon arrival they found only continued suffering, and, to add insult to injury, a land tenure and subsistence crisis precipitated by the Reserve.

Campesinos proposed forcefully that the Reserve breached a social contract between the state and campesino community, a contract that combined land and development aid to assist campesino subsistence. Outlined in Article 27 of the Mexican constitution, this contract mandated land distribution in the form of *ejidos*, villages managed as common property (see below and chapter 3), and agricultural support to Mexico's small-scale farmers. These guarantees were in effect until 1991, when authorities altered the legal framework of Mexico's agrarian structures (see chap. 5 for more on these issues). Despite these changes, people in Calakmul, like campesinos elsewhere in Mexico (Collier 1994), continued to hold the state accountable for these promises.

Campesino anger about the Reserve rested on the way protected areas broke with Article 27. First, the Reserve took land out of the agricultural base. In addition to eliminating a source of future farmland, in the early days of the Reserve, a number of villages were threatened with relocation when it came to light that Reserve borders accidentally included land in the hands of campesinos. Campesinos knew little of how relocation might contradict the collaborative goals of a biosphere reserve. Instead, activists focused on how relocation required that the state contradict its ideal role by taking land away from campesinos to whom it had already given title (most cases were later settled in favor of campesinos).

Second, the Reserve's existence meant stricter enforcement of regulations prohibiting hunting and the felling and burning of forests. Again, campesinos knew little of a reserve's development aspects. The Reserve was presented, first, as a threat to campesino livelihoods. In the early 1990s, residents reacted militantly to Reserve policies, saying they were ready to murder anyone who presented him or herself as an "ecologist."[3]

The emotional and moral weight campesinos attached to Article 27 could be elusive to someone such as myself, an urbanite who has never worked the land or faced real food scarcity. After awhile though, it struck me that I could understand at least part of this polemic by comparing Article 27 to the importance of free speech in the United States. The fact that people argued about it continuously showed the extent to which Article 27 and its ideals were indispensable to local political life and to campesino ideas of what it meant to be part of the Mexican nation.

In 1994, Reserve and Council staff told me that early opposition to the Reserve was so strong, the government feared a rebellion like that of the Zapatista army, which began in January of that same year. Although the Zapatista action occurred five years after the Reserve's declaration, in the event's retelling, the guerilla movement had parallels in Calakmul. Opposition to the Selva Lacandona reserve in Chiapas galvanized campesinos in that state and contributed to the formation of the Zapatista army (Collier 1994; Leyva Solana and Ascencio Franco 1996). The indigenous character of the Zapatista uprising would also prove a challenge to ruling authorities at Calakmul. Both the Zapatistas and campesinos in Calakmul asserted that government neglect forced them into enduring poverty and rebellious political opposition. This retelling, however, obscured the way the conservation backlash at Calakmul, in contrast to Chiapas, received special government attention. Also, Chiapas offered examples of more than political rebellion. Frontier Chiapas had been home to a powerful campesino union that effectively acted as an autonomous, local government (Leyva Solano 2001). Reserve Director Acopa, a native of Chiapas and close observer of events there, may have had such a group in mind as he helped shape reaction to Calakmul's conservation backlash.

Acopa came to Calakmul as an organizer with the federal government's Programa Nacional de Solidaridad, or PRONASOL. This agency, originally, had little to do with conservation. Acopa was working to build a local group (the Regional Council) through which PRONASOL could channel development funds aimed at a variety of local needs. PRONASOL's development aims became jeopardized by the conservation backlash. In response, Acopa tapped into anti-PRI and anticonservation sentiment to renegotiate Calakmul's overall relationship with federal authorities. Campeche's 1991 gubernatorial election served as a platform for this renegotiation. In return for supporting the PRI candidate, the residents of Calakmul—through the PRONASOL-funded Regional Council—would receive the development funds they desired. They would also find relief from relocation threats. One of the Regional Council's first board members described this votes-for-development deal:

> We wanted to form a group that could sell its [farm] products with the aid of technical advice. But then came the problem of the Reserve and that in 1990, we learned some people were inside it. When the first investigators came, birders and all those people who go into the forest, we realized there were campesinos inside the Reserve. SEDUE said they had to leave, and they began to hold meetings with villages. In that time . . . ecologist[s] . . . went to the village of Altamira for a meeting and there the people told the ecologists that if they weren't smart, they were going to be lynched. The Regional Council talked with the government. [We said] it wasn't right, that if the ejidal decrees were from before the Reserve's, you cannot place one decree on top of another. The Governor said, "I promise to bring the President here, but you all are going to work out this problem with him, that you don't want to move and that you want to care for the Reserve."

Campesinos in Calakmul did vote for the PRI candidate, after which President Salinas de Gortari personally visited the region. In a speech to hundreds of people, he promised programs that would contribute toward a "productive ecology." He also repeated the charge that farmers "care for the Reserve." In practice, this caring entailed financial support for the Regional Council, monies that underpinned a list of conservation-development projects. The Council, technically a nongovernmental organization, soon managed a budget rivaling that of any government office in southeastern Campeche. By 1994, the Reserve and Council's total annual expenditures likely neared US$1 million, funds aimed principally at 15,000 people living along the Reserve's eastern border. Deocundo Acopa oversaw these expenditures after he left his position with PRONASOL to become the Reserve's first director and official advisor to the Regional Council.

The Reserve-Council alliance linked the Biosphere Reserve and surrounding communities in a way that aimed to encircle the Reserve, not with fences, but with campesinos willing to defend its existence. To these ends, the Reserve and the Regional Council became virtually indistinguishable. During Acopa's tenure, nearly all Reserve funds in support of conservation-development projects were channeled through the Council. Acopa lent Reserve ingenieros to Council projects on a full-time basis. He hired Council members in various capacities, and lobbied for Reserve entrance fees that would support Council projects. Acopa relished Calakmul's personalized politics and soon became the most powerful government officer in southeast Campeche, earning the nickname *el tigre de Calakmul*, the jaguar of Calakmul. His use of patron-client norms always sat alongside the Council's democratic structure, a contradiction he finessed by highlighting his role as a giver of advice (*un asesor*). While Acopa was a consummate cultural broker, his authority, and by extension the Regional Council's, also drew heavily on the finances he commanded.

Most of these monies were government funds, but the Reserve-Council also cited sponsorship from the World Bank's Global Environmental Fund and Canada's Eastern Ontario Model Forest, as well as indirect support from the U.S. Agency for International Development. From this point on, I use the words *environmentalists* and *conservationists* to refer generically to Mexican and international associates of these groups. Their physical presence in area ejidos was extremely limited. Supra-local agents, however, did visit Reserve and Council offices, sponsored conferences, and made their opinions known in evaluating how their money was spent. Supra-local environmentalists were energetic contributors to policy discussions surrounding Calakmul's conservation-development agenda and helped create a specific local atmosphere (see Acopa and Boege 1998). In fact, Reserve Director Acopa saw the Reserve-Council alliance at odds with a certain wing of the international environmental movement that, he believed, would cut campesinos out of any conservation formula and impose a rigorous separation between local people and the Biosphere Reserve.

All this activity and discussion took place at a time when little was known about either Calakmul's ecology or the viability of the Reserve-Council's conservation-development programs. Policy makers and environmentalists certainly understood the broad outlines of area ecology, as I describe them below. Detailed understandings of ecological dynamics, however, were absent. Acopa and fellow managers (including international donors) admitted the conservation-development programs they sponsored were experimental. Nobody knew if the programs would increase forest cover or improve campesino livelihoods. People anxious to see the Reserve-Council alliance succeed cast this experimentation as "innovative," noting there were few examples of successful, participatory sustainable development to be found anywhere. The dearth of ecological knowledge may have helped this spin. Not knowing the details of local ecology allowed people to build multiple, sometimes conflicting, relationships and land management programs around the same natural resource base.

Vegetation, Ecology, and Climate in Southeast Campeche

Crossing the center of the Calakmul Biosphere Reserve, the highway from Escárcega city to Xpujil traverses some unsettled terrain. The road climbs briefly as it nears Xpujil and the low lying hills and platforms, the *meseta baja de Zoh Laguna*. Whenever I drove this stretch, I saw a dark figure flash across the asphalt, usually a coati, or tayra, a member of the weasel family. The Reserve's uninhabited feel conjured thoughts of pristine, primitive forests. A keen sightseer, however, might note that Calakmul's trees were relatively thin, suggesting a fairly young forest. This was not the lush and verdant forest travelers read about in rain forest guides. An international conservationist once remarked to me that Calakmul, with its scrappy feel and paucity of magnificent views, was his least favorite stop on travels that brought him to Mexico's most beautiful places.

Calakmul's principal difference from the stereotypical verdant rain forest is that, as a seasonal tropical forest, it experiences marked dry periods (Whitmore 1990). In November, Calakmul's trees are largely bare of leaves. November also heralds Calakmul's coolest days. During December, January, and February, temperatures in Calakmul near freezing. These are the months of least rainfall, but a dense fog blankets the area in the early mornings. During these months, I often awoke to the sound of moisture dripping from the trees, only to find the fog, not a rainstorm, responsible for the dampness. April, May, and June are Calakmul's hottest months, when temperatures reach as high as 106° F. The rains usually begin during these months, but rainfall at Calakmul is notoriously unpredictable. My research began during the tail end of a drought year when many families had no agricultural harvests whatsoever. A year later, I left Calakmul after repeated hurricanes flooded temporal streams, roads, and crops. Rainfall data from 1958 to 1991 shows a maximum annual rainfall of 1,624 mm and a low of 593 mm, with a mean of 930 mm (Folan et al. 1992). During one out of every four to five years, annual rainfall drops below 800 mm, causing shortages in water supplies and crop failure (Boege 1995). With no permanent streams and seasonally flooded forests insufficient to household needs, water management at Calakmul was a chronic concern. Where outsiders viewed forest cover as Calakmul's chief environmental

Table 1.1 Tropical Forests of Southeast Campeche

Type	Description
High evergreen	Canopy greater than 30 meters
High semi-evergreen	Canopy 25–35 mts; 25–50% leaf loss in dry season
Medium semi-evergreen	Canopy 15–30 mts; 25–50% leaf loss in dry season
Medium sub-deciduous	Canopy 15–30 mts; 50–75% leaf loss in dry season
Low semi-evergreen	Canopy < 15 mts; loss in dry season
Low sub-deciduous	Canopy < 15 mts; 50–75% leaf loss in dry season
Low floodplain	Low to medium forests with clay soils
Savannah floodplain	Grassy cover

Sources: Boege 1995; Ericson 1996

issue, campesinos would likely rejoin they were more concerned with water management.

Rainfall variability affects forest composition in a place that has been intensively exploited throughout the past century. Researchers generally characterize southern Yucatán forests according to height and amount of leaf loss in the dry season (see table 1.1). Maps in the 1950s uniformly described Calakmul's jungles as high semi-evergreen (Miranda 1958). In contrast, maps dating from the late 1980s and early 1990s show a more varied forest cover, alternating between medium (15–25 meters) and low heights (less than 15 meters) in which dry season leaf loss affects 25 to 75 percent of area foliage (García-Gil and March 1990). This change is partly the result of logging practices that markedly transformed Calakmul. During the 1980s, regional sawmills ceased operation because of a lack of quality timber in area forests. Botanists working in the early 1990s encountered a forest lacking older trees. Photographs from the 1950s show a forest housing taller trees of greater diameter than can be found today (Beltrán 1958). Ruminating on these pictures in 1995, botanist and Assistant Reserve Director Esteban Martínez questioned whether the potential for botanical growth at Calakmul could be determined from today's forest cover.

Calakmul's patchwork forest mirrored land cover throughout Campeche, a state historically dependent on a forest economy (table 1.2, although see Hostettler 1996, for assertions that state authorities overestimate forest cover). In the early part of the century, Calakmul's *chicozapote* trees (*Manilkara zapota*) provided *chicle* to feed the craze for chewing gum then sweeping the United States. During the second half of the century,

Table 1.2 Estimated Forest Types and Land Use for Campeche State, the Calakmul Biosphere Reserve, and Settlements Home to Reserve-Council Activities

Forest/Land Use	State	Reserve	Settlements
High evergreen forest	1%	5%	6%
Medium semi-evergreen forests	49%	50%	20%
Low semi-evergreen forests	9%	35%	10%
Secondary growth (*acahual*)	22%	0%	43%
Agriculture, pastures, water, population centers, etc.	19%	10%	21%

Sources: Stedman-Edwards (2000); *Calakmul Model Forest: Productive Ecology Proposal* (Ottowa/Mexico City: Ministry of Supply and Services; SARH, Subsecretaria Forestal, 1994)

logging for valuable mahogany (*Swietenia macrophylla*) and Spanish cedar (*Cedrela odorata*) dominated Calakmul's economy. By the mid-1980s, these species were exhausted, and people in Calakmul turned to less desirable woods, which they sold for railroad ties. Although logging continues today, Calakmul's forests now contain mainly trees for domestic use by area residents, who struggle with the legacy of earlier forest industries. Calakmul has never had a well-diversified economy. With the demise of logging, people focused their labor on farming for both subsistence and cash income. Calakmul's soils, however, are generally thin and make for poor agriculture.

According to the Mayan classification system used throughout the peninsula, the predominant soils in southeast Campeche are *tzek'el* and *pus lu'um*, soils whose calcium content and rapid loss of moisture can result in meager harvests (Gates 1993; Robles Ramos 1958). Moving off the meseta toward the east, *kan-kab* and *ya'ax-hom* soils are present, soils that offer greater agricultural productivity (Aguilera Herrera 1958). In chapter 6, I show how this difference underpins both a range of subsistence possibilities in Calakmul and people's dependence on development programs.

This sparse ecological knowledge accompanied the Reserve's declaration and, by 1995, knowledge of Calakmul's environment had not changed significantly. Leaders at the Regional Council did tout the existence of one ecological study conducted in the early 1980s. That research focused on logging practices and betrayed rapacious deforestation by local timber companies. At then rates of harvest, Calakmul's forests would supposedly be decimated by the early 1990s. The location of this document is not known, but its singular existence demonstrates the scant scientific foundation to early conservation policies at Calakmul (see also Toledo 2000). Social scientists and Calakmul's conservation-development staff worked mainly with ecological information reported in a few state publications (including the Reserve's first management plan, Folan et al. 1992), documents emanating from forestry programs in neighboring Quintana Roo state (Primack et al. 1998), and a thorough, if somewhat dated, review of peninsular ecologies (Beltrán 1958). Both governmental and nongovernmental agencies agreed that an improved understanding of Calakmul's ecology was crucial to designing appropriate development programs. At the same time, groups like the Council, PRONATURA, and Calakmul Model Forest were under pressure to conduct research that demonstrated to donors their programs' ecological viability. This catch-22 took place at a time when Mexican and international academics began to add their additional layer of research.

This growing body of research showed how the variety of local ecologies at Calakmul meant communities differ significantly in the resources at their disposal. In some ejidos, water scarcity has never been a concern. These communities contain large lagoons or are located where rainfall is more abundant. Other ejidos are entirely dependent on the water brought to them by municipal trucks. Some Calakmul communities offer farmland fertile enough that people have few fears of food scarcity, while other villages offer farmland that barely merits the work people put into farming. Some of Calakmul's ejidos house tens of thousands of hectares of forest, lands designated not for farming but extractive activities. In these places, a forest economy combining logging and chicle extraction is a viable option for ejidal residents. Other communities have relatively little forest holdings, and managing these lands for forest activities (as the Reserve-Council proposed) is not economically feasible. Variability in village land bases arose during Calakmul's history of colonization and community formation. I explore this history in chapter 3. Conservation at Calakmul, thus, lies in the intersection of regional events and ecologies, people's daily lives, and the national and international policy settings.

Sorting through this combination of conservation as both the direct and indirect ways people work with the environment, I note that conservation practitioners at Calakmul were of two minds regarding the usefulness of a biosphere reserve to protect forests. I describe this ambivalence and my own location in this social world in the remaining pages of this chapter. I went to Calakmul to examine the impact of the Reserve on the lives of local people. I learned that the programs described above, both their initiation and abandonment, could be understood only by taking into account campesinos' broader lives and, most critically, their relationship to government authorities and their designation as "poor."

I proceed with a snapshot of how today's traveler might encounter Calakmul. Because of the demise of Calakmul's conservation-development agenda (described in chap. 7), tourists are unaware of the activist history behind today's depiction of Calakmul as an "ecological" region. I then move to a description of my own arrival to Calakmul. Here as well as later, I draw attention to my changing understanding of the issues under consideration. I wrote this way keeping in mind the environmentally aware reader, a person interested in getting beyond surface descriptions of poverty and tropical forest protection. All too often, stories in popular media and publications put out by environmental groups hail conservation successes and failures. Rarely, however, do we have the opportunity to hear about the people who live these events, and how complicated their experiences of conservation can be.

Calakmul for Ecotourists

When I visited Calakmul's market town of Xpujil in 1999, many of my friends from Calakmul's conservation-development agenda had moved on, but I was impressed by the community's newfound dignity. Xpujil was still as I remembered it—a sweltering, tropical crossroads, alternately dusty in the dry season and flooded in the rainy season. If the town has any fame, it is probably confined to long-distance truckers who stop for a meal and a visit to the town's brothels. But, since my research in 1995, numerous restaurants and shops had sprung up catering to area swidden (or slash-and-burn) farmers and a growing government bureaucracy. In 1996, Xpujil became a *cabecera municipal*, a capital for the county or municipality of Calakmul. Xpujil's growth rested on the municipal funds now entering this corner of Campeche state. The municipality shares a name with the Calakmul archaeological site. Surrounding the site, and comprising roughly half the municipio's land, is the enormous Calakmul Biosphere Reserve. The Reserve is the reason for the county's existence. (From here on, I use "Calakmul" to refer to the area inside municipal limits and "Reserve" to denote the Biosphere Reserve.) Hopes for regional development are now pinned on tourism to the Reserve and local archaeological sites. Xpujil hoteliers and restaurant owners work to position the town as an entryway to forests and Mayan ruins. Meanwhile, Campeche state legislators claim Calakmul is the country's first "ecological" municipality (*Diario de Yucatán*, December 31, 1996).

Calakmul's distinguishing mark is, supposedly, a sustainable economy that protects area forests. A forest economy is readily apparent, but not the one sought by earlier activists. Locals (illegally) offer to sell infant coati and parrots to tourists sitting in the open-air restaurants attached to budget hotels. T-shirts touting the region depict jaguar and deer alongside one of the many ruins that dot the county. Municipal trucks, buildings, and a few taxicabs are painted with a jade mask found at the Calakmul archaeological site. This "Lord of Calakmul" is now mascot and marketing gimmick, a brand used to convey the area's distinction to tourists and local people alike. With ongoing construction of higher end hotels (tellingly, financed by urban investors, located outside Xpujil, and staffed by recruits from distant cities), Calakmul's transformation from a forgotten frontier to a jewel in Mexico's plans for nature and history tourism may yet happen. Already, Xpujil's bus station offers Mexican tourists—the majority of tourists who visit Calakmul—a visitors' information center. And, U.S. environmentalists use Calakmul's expanding tourist infrastructure to conduct fund-raising tours.[4]

This emphasis on an Xpujil-based ecotourism counters the conservation-development agenda of the early 1990s. In chapter 7, I describe the events that sharply curtailed conservation-development. At the time, tourism was viewed as only one strand in a diverse economy connecting people and ecology. The town of Zoh Laguna, not Xpujil, was the seat of this broad-based agenda. Researchers (like myself), development agents, and Reserve-Council ingenieros viewed Xpujil as a déclassé alternative to Zoh Laguna's quaintness. We went to Xpujil to shop or visit a doctor, but retreated to Zoh Laguna's shady, clapboard homes. Zoh Laguna was once a company town, run by sawmill operators who, in the 1950s, provided residents a movie theater, a school, a baseball team, and a hospital. Calakmul's conservation-development community related better to this prosperous past than to Xpujil's.

The rivalry between the towns of Zoh Laguna and Xpujil was part of a more serious argument. Xpujil tended to house Mexican federal agencies. Zoh Laguna housed the headquarters of the Reserve, PRONATURA, and Calakmul Model Forest. Confusingly, the Xpujil Regional Council also had its headquarters in Zoh Laguna. (I interpret this as a simultaneous acknowledgment and antagonism toward power holders; see chapter 3.) In contrast to the federalism symbolized by Xpujil, groups in Zoh Laguna sought to encourage local control, if not ownership, of natural resources. The distinction between Xpujil and Zoh Laguna, thus, rested on whether state power would build on local power structures or on a burgeoning federal bureaucracy. Would state agents alone determine

Calakmul's future, or would a public-private consortium of campesinos, environmentalists, and state agents prevail?

Superficially, my 1999 visit suggested state agents had gained the upper hand in Calakmul. For me, the most marked sign of change was at Doña Belén's restaurant in Zoh Laguna. (In Calakmul, "Don" and "Doña" are terms of address meaning Mr. and Mrs.) Before, her tables were a bustling meeting ground for all kinds of professionals interested in Calakmul's ecology. People joked someone could study regional conservation without ever leaving the restaurant. In 1999, Doña Belén's tables stood empty, and her new restaurant in Xpujil catered to campesinos. The powerful Regional Council had diminished from thousands of members to a skeleton staff. Collaborating with the Reserve and Calakmul Model Forest, the Council had built an herbarium where researchers could protect computers in a rare, air-conditioned room. Inside the herbarium, equipment for geographical positioning helped campesinos delineate the borders to their ejidos with precision. Adjacent to the herbarium was a botanical garden, where local plants, including delicate orchids, were carefully marked. The garden was part of an environmental education program in which school children might follow its shaded paths to a small zoo. Zoo animals represented regional wildlife. In 1995, children might pet a purring puma or push away the wild pigs that tagged people's ankles. By 1999, weeds had all but obscured the herbarium. Of the zoo's animals, only the jaguar and two pumas remained. Someone had poached the red deer.

Having worked hard in 1995 and since to decipher politics surrounding the Calakmul Biosphere Reserve, I first worried these changes might suggest my efforts were in vain. All that I knew seemed to have vanished rapidly. But, within a nostalgia for things as I knew them, I saw more probing questions about the speed of development change and the depth of conservation-development ideologies. Was conservation linked to development's star in a way that conservation became a passing fad? Or, did something else explain the furious adoption of conservation programming along with its quick dismissal? As a story in which land provides a constant backdrop to numerous kinds of power struggles, Calakmul shows how ecology and environmentalism both inform and are held hostage by power struggles.

One Researcher, Then Many

Answering these questions required bringing my personal history to bear on the ambivalent ways people in Calakmul reworked environmentalism. I once teased a Reserve ingeniero as he set about eating a dinner of

Paca agouti, a prized but illegal game meat. He flashed me a mischievous smile as he said, "Hey, I'm a forester, not a biologist! So don't you touch a tree, or I'll get you in trouble." I laughed at the joke that would likely unsettle colleagues who provided my long distance introduction to Calakmul. I first heard of Calakmul while working as a young secretary, fundraising for The Nature Conservancy's Latin American programs. At the time, I was much like the nineteenth-century Frenchman Henri Rousseau, whose tropical painting covered my graduate school ecology text. I used luxuriant depictions to describe, in publicity materials and proposals, places I had never seen. I was anxious to move beyond the secretarial position, and since most people in authority had advanced degrees, graduate school seemed the right path. But, graduate school in which field?

As I conducted an informal survey about conservation's most pressing issues, various professionals talked about the need to consider anthropology and the role of local people in conservation agendas. My Washington, D.C., experience in the early 1990s coincided with critiques that, in the developing world, protected areas were oppressive measures that often required removing people from ancestral homelands and denying them access to the natural resources they needed to survive. Environmentalists working internationally were concerned about a growing conservation backlash (Adams and McShane 1992). Sustainable development and community-based initiatives were promoted as solutions not only to the skepticism characterized by the paca-eating forester, but also the worry that protected areas can deprive people of their livelihoods (Ghimire and Pimbert 1997; Western and Wright 1994). To undertake these new directions, conservation groups, staffed mainly by physical scientists, needed expertise with people and cultural diversity. Thinking I might provide that expertise, I entered graduate school. My undergraduate studies had stressed social issues of peace and justice. As I entered the next stage of my academic career, I questioned how these aims fit with environmental protection.

My first trip to Calakmul alerted me to the site's importance. I lucked onto the presidential visit described above, when Salinas de Gortari sealed the conservation-development deal that would be a main point in my research. In comparison to the strenuous isolation of other research sites I explored, Calakmul offered a living standard akin to car camping. The presence of a university-trained, ingeniero staff attached to the Reserve and Council—nearly all men, some of whom proved uncomfortably keen on helping female researchers—meant facilitated access to area communities. With a mixture of serendipity and political acumen, I committed to research at Calakmul.

As it turned out, this commitment was really a negotiated contract. The Reserve Director, Deocundo Acopa, assigned researchers a particular role in the conservation-development agenda and, by the mid-1990s, had begun encouraging the work of Mexican and foreign academics. In return for logistical help, Acopa believed an academic's job was to provide training and employment for campesinos and, emphatically, to make our research results available locally. On the one hand, academic research was supposed to contribute to campesino reflections on the causes and solutions to their social problems. On the other hand, these demands were clearly nationalistic. I felt the weight of Mexican resentment toward its powerful neighbor. "You came to harvest," a colleague accused me, suggesting I was not that different from U.S. citizens of Calakmul's past (chap. 3), eager to profit from other people's environmental work. If only symbolically, my association with an imperialist power threatened Reserve-Council managers in their struggle to control Calakmul's future. U.S. researchers sat on a continuum with foreign NGOs or Mexican federal authorities who, purportedly, took their cue from the U.S. Forest Service. Campesinos suspected these people worked at the behest of powerful interests. Because of this, Reserve-Council managers demanded I capitulate to their goals of campesino empowerment. My political inclinations were similar enough to that of Reserve-Council managers that I was comfortable with the content of their demands. The tone of these requests, however, was disturbing. The emotional pressure would be indicative of the force the Reserve-Council could bring to bear in realizing its agenda.

In the midst of this disquiet, Reserve-Council ingenieros introduced me to the villages of Orozco and San Lorenzo, where I asked permission to conduct my research before village assemblies. After brief discussions, which mainly centered on where I would live and what family might help me with cooking, both ejidos accepted my proposal. I promised to deliver copies of my finished research to village authorities (accomplished in 1999), and I made a small contribution to village funds. Later, I learned that even though the particular ingenieros I worked with were well regarded, people living in Calakmul were highly skeptical of all outreach staff. Campesinos were accustomed to visits by state ingenieros—biologists, agronomists, veterinarians, and others who oversaw an array of development programs that went well beyond what the Reserve-Council had to offer (see chaps. 4 and 5). Critical to campesinos' access to development aid, ingenieros stood in a position of authority toward campesinos in a highly interdependent relationship. Ingenieros needed campesinos as much as campesinos needed ingenieros. Without campesinos, ingenieros, whose work entailed addressing questions of poverty, would be without a job. Orozcans and San Lorenzans resisted this hierarchy by commonly complaining about staff whose basic understanding of agriculture and ecology was deficient. More seriously, campesinos decried ingenieros who turned development programs into an opportunity for extortion. People remembered ingenieros who arrived to promote some government project, only to demand campesinos cook them an expensive meal or charged campesinos for invented costs. Despite these problems, campesinos regularly acceded to whatever program technical staff offered. They did so to cultivate the appearance of conviviality and assure a continued flow of development aid. They also feared retribution if they did not comply with staffers' requests. Once the ingenieros left the village, Orozcans and San Lorenzans implemented projects as they saw fit.

These complications meant that my acceptance by Orozcans and San Lorenzans did not automatically translate into endorsement of my research. Furthermore, I presented a problem for people who depended on the brevity of ingeniero visits to rework conservation-development projects. I had entered people's private spaces of resistance. Orozcans and San Lorenzans, who might present themselves as environmentalists to outsiders, had to choose whether to maintain this charade throughout my stay. I quickly took pains to express my political solidarity with the people of both communities. While in my mind I had not set aside entirely my environmentalist sentiments, my growing involvement with the lives of Orozcans and San Lorenzans led me to deeper questions about ethics and environmentalism.

For reasons of their own, Orozcans and San Lorenzans dealt with me differently. Village leaders in Orozco, indeed, opted to put forth a show of environmentalism. The strains of doing so grew as my stay in Orozco stretched out to eight months. This display was necessary because Orozcans were highly dependent on the financial aid offered by the Reserve and Regional Council. Furthermore, Orozco's leaders were a fractious group, all trying to assert their own ideas of order in a village deeply divided by ethnicity and wary from their ejido's history of social strife. The environmentalist posturing was a way of putting off an outsider who might delve into social wounds and otherwise make trouble. For my part, I worked carefully to remain nonaligned in Orozco's disputes, and I tried to make sure my presence would not cause them trouble with outside agents.

San Lorenzans were not in as precarious economic or social circumstances, and I soon achieved easygoing relationships in the community. San Lorenzans were open about a bitter dispute that had divided ejidal members in the months prior to my arrival. I solicited advice from village leaders about how I should handle their differences. Refreshingly, they responded, "This is our argument not yours, so it shouldn't affect you." Even though I would have many conversations about this dispute, San Lorenzans were true to their word. They never pressured me to take sides. My four months in their community passed quickly. Environmentalism, however, was a touchier subject, because San Lorenzans were avid hunters. Remarkably, hunting became a plank upon which San Lorenzans and I were able to build friendships.

I really do love wild animals, and once people saw my excitement, they began to invite me to see their latest capture or kill. I had been repaying people's kindness with family photographs and soon found myself taking trophy portraits. My specialty became men standing beside dead animals, and I learned a lot from these pictures. I learned that fox and ocelot still entered settled villages. Armadillo can turn up in a cornfield as easily as deer and paca agouti can, but the stealthy tayra rarely comes under fire. I learned that shooting monkeys, let alone eating them, was highly controversial, because the monkeys' human qualities disturbed people who worried they were killing one of our own. Most important, I learned that in the charged atmosphere surrounding conservation, I could find common ground between myself and campesinos. People never forgot I was a strange *gringa* woman, financially independent, and much too old to be unmarried—"And, you've never even had one child?!" one man asked me disbelievingly. The force of my oddities should become clearer in the following pages as I explain the importance of nationalism, social class, gender, and family at Calakmul. Over time, however, in the give and take of daily life, our respective mettles became evident, and we grew into relationships, as rich and complicated as human relationships are everywhere.

Because of the sensitive position of Orozcans and San Lorenzans within conservation-development regimes, the usual reporting that obscures personal identities takes on greater urgency for them. I have changed the names of all people and towns, except for those of the Reserve director, the Reserve's assistant director, Doña Belén (she appreciates the publicity), Xpujil, and Zoh Laguna. I have been aided in these protective efforts by the passage of time. Central characters who appear in these pages have moved to new locations. Central events and issues have been transplanted. I chose to write in the past tense to reinforce my reporting being situated in a time now gone.

The days I describe, nonetheless, contain an enduring relevance. They explain how particular paths of conservation, development, and peasant empowerment materialize and how these paths become transformed. As a relevant aside, these days also explain how particular paths of academic research materialize. Although in 1994 just a handful of researchers were working in Calakmul, the area has since undergone a veritable explosion of investigation. By the late 1990s, researchers from at least thirteen Mexican and U.S. universities worked in Calakmul, including two schools that sponsor large-scale, multidisciplinary initiatives. Nearly all this work touches on environmental themes. To a large extent, this research also focuses on communities east of the Calakmul Biosphere Reserve where the Reserve-Council alliance was most active. The narrowness of this topical and geographical focus carries great risks in knowledge production. Some explanations for environmental change, or even the relevance of that change itself, may appear more weighty than a broader perspective warrants (Sophie Calmè, personal communication 2001). In making a grand show of conservation, the Reserve-Council alliance put this dynamic into operation and continues to shape people's thinking about Calakmul in implicit ways. Another aspect of the alliance, however, has not endured. In chapter 7, I will show how the alliance's message of campesino empowerment has been muted in the trend toward large-scale ecotourism and bureaucratic governance, as well as this intensive monitoring by academic researchers.

An Outline

Throughout the book I explore questions of conservation and development from two perspectives. In the first perspective, in chapters 3, 6, and 7, I use a regional lens to look at how people used conservation to create Calakmul as a coherent political entity where none previously existed. Calakmul's current residents are pioneers on an agricultural frontier. Over the last forty years, they colonized area forests in search of economic security and improved living conditions. I develop the second perspective in chapters 4 and 5, and again in chapter 7, where I focus on the personal histories that brought people to Calakmul, aspects of community life that shape their daily lives, their farming practices, and their immersion in development programs that fail to resolve their economic frustrations. In particular, I consider the lives of people living in the pseudonymous Orozco and San Lorenzo, two of Calakmul's ejidos. The ejido is a particular kind of common property regime in which landed farmers have broad decision-making authority regarding their natural resources and internal political life. The designation of Orozco and San Lorenzo as ejidos deeply affected residents' position within a triangle formed by themselves, state authorities, and the local environment. I further define the ejido in chapter 3 and consider its impact all through the text but especially in chapter 5.

I draw most of my material from the fourteen months I spent in 1994 and 1995 shuttling among Orozco, San Lorenzo, and the town of Zoh Laguna, headquarters of the Reserve-Council alliance. Across these sites, I watched how conservation was alternately pervasive and absent in people's lives, how campesinos variously adopted an environmentalist pose, ignored conservation objectives, and reshaped environmental aims to fit their own ends. Following brief visits to Calakmul in 1996 and 1999, I returned in 2001 to survey 150 households in ten communities. In the text, I use this latter period to place Orozco, San Lorenzo, and the events of 1994–95 within a broader historical and ecological context.

Most of the material on conservation-development comes toward the end of the book. This structure is purposeful. I believe conservation-development can be made sense of only in the context of people's broader lives. My grounding in phenomenological anthropology explains this position, but phenomenology also forced me to consider additional theoretical explanations for conservation-development, as I explore in the following chapter.

2

Theorizing Conservation and Development

I tell my introductory students that anthropology asks that we walk more than just a mile in another's shoes. Anthropology entails seeing the world from another's perspective, taking into account as much as possible that person's history, learning, and experiences. Phenomenological anthropology theorizes what we might find in this exercise. The theory moves between noting how people act on the world and are, in turn, influenced by that same world. "Each person is at once a subject for himself or herself—a *who*—and an object for others—a *what*. And though individuals speak, act, and work toward belonging to a world of others, they simultaneously strive to experience themselves as world makers" (Jackson 1998:8). Upon entering a social setting, then, anthropologists must begin to tease out this give and take. What happens when a group of people—with different histories, knowledge, and experiences—tries to create different kinds of social worlds in the same geographic place?

In some ways, that is exactly what was happening with conservation at Calakmul. At the same time, a social world already existed in the region, and these ideas, events, and people became my point of departure. I originally set out to Calakmul to conduct a study in ethnoecology. I would compare different understandings of ecology and environment. What was intended to be a dissertation thesis turned out to be just one chapter and later a published article (Haenn 1999). The social world surrounding conservation in Calakmul was deeply political, and I would have been a poor anthropologist, indeed, if I failed to follow the lead of the people I came to learn from. It is not that ethnoecology was unimportant to Calakmul's conservation scene. The political issues were just so salient as to demand most of my attention.

It is important to remember this point throughout this chapter. Here, I locate Calakmul within anthropology and studies on people and protected areas more generally. In choosing to frame my work within some people's writing rather than other's, I began with what I learned from a year's living in Calakmul ejidos, including countless formal and informal interviews, dozens of ejido and Reserve-Council meetings, and the informal asides offered at dinner, over a soda, or on drives between towns. I did not go to Calakmul looking to prove conservation was political. In fact, my training emphasized the economic issues that arise in chapter 6 and ecosystems theory, a direction almost entirely absent from this book. When I returned from Calakmul, I struggled to find a theory that adequately addressed the political accounting conveyed to me by Reserve Director Acopa and residents of Orozco and San Lorenzo. Some of the most helpful writers in this regard published years after my field research. Thus, I came to consider conservation as a postcolonial act of state formation post hoc. I offer this theory at the beginning of the book, because I believe it will help make sense of the many strands of information readers must bear in mind to grasp the complexity of Calakmul's conservation setting.

A Renovated Ecology

Theory in human-environment relations, like conservation-development, underwent marked transformations in the 1990s. Overall, theorists added to earlier approaches that tended to focus on small groups of people living in rural areas, often depicting these groups as embedded within local ecology dynamics (Rappaport 1984). As anthropologists grew to elaborate local people's connections to national and international structures, these telescoped descriptions became harder to sustain. Researchers increasingly recognized that typologies linking ethnic groups to particular environmental activities and ecologies—built around a four-part classification that included hunting and gathering, pastoralism, small-scale farming, and industrialized society—were not exclusively products of politically neutral processes or even environmental exigencies. Instead, people's relations to the environment were viewed as multifaceted, with roots in political histories and power structures, both of which were informed by cultural differences (Descola and Pálsson 1996; Escobar 1999; Li 1999; Rocheleau et al. 1996; Wilmsen 1989). In anthropology, this cultural emphasis on power, identity, and history was criticized by researchers who lamented a loss of ecological depth (Vayda and Walters 1999). Geographically and socially expansive approaches seemed to leave behind the environmental constraints evident when researchers examine the direct, physical connection between people and the environment. Furthermore, to the extent that anthropologists were interested in ameliorating environmental problems, these newer studies implicitly doubted people's role in determining environmental outcomes. They showed how people who directly act upon the environment might find their work captive to distant decision makers (Stonich 1993).

These debates have challenged theorists of human-environment relations to develop a comprehensive answer to a series of questions. How is the environment both an entity outside human society with which people reckon and the product of how people think and relate to one another? (See Milton 1996.) How should theorists prioritize the variety of ecological, ideological, social, political, economic, and historical factors contributing to any given environmental situation? (See Bebbington 1999.) How might we better define both what constitutes environmental degradation and solutions to environmental problems? (See Fairhead and Leach 1996.)

My earlier forays into these questions sought answers in political ecology. For this text, I have turned away from an explicit focus on political ecology, struggling, as Brosius does (1999), with the different orientations that share the name. Where political ecology draws on both political economy and poststructural concerns, I have sought a way to unify these while avoiding certain weaknesses in the theory. Paulson, Gezon, and Watts describe these debilities as "a weak specification of political economy and the political, its sometimes vague [reference] . . . to exogenous forces . . . [as well as] uncertainty and debate about the nature and place of politics in environmental analysis." (2003:209) Circumstances at Calakmul resolved these issues while presenting a further, pressing complication that seemed outside political ecology's immediate concerns of who influences whom and how both power and nature become constructed in certain contexts.

I found environmental problems may be defined and acted on in ways that vastly complicate their resolution. Paradoxically, this outcome is a mark of successful global conservation initiatives. These initiatives have positioned forest protection as a vital element within multiple political frameworks, such that environmental ideals and practices now structure those relations (Peluso 1992). When environmentalism becomes a pillar within power relations (a source of authority, prestige, and influence; see Paulson et al. 2003), people may resist resolving the ecological tensions on which power (and its contestation) rests. My point here is a bit different from those who have argued a "green imperialism," that environmental protection works to subjugate certain classes (Grove 1995; Shiva 1988). I add to the possibility of subjugation the observation that, in any given conservation setting, few people may be interested in actual environmental protection, while many people may use the *idea* of protection to further other aims. Conservation then becomes omnipresent, in the way people talk and relate to one another, but absent in practice. Meanwhile, this omnipresence has concrete environmental effects. In light of this, I add

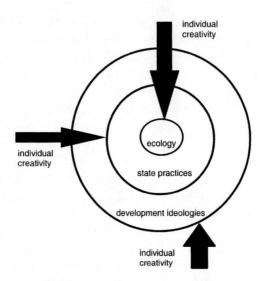

Fig. 2.1. Schema of theoretical overview.

to the questions noted above: what paths of political organization and environmental discourses lead people toward or away from environmental solutions?

Figure 2.1 presents a schema of my response to this dilemma. Harking back to material presented in chapter 1, I begin with theories of state formation. Conservation was intimately tied to bolstering the state's presence in Calakmul, but this was not a seamless process. State agents were forced to employ conservation-development to counter local opposition to conservation. Policy makers at Calakmul were not unique in mapping conservation onto development. In his critique of the global move toward conservation-development, Oates describes environmentalists as falling "in love with economic development" (1999:43). Thus, after considering state formation, I explore the implications for both states and conservationists in taking development (even in the guise of sustainable development) as their raison d'être. Finally, I concretize these points in people's everyday lives, while noting the possibility for creative change. I do so by returning to considerations of phenomenology and "figured worlds." It goes without saying that as an anthropologist I view this four-part configuration of ecology, state, development, and creativity as profoundly affected by culture. Elaborating the cultural quality of these phenomena at Calakmul, and the role of cultural differences in conservation-development settings, lies among my central tasks.

State Formation

Although private individuals (in national and international NGOs) set conservation in motion at Calakmul, environmental activities there have largely been a domain of the state. In this sense, environmental research must reckon with the state as a cultural construction, in which environmental management somehow becomes part of the state's mandate (Scott 1998). People living today often take for granted the existence of state governments, but, for most of human history, states as such did not exist. In figuring out exactly how states get invented, researchers of state formation describe a need to explain *"forms of rule and ruling* [in which] key questions then become NOT *who* rules but *how* rule is accomplished" (Corrigan 1994:xvii, emphasis in original). Theorists of everyday forms of state formation go about this task by moving beyond the notion of power as a series of tactical maneuvers or the result of certain political structures (for example, democratic, authoritarian, etc.). Everyday forms of state formation consider culture as a central issue within governance (Joseph and Nugent 1994). These researchers look at symbols, meanings, and activities of everyday life and how these contribute to and reflect engagements between state and citizenry. Through these engagements, people become active participants in state formation. For my purposes, this raises the question: How have particular policies and moral prescriptions been changed by rural Mexicans? (See Vaughan 1999.)

Although, on the one hand, state practices must appear uniform to provide national coherence, on the other, local governance displays a range of symbolic and practical interactions between state and citizens. Lomnitz-Adler (1992) posits a theory that connects this local activity to cultural life more broadly. He depicts various "culture regions" where the intersection of physical geography, power structures, and communication patterns produces distinctive cultural settings. Regions are part historical artifact. Over time, people accumulate certain ways of interacting. They use speech and symbols that are locally recognizable, but these may not be so transparent to outsiders. This communication and symbolic work can build on historical differences in power (the difference between social classes or between ethnic groups) and keep those differences alive over time. While we can think of a power-communication structure as encompassing a certain group of people, when mapped onto the physical terrain, these structures separate one geographical region from another. These distinctions explain why we think of northern Mexico as different from southern Mexico and why we draw the line where we do (somewhere south of Mexico City). Power-communication structures set apart the

Yucatán peninsula from other indigenous areas, for example, in the Mexican states of Oaxaca and Chiapas.

Thinking about Calakmul as a regional culture helps explain the challenges governing authorities found there. With its mix of newly arrived migrants, Calakmul did not offer readily available speech and symbols with which authorities could work. These intangibles were, nonetheless, highly necessary. Peopling a frontier is not enough to create borders or establish a territory to govern. Authorities must find within people themselves the basic elements for state building (Azuela 1989).[1]

How might state agents identify and harness local norms and symbols from which to build their operations? The task here was twofold: to gain sufficient legitimacy to rule and create a governing structure that could manage dissent. Building a unified, manageable society is a problem for both state authorities and the subjects they would rule. Persistent contradictions, of the kind evident in chapter 1, weaken power structures. One resolution to this problem is the implementation of hegemonic systems that address domination *and* resistance, systems that make sense of both the state's coherence and its cleavages (Roseberry 1996). In these cases, protesters and resisters adopt the language and tools of dominators "in order to be registered or heard. . . . But [one] must stress the problematic and fragile character of such frameworks" (ibid.:81). Once conservation was thrust upon them, people in Calakmul adopted the language of environmental protection, but this process included slippages as well as people's creative reworking of environmental issues. Environmentalism, in its guise as state formation, was a work in progress whose conclusion in 1995 was unknown.

State building at Calakmul was complicated further by two points. The first entailed competition between Campeche state and federal authorities. Although I do not delve into the role of federal agents in this book, both entities used conservation to bolster their separate spheres of influence. The federal funds channeled through the Reserve challenged Campeche state's claim to rule Calakmul's territory. The Reserve itself was touted as a rare example of state-federal collaboration in protected area management. But, this partnership structured rather than resolved bureaucratic competition. Rivalry between federal and Campeche authorities also took place in reference to Calakmul's people, whose strongest identities were not tied to Campeche or to the Mexican nation, but to their home states and their status as campesinos (an identity that lent itself to a federal affiliation; see chaps. 4 and 5). Critically, constructions of state and environment at Calakmul took place in the context of a *fractured* state.

In Jeffrey Rubin's words, a fractured state operates through "a multitude of regional arrangements—each a distinct combination of bargains, coercions, and alliances—that together reinforced the power of the center in broadly similar ways" (1997:13). Rubin's writing resonates with the notion of regional culture by pointing to the spaces where localism thrives, the spaces where "the presence of the state has been uneven and incomplete across both geography and political life" (ibid.:12–13). We will see numerous examples of these spaces in the chapters to follow.

The second complication in state building at Calakmul centered on how to position area ecology in these emerging power structures. To the extent that regional cultures are rooted in specific places, they build on and incorporate specific ecologies. As a result, state processes include simultaneous efforts at resource exploitation and the symbolic construction of nature. In other words, state formation requires the cultural construction of nature as a way to control specific territories and as a way to bind people within those territories to regimes of power (Escobar 1996). The shift in Calakmul from a political economy built on forest extraction and swidden farming to one built on sustainable development required a change in both ecological definitions and people's identities in relation to the environment. Policy makers self-consciously attempted to steer this change. Campesinos, however, resisted vigorously identities and practices associated with conservation. This resistance had an impact. State agents were not entirely free to define nature or people as they wished. Instead, authorities were forced to appeal to conflicting constituencies by sustaining contradictory constructions under the conservation-development rubric. These contradictions produced a cacophony at Calakmul, which the Reserve and Regional Council ordered by loudly proclaiming how conservation was really about something else, say, political control, campesino empowerment, or development aid. The latter held special appeal. Despite their different notions of environment, state agents, campesinos, and environmentalists shared a belief in the value of economic development. Sustainable development briefly worked as a "metafix" at Calakmul (see Lélé in Dobson 1998:33), thereby placing conservation squarely within a very complicated, contentious state-campesino relationship that hinged on campesino poverty.

Poverty, Development, and Contradictions in State Formation

Throughout the 1990s, government agents touted economic development as their primary achievement in Calakmul (Pino Castillo 1998), a tendency that continued even as the conservation-development agenda fell into decline. Authorities congratulated themselves on an expanding water infrastructure, paved roads, schools, and health clinics. Each success carried a note of caution. Campesinos remained poor, and there was still much to be done. Development's role as a primary axis connecting campesinos and state agents had much to do with Article 27 and an enduring social contract that endorsed a welfare state. At the same time, this nearly single-minded preference for development seemed curious given Calakmul's many pressing social issues. Throughout the book I will point to the issues of intracommunity conflicts and high rates of local violence. During 1994–95, murder rates at Calakmul were 2.5 times the national rate.[2] State agents rarely tackled these questions. Where development monies and successes were reported in Regional Council assemblies, local newspapers, and various state and NGO documents, finding data on public safety required some sleuthing. State authorities seemed to have narrowly defined their mandate, leading me to question both why this was the case and its implications for human-environment relations (see also Ferguson 1990).[3]

In thinking through this enigma and its relevance to conservation, I drew inspiration from theories of postcolonialism. The application of postcolonialism to a Mexican context requires careful attention. Klor de Alva asserts that theories associated with the independence of Asian and African nations do not easily apply to Latin America (1995; see Young 2001 for an overview of postcolonial theories). Among his arguments, he notes that agitators for independence elsewhere positioned themselves against their Western rulers. In Latin America, post-independence leaders continued to look to the West as a model, while recreating colonialism within indigenous and other marginalized groups. Certainly, Calakmul's role as a provider of resources and labor supports the notion that its relationship to Mexican authorities is more colonial than postcolonial. Nonetheless, I view postcolonialism as a useful tool for thinking about the diverse tensions at play within Calakmul. As Calakmul moved beyond its colonial role to what Klor de Alva might call its incorporation into an imperial order (ibid.:266)--one that demanded cultural transformations (via environmentalism) as well as political integration—the Reserve director who brokered this shift did so with the revolutionary notion that campesinos, not the state, would gain the upper hand. The director's hybrid development, ecological, and political ideas (see chap. 7) positioned him as a postcolonial figure. He provided a postcolonial hallmark to a place that otherwise exhibited power relations that did not fit easily into categories of "colonial," "postcolonial," or "imperial."

One such discomfiture lies in how to locate Calakmul's settlers in such a configuration. As we saw, the Reserve precipitated a kind of settler rebellion at Calakmul. However, unlike colonial settings where people agitated for political independence, people in Calakmul fought for a more intensive campesino-government relationship, one that fulfilled the promises of Article 27. In considering the interaction between social and biophysical processes over time, Sluyter views theories of postcolonialism as an apt framework (2002). At Calakmul, however, an existing state's use of environmentalism in the construction of a new state apparatus may fall outside the temporal framework of postcolonialism.

I found a more fruitful application of postcolonial theories in the work of Akhil Gupta. Gupta accords a central place to development activities and discourses in the work of state agents who seek to rationalize the state's existence and build a bridge between state and citizen (1998). Gupta asserts that state authorities have used development projects in their quest for legitimacy and their desire to win over highly skeptical constituents. From this perspective, state formation on Calakmul's frontier may not be as novel as its proponents asserted. According to postcolonial thinkers, state actors do not operate in a vacuum but, instead, draw on known development formulas. These formulas already contain certain power configurations (Escobar 1995). Rather than have a liberating effect or change political arrangements, new kinds of state formation can reorient people within existing power structures. Approaching state formation as a reorientation allows me to explore the way people used ecology to think both with and against the state. In the case of Calakmul, this reconfiguration resulted in continued campesino subordination, even though many people worked against such an outcome.

Assertions of campesino subordination require strong corroboration, and in a moment, I provide preliminary evidence for this assertion. Prior to that, it is important to note how the contradiction between purportedly novel political arrangements (postcolonial) and enduring power relations (colonial/imperial) connects to additional incongruities and a social life permeated by contradictions. If conservation initiatives gave new material to existing power regimes, these contradictions served as a basic medium through which authorities and campesinos reckoned with one another. Contradictions provided a space in which both Calakmul's people and certain administrators were able to counter conservation's authoritarian tendencies (cf. Bebbington 2001).

Among these oppositions, one issue that stood out was the tendency to describe campesino subordination with the words *jodido* and *fregado*.

Literally translated as "fucked" or "screwed," in different contexts, these words might describe people as "poor" or stuck in a situation that is difficult to improve, a "shit hole." The phrases peppered the conversation of campesinos and state agents alike to describe campesinos as part of Mexico's lowest echelon (see also chap. 5).

Postcolonial theories helped me look beyond the apparent truism of campesino poverty to examine how constructions of poverty may reinforce power divides and hold certain ecological consequences. For example, Gupta notes colonial regimes rationalized their rule by fostering "modern" values and activities in purportedly "backward" areas. This sentiment became transformed in the postcolonial era as newly independent states (and their financial backers in international arenas) worked to "develop" areas and peoples considered "underdeveloped." Distinctions between "developed" and "underdeveloped" were not just economic, but also required identity differences. In the postcolonial condition, Gupta notes, poor people identify themselves as left behind and this affects "who people think they are . . . and what they can do to alter their lives" (1998:ix). By extension, constructions of poverty (and its counterpart, wealth) affect how we think about the environment and the possibilities we see for environmental change.

The United States is saturated with development ideology and notions of never-ending economic growth, such that it can be hard to imagine poor people feeling other than left behind (Escobar 1995; Lutz and Collins 1993). It can be difficult to imagine that life without a wealth of material goods does not necessarily lead a person to identify as poor. Once, however, driving home from work, I listened to a radio show report a heartfelt story that underscored this possibility. The story addressed a U.S. corporate executive who had recently sold his business and distributed a portion of the proceeds to his employees, an average of US$233,000 each for 550 people. The journalist pressed the man for his personal background, asking if he had grown up with money. The executive sounded uncomfortable with the question: "I thought we had a lot of money. I thought we were very wealthy people. We didn't have any electricity or running water, but we had everything everyone else in the neighborhood had. We were farm kids and were very happy and very fortunate to have had wonderful parents" (*All Things Considered*, August 2, 1999). For the most part, readers might find it unusual that a family without electricity or water would consider itself wealthy. The executive's atypical quality in this regard suggests the power of development ideologies in shaping people's feelings about themselves and others.

Anthropologists observe that, while people have always recognized wealth differences, identities of underdevelopment are increasingly the norm. This is especially true among people who, for decades, have been subject to a state that structures both poverty and economic development in ways that rationalize the state's existence (Ferguson 1999; Gupta 1998). State authorities may, for example, link membership in the nation-state vis-à-vis socioeconomic status. In the Mexico case, we need only to look to revolutionary history, when the birth of today's Mexican state (circa 1920) hinged partly on improving conditions for *Los de abajo* (Azuela 1927), the underdogs or the underlings. At Calakmul, the phrase resonated from political speeches to schoolchildren's recital contests. Throughout the twentieth century, Mexican state agents attended to revolutionary promises by extending numerous aid programs to campesinos. These programs failed to fully incorporate campesinos into market economies. But, they have heightened people's consciousness regarding their status as "poor," while creating a new economy in which people are forced to rely on a mixture of subsistence work, wage labor, and state aid (Collier 1994; Otero 1999).

It is important to note that people's participation in this mixed economy and its associated identities was not entirely voluntary. At Calakmul, campesino involvement in development programs was technically voluntary, but local ecologies and larger, macroeconomic issues did not allow people the freedom to opt out of a cash economy (see chap. 6). Engaging development programs had become a necessity for small-scale farmers whose work had been continuously devalued in state preferences for an industrialized economy. Between 1994 and 1999, the price of corn in Mexico, the staple food in Calakmul, dropped 45 percent in real terms (Correa 2001). This devaluing of farm products means Mexican peasants are under continuously heightened pressure to raise the cash necessary to send children to school, cover health-care costs, and purchase consumer items. As they combined subsistence and wage work, people in Calakmul were not unlike other peasant families who supplied cheap food and surplus labor to national and international markets. They also shared with other peasants the extent to which state activities brokered this exploitation (Gupta 1998). In the late 1990s, for example, Campeche's governor exhorted campesinos to solve the problem of their poverty by abandoning farming and joining Campeche's *maquiladora* (low-wage, factory) workforce (Cahn von Seelen 2004). But, people in Calakmul report that low wages and overall job scarcity leave the direction of such change unclear. Authorities, meanwhile, give few assurances that by abandoning their farming, campesinos will be able to improve their standard of living.

Despite these complications, development as a rationale for nation-states retains its appeal. In addition to bridging diverse social groups, development theories helpfully provide a course of action that, supposedly, leads to predictable ends. Once economically depressed areas adopt the purportedly successful policies and activities of more advanced economies, wealth creation should follow. In practice, such replications are fraught with problems. Setting aside the question of whether policies are applied in good faith (see chap. 1), federal, state, and international policies undergo significant transformations as they pass through the filters of regional cultures. At the local level, imposed definitions encounter existing meanings and the result can be a series of inconsistencies. At Calakmul, these contradictions multiplied when development ideals met the demands posed by environmentalism and peasant expectations of state behavior.

In its formulaic quality, conservation is akin to development. Protected areas offer a defined course of action that should lead to environmental protection. Consequently, observations that protected area formation and management mimics the colonial order have become commonplace (Brandon et al. 1998; Neumann 1998). Given the many dimensions of power, however, we can consider additional connections between power and environment—as sites of performance, as sites for cataloging and domineering through knowledge, as sites of instrumental power, and as sites where people's chimerical narrations establish a hall of mirrors that deflects definitive statements. Making all this manageable in writing, as well as in theory, has proved challenging and requires some elaboration.

Agency in Writing and Theorizing

Reflective of broader movements in human-environment theory (see Sluyter 2002), anthropological thinking about power and ecology has largely focused on instrumental questions of political economy (Durham 1996; Schmink and Wood 1987; Stonich 1993) and, more recently, on the meaning structures surrounding environment and environmental management (Brosius 1999; Escobar 1999). As I mentioned earlier, these differences are not necessarily incompatible. Both approaches are necessary to explain events at Calakmul, where social life included heavy doses of rhetorical flourish. Understanding environmentalism thus required an exploration of both the intersection and distinction between environmental actions and environmental talk. Describing this range, however, is new to anthropological reporting, and the breadth of material involved presents particular difficulties in writing and theorizing.

To respond to this quandary, I followed an actor-centered approach. That is, to the extent possible, I structured my writing around what people told me and what I observed rather than sought adherence to some theoretical concern. This narrative structure fit the mood at Calakmul. The hearty characters who appear on these pages likely would have little truck with writing that failed to place their initiative center stage. Emphases on personal history, ejidal life, and economic issues reflect local concerns, although campesinos would likely add family and religion as topics central to their lives. In the conclusions, I suggest how an actor-centered approach is useful to remedying some of conservation's injustices.

Because conservation is an international affair, an actor-centered approach would take me only so far (see West 2000). Even though conservation could have considerable impact on their lives, campesinos were largely unfamiliar with conservation ideas and networks beyond proscriptive laws and local programs. Here, I had to pull together ideas, viewpoints, and activities that were in tension with one another, even if, locally, they were not always verbalized as such. This task extended to exploring regional history, noting variable ideas of farming, and documenting the financial impacts of different aid programs, as well as describing regional and supraregional conservation issues. For these topics, I depart from local narrations and provide standpoints that are more explicitly my own.

Tacking between an actor-centered and analytical approach, I mimic some of the tensions found in conservation-development, and I invite readers to use this structure to explore the stresses of a multicultural conservation setting. Although they did not view themselves as masters of their own destiny, campesinos often took pride in the intellectual skills and strength of character they brought to life's obstacles. Their sense of agency and a future that is essentially unknowable coincided with Janet Finn's description of "people as works in progress, shaped by attachments, aspirations, interests, and the rhythmic practices of daily life" (Finn 1998:14). We can compare campesino agency in respect to government agents to Finn's characterizations of copper miners and mining corporations, where: "Agency must be understood in terms of the intimate contradictions and confusions posed by mining life, where residents were both beneficiaries and victims of corporate largesse and exploitation. Lessons of agency are embedded in the stories of bravado that mask life's real dangers. Likewise, agency is encoded in the stories of crafts(wo)manship, the creative making of self and circumstance out of the material at hand" (ibid.).

My and campesino stories are sure to find dissent among some readers. Responding to a reading is, itself, a form of agency, although one not widely shared in Calakmul (where many adults are functionally illiterate). Readers and campesinos, however, do share a common agency. The critical eye readers bring to this text is similar to the critical eye campesinos brought to conservation. As readers evaluate the material in this book, they might ask what the *experience* of critical reading teaches about campesino responses to conservation. I further address reading as a conservation strategy in the book's conclusion.

The Shape of Campesino Agency

Conservation programming brought to Calakmul new material for the crafting of self and circumstance. However, this material did not stand alone. Instead, it became intertwined with existing material, especially ethnicity, gender, family, ejidal norms, state-campesino relations, and local environmental activities. As works-in-progress, individuals encounter existing social and ecological realities, but they do not encounter all possible realities. Instead, from their particular social positions, people encounter a limited range of realities and work to order these in a way that allows protagonists an element of control over their and others' behavior. Holland et al. (1998) describe these ongoing encounters between personal experience and social realities as comprising an individual's "figured world." Bringing together Jackson's work in phenomenology with Holland et al., we see how, within figured worlds, "*control, right,* and *power* . . . [are] issues of existential mastery before they are matters of economic or political advantage" (emphasis in original; Jackson 1998:21). Larger political processes can reflect these more personal desires and speak to the anxiety people feel regarding basic life questions. Such anxieties are especially pertinent in subsistence economies, where future survival is far from assured. Lest readers mistake the notion of "order" for "orderliness," it is important to note that actors may negotiate the gap between their personal desires and the world they encounter in a variety of ways. As we will see, paradox, ambiguity, and disorder, as well as simultaneous acts of cultural construction, deconstruction, and reconstruction are all relevant tools in this regard.

Although aimed at explaining social relations, ideas of figured worlds and world making withstand an ecological reading. These notions can underpin an approach to ecology that oscillates between the oppositions that currently characterize human-environment theory, between stewardship and powerlessness, between human-environment relations as subject to ecological norms and as subject to social norms. Rather than reconcile these dichotomies, in practice people move "between these domains, playing them off against each other, negotiating the troubled boundary between them" (ibid.:20). Recalling this chapter's opening discussion, we see this oscillation in cases where people alternately view ecological qualities as impersonal objects and as imbued with "subjective meanings and social destinies" (ibid.:9; see also Milton 1996). Environmental issues may be marshaled to serve political ends, while environmental practices simultaneously follow a different logic of ecological precepts. Environmental cosmologies may, at the same time, exist within a separate framework still. These configurations are not always neatly bound, and, although researchers may discern patterns in human-environment processes, a summary coherence to ecological settings may be fleeting at best.

Return to Ethnography

My approach to agency suggests that power is unavoidable and diffuse, and is generated from multiple points. This idea differs markedly from the way people in Calakmul viewed power. They saw it as a limited good. Campesinos believed people gained influence and wealth at the expense of their neighbors. In the least, an individual's rise to prominence held the possibility of decreasing similar opportunities for others. This notion may be characteristic of a patronage society, in which patrons dole out benefits to a restricted group of clients. For clients, personal advancement rests on monopolizing connections to a patron. However, people did not always view this power structure as limiting their personal agency. Instead, ambitious individuals viewed patron-client ties, especially their tendency to be carried out behind closed doors, as sites of creativity. Many campesinos jockeyed to position themselves advantageously within the changing political realms brought about by conservation programming. They speculated endlessly about who was building ties with whom and whose public, political life masked private dealings. Campesinos tended to channel their political activity through campesino organizations, and after demonstrating the importance of these groups, in the conclusions I note future paths of natural resource management that these groups are shaping.

If power and its accompanying wealth existed in limited supply, campesinos agreed that government authorities held a majority share. In this sense, conservation presented familiar conundrums that rest on decades of state interference in the rural sector. How would these new directives affect people's subsistence and relations with ejidal neighbors? How could campesinos use their practical and symbolic connections to the land to tap into government resources while keeping at bay predatory

government practices and (what they perceived as) nonsensical environmental directives? Identity will prove the main link connecting campesinos and state agents, but campesinos have multiple identities, which
premised some groups of people in these relations.

Environmental historians describe this interaction between ecology
and society in deceptively simple terms, as a give and take. People are
presented with an ecological setting that they modify. This modification
has repercussions to which people respond. Responses again cause modifications to which people react, and so on (Schoenbrun 1998). In my
account, I situate postcolonialism, state formation, and agency in the
midst of these interactions. Migrants new to Calakmul struggled with this
give and take, as they learned to work within a new ecology and a new
society, and as they filtered this information through their past experiences (see chap. 4). Despite its frontier character, Calakmul did offer a
historical legacy that framed this learning and subsequent land use negotiations. My analysis of that legacy underscores a fear-filled atmosphere
surrounding power and environment and challenges the notion that campesinos are the only cause of deforestation.

3

Conservation's Hidden History

My history of Calakmul not only sets the stage for migrant encounters with local ecology. Through the account I question the effects of history making on state and environmental practices. I first learned about Calakmul's history from Reserve and Council ingenieros. I also interviewed the peasant leaders who created Calakmul's conservation-development pact. This introduction was similar to that offered to international conservation and development agents. Sitting at Doña Belén's tables or accompanying ingenieros to ejidos, I learned a kind of official version of Calakmul's history, one that rationalized the Reserve-Council alliance. People commonly described Calakmul as a "frontier," forgotten by Mexico's government, until the advent of the Biosphere Reserve.

Although home to pre-Columbian cities, these people said, Calakmul was depopulated for centuries until the 1920s. At that time, Calakmul's trees provided U.S. markets with chicle, the essential ingredient in chewing gum, and people, mostly men, came to the region as chicle tappers. In the 1940s, Calakmul's economy turned to logging, after chicle's boom abruptly ended with the invention of a synthetic substitute. Logging continued into the 1980s, but beginning in the 1960s, swidden farmers moved to Calakmul. Campesinos compensated for poor harvests and earned cash by selling wood to the timber companies. This relationship was contentious, and campesinos complained they were underpaid. Campesinos began to organize for change. In the 1970s, they formed the Union of Forested Ejidos. In the 1980s, this group transformed into the Union of Maya People. Labeled communists, Union organizers came under attack by timber barons. One of the Union's activists received threats from the army. At the same time, Union members had connections to national-level organizations. Through these groups, peasant leaders reached sympathetic governing figures. They delivered to Mexico's former president Miguel de la Madrid and his successor, Salinas de Gortari, copies of a scientific report on deforestation in Calakmul. The report found that, if sustained, logging rates of the early 1980s would leave Calakmul without a standing forest by 1995. Around this report, Calakmul's campesinos built a relationship with Salinas, who entered office in 1988. This relationship culminated in the votes-for-development deal, when the Union of Maya People was renamed the Xpujil Regional Council.

This snapshot fast became Calakmul's official history as researchers, environmentalists, and others solidified an oral account in published writing (Boege 1995; Ericson et al. 1999; Haenn 2000; Stedman-Edwards 2000). The story suggests a series of boom and bust cycles culminating in environmentally destructive farm practices. Interestingly, this story of boom and bust resonates with the histories of other places similarly marginalized within global economies (Muratorio 1991; Wilk 1991). Do market connections provide a uniform history to these distinctive places? Or, is something else happening? (See also Fairhead and Leach, 1996.)

On closer examination, I found the official history curious for the contradictions it presented. Over the course of the narrative, Calakmul's ecology, formerly an aggressive opponent in campesinos' working lives, became a fragile entity in need of protection from those same campesinos. This new environmental definition sat alongside a new campesino subjectivity. Peasants, once considered defenders of area forests, became stubborn culprits in deforestation. With its social evolutionary tones, the official history depicted this change as a natural outcome of historical processes. In this sense, the history conceded deforestation as inevitable. Having watched the history arise out of the Reserve-Council alliance, I do not believe this was the authors' intent. Instead, I see in this history an attempt to make the *state's* presence, as well as its accompanying prerogative over Calakmul's lands, unavoidable. Reserve and Council staff were left to deal with the social and environmental implications of this endeavor.

I base these conclusions on a reconsideration of Calakmul's history in light of published materials and oral histories. The information in this chapter rests substantially on the 2001 survey of Calakmul communities. Comparing these findings with the official history, I see important points of disagreement and obfuscation, especially in regard to the state's role in affecting environmental change. Rather than stand as a simple corrective to the official history, these other perspectives serve to deepen our understanding of historical processes. They demonstrate that people have long had conflicting ideas about social and human-environment relations at Calakmul.

Calakmul's Pre-Columbian and Colonial Past

Because oral histories begin with Calakmul's pre-Columbian past, I give brief attention to this period before turning to colonial times. This is a cursory exploration. I do not pretend to do justice to the complexities I address. Instead, I hope this excursion raises further questions about

Calakmul's history and past ecologies. As academics and conservationists try to imagine alternative socioecological futures, it is worth exploring history's rich material for that imagining.

In the official history, the archaeological record offers intriguing questions about how Calakmul might support large numbers of people. By the time of Spanish arrival to the Americas, urban Mayan societies had passed the height of their influence, when tens of thousands of people lived in what is now southeast Campeche (during A.D. 550—770; Adams 1985). Abundant pre-Columbian ruins testify to these people's ingenuity and organizational skills. However, the centuries prior to the Spanish incursion saw a dramatic decrease in the number of people living in Calakmul. The reasons for this decline continue to be debated, but archaeologists suggest a mix of factors that include climate change, natural resource degradation, warfare, and the vulnerability of urban rulers. The role of each of these factors may never be known. Readers might consider relevant writings in archaeology and historical ecology (Graham 1998; Turner et al. 2003). By the time of the Spanish conquest, the archaeological site of Calakmul served ritual functions, but few, if any, people lived there. In areas that now constitute the Reserve's eastern and western borders, indigenous populations were present throughout the Spanish colonial period. Because of better documentation available for the eastern portion, where the Reserve-Council was most active, I concentrate on this area.

The eastern edge of the Reserve appears in historical documents under the name La Pimienta, home to a group known as the Cehach (Antochiw 1994; see fig. 3.1). In the early 1600s, residents of La Pimienta may have numbered 20,000 (Antochiw 1997). Spanish authorities repeatedly tried to conquer La Pimienta for numerous reasons. Southern peninsula forests housed trade routes connecting central Mexico with Guatemala and Honduras. Writing in 1639, the Spaniard Leon Pinelo expressed the need for a military campaign to gain control of commerce then in the hands of independent Indians (Leon Pinelo 1958). Indigenous groups traded in forest products such as wax and cacao, but these same forests held an ambiguous value for Spaniards. This ambivalence lies in what Dumond describes as Spanish notions that southern forests were economic surplus (Dumond 1997b). Although they coveted a few forest goods, Spaniards otherwise saw forests as barren and uncivilized. They viewed the fact that Indians lived in the forest as evidence of native barbarism (Jones 1989). This mutual identification of forests and forest peoples as wild would endure well into the twentieth century (Taussig 1987). People in Calakmul would use the imagery to comment on their own fears of

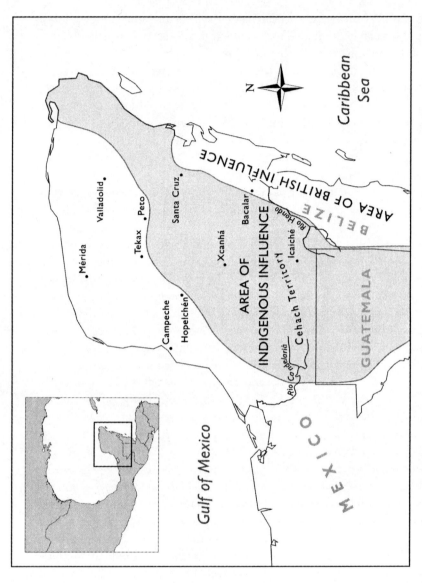

Fig. 3.1. Areas of political influence on the Yucatán peninsula, 1680 to 1850, with current political boundaries (modified from Farris 1984).

the repressive aspects of their migration. During the colonial period, the connection spoke to the antithesis autonomous Indians posed to Spanish colonial aims. Until the early 1700s, indigenous people escaped Spanish domination and forced labor by fleeing to politically independent forested domains (Farris 1984).

Calakmul's forests never isolated indigenous people. Indeed, in 1700, Cehach representatives would act as guides to Spaniards in their campaign against the Itzá kingdom located just south of Calakmul in what is now the Guatemalan Petén (Jones 1999). Forests helped structure certain kinds of connections between indigenous people and their would-be colonizers. For example, indigenous people on the Caribbean coast feared British loggers as well as pirates. Both groups sacked native villages and conducted slave raids. A British presence opposed both indigenous and Spanish claims to southern peninsula forests. An end to this three-way struggle would be crucial to Calakmul's incorporation into the Mexican state.

Calakmul and Yucatán's Caste War

Few publications address Calakmul prior to the mid-1800s. The period following this time, however, has received much attention for its connection to a watershed event in Yucatecan history. Mexico was now an independent country, where regional conflicts bespoke the enduring and contested quality of local power structures. In the case of Yucatán, these tensions found an outlet in the Caste War, fought mostly between 1847 and 1855 (Reed 1964). Following the Caste War, Calakmul would display the fragility of the new nation-state, as well as the bargains with regional power holders that enable federal influence.

Centered on the northern half of the peninsula, the Caste War saw Yucatec Maya battle Spanish-speaking elites. While historians depict an exploitative plantation economy as the war's impetus (Dumond 1997a; Reed 1964), the war's name connotes popular understandings. Mayan people aimed to overthrow a status quo built on ethnic difference. Most of the fighting took place in what were then the outer limits of Spanish-speaking society, the areas north and northwest of Calakmul near Peto and Tekax (see fig. 3.1). Elite failure to conquer fully these areas likely affected their ideas of the forests that lie beyond. As the war ended in a stalemate (Dumond 1997a), Spanish-speaking combatants and their Maya supporters were confined to the peninsula's northwest. Mayans in these areas later became slaves to local plantations. Rebel Maya retreated south, including to the area now bordering Calakmul's Biosphere Reserve.

Among the new southerners, historians distinguish three groups.

The most famous retreated to Chan Santa Cruz, currently the town of Felipe Carrillo Puerto in Quintana Roo state. A second group clustered around the village of Ixkanhá near the Reserve's northeastern corner. Finally, a third group joined residents of La Pimienta to form the village of Icaiché (ibid.). All three groups were sovereign over the lands they claimed. Santa Cruz and Icaiché Maya repeatedly raided British Honduras and received logging fees from British companies. These raids were part of a perpetual instability among the rebel groups, the British, and the Mexicans. Mexico continued to make territorial claims to British Honduras and provided the Icaiché with weapons to harass the British. The British, in turn, armed the Santa Cruz Maya, who acted aggressively against Ixkanhá and Icaiché. This geopolitics continued for more than half a century. Only with the advent of the chicle industry in the twentieth century did the peninsula's balance of power change (Baranda 1873; Dumond 1997a; Sullivan 1989).

Given assertions in 1995 that Calakmul was depopulated until the early twentieth century, it is worth asking how many Maya lived in Ixkanhá and Icaiché. What happened to these people? Dumond reports 8,000 to 10,000 people living in these communities around 1885, although state estimates inflated the total to 15,000. Dumond also describes these populations as fluid and under considerable demographic pressure. In addition to the tensions of war, rebels had to deal with diseases such as smallpox, malaria, and hepatitis (Dumond 1997a, 1997b).

Despite these pressures, rebel Maya retained their independence into the 1900s. Their decline was possible only when Mexico signed a border treaty with the British. Mexican authorities were motivated to make peace by companies seeking timber on indigenous lands. The treaty stemmed Icaiché raids, while the new alliance gave British loggers a means to stop paying rents. This turn of events suggests the development of a nation-state was not sufficient to end indigenous autonomy in Calakmul. Mexico required an international order of nation-states to subjugate autonomous peoples.[1]

The people of Ixkanhá and Icaiché were then subject to a gradual, often ineffectual, bureaucratic conquest. In a strategy that would resurface during the 1990s, authorities built roads to connect rebel settlements to areas under Mexican control (Dumond 1997b). A government reorganization created a municipio out of Ixkanhá and Icaiché, thereby undercutting the indigenous generals who formerly commanded the areas. Even still, state agents could be ambivalent in following through on their aims. Dumond describes how, in 1885, the people of Ixkanhá built a school in anticipation of a promised teacher whom authorities never commissioned (Dumond 1997a:118). Campeche authorities, who would have overseen this bureaucratic conquest, were likely hampered by their sense of a state in demographic crisis.

Officials of Campeche, always one of Mexico's least populated states, worried about their state's few inhabitants. The Caste War had halved Campeche residents to 89,000 (Martínez Alomía 1991). Plantation owners complained of too few workers to staff haciendas. Campeche pundits fretted about a lack of local industry, out-migration by the state's youth, and their failure to produce a professional class. One group even lobbied to have Campeche declared a federal territory to bolster the state's finances. Opponents of the proposition countered the state had a sufficient population. The problem lay in population dispersion, including those Maya in territory outside state control. This faction argued for a "self-colonization" (Sierra 1991:310) to utilize the state's "rich natural products" (Martínez Alomía 1991:207). These plans had few direct results but presaged state support for the chicle industry, which would attract powerful outsiders while resolving questions of finance and territorial control.

Although most of Calakmul was unoccupied when tappers arrived, newspapers from 1935 show the Icaiché, at least, continued to control desirable territory. In the early 1930s, Icaiché's leaders still received rents from logging companies (*Quintana Roo: Album Monográfico* 1995). Mexican agents visited Icaiché as dignitaries visiting a foreign country. Yet, also in 1935, newspapers report the Icaiché willingly abandoned their homes to escape the "wicked exploitation" of chicle contractors (ibid.:218). They moved to a town that, as part of a government resettlement scheme, held the promise of running water and schools. In this way, Icaiché's people appear as both fiercely independent and passive victims of the chicle industry. Could the Icaiché really have acted of their own accord in surrendering independence and claims to vast forests? Dumond (1997b) writes the group was forcibly removed, after which the Icaichés' home became a shipping point for chicle. In the 1990s, a tapper recalled the site's size. Much bigger than a camp, he said, Icaiché was a town.

Calakmul and Chicle Colonialism

Events at Icaiché coincided with Calakmul's expanded incorporation into global economies. Chicle extraction alone was not responsible for this change. Even though Calakmul's official history depicted chicle and timber extraction as two discrete periods, people living in the area since midcentury report the continuous coexistence of chicle tapping, logging, and farming. Published accounts further describe chicle's boom as financed by U.S. companies who, since the late 1800s, held timber concessions in Campeche (Ponce Jiménez 1990). These perspectives of blended regimes suggest successful market incursions in Calakmul required a multifaceted assault. While this process might be summarized within the rubric of globalization, the very term *globalization* can obscure the variety of beliefs and social arrangements that make such processes possible (Escobar 1999). The official history distinguishes between chicle and timber for a reason. Teasing out the industries' distinctions, we see the variable connections between power and environment.

When the U.S. fad for chewing gum took off in the 1910s, Mexico became the world's largest producer of the resin and Campeche its most productive state (Konrad 1991). Commonly believed to relieve tension, gum was included in the rations of WWI soldiers. The U.S. Department of Defense retained a role in chicle exploitation through WWII, when it became the world's largest purchaser of the resin (Ponce Jiménez 1990:5–9). Just as WWII brought chicle production to all time highs, research saw the development of a synthetic substitute for chicle. By 1947, Campeche and Calakmul's chicle-based economy came to an end.

During the thirty years prior to 1947, Campeche was essentially a colony of U.S. gum manufacturers. As much as 95 percent of Mexico's chicle harvests were bought by U.S. companies. These same companies, such as William Wrigley Jr. and Leaf Gum Co. of Chicago, held chicle concessions and financed Mexican contractors to carry out harvests. In doing so, chicle companies amassed vast land holdings. In 1940, a single U.S. company controlled more than 1,140,000 acres of forest (ibid.), an area two-thirds the size of the Calakmul Biosphere Reserve (1,787,000 acres). The industry's influence was formidable. In 1940, taxes from chicle tapping contributed 63 percent of Campeche state revenues (Ponce Jiménez 1990:36).

In her assessment of the industry, Ponce Jiménez describes negligible state intervention in chicle operations before the mid-1930s. At that time, changed federal policies declared chicle a public resource and mandated the creation of cooperatives that would implement extraction "under the protection and guidance of the federal government" (ibid.:25). U.S. companies named themselves managers of the cooperatives and little changed. In the following decade, a more powerful federal administration, under President Lázaro Cardenas, strengthened the cooperatives. Cardenas linked these changes to the expropriation of U.S. concessions. As part of a national land reform initiative (most famous for the distribution of ejidal lands), concessions were assigned to tappers' cooperatives (ibid:30). Some of these concessions would later form the core of the Calakmul Biosphere Reserve. The reforms, however, were necessarily limited as U.S. companies remained the product's sole buyer.

Beginning with the chicle period, researchers have access to firsthand accounts of forest life in Calakmul. During peak years of production, as many as 20,000 *chicleros*, men who tapped chicle, along with the women who cooked for them, descended into Campeche's forests (ibid.:13). Chicleros kept town residences but spent as long as nine months of the year in forest camps. The *centrales*, where chicleros built airplane landing strips, storage houses, and offices, were more or less permanently occupied. Xpujil was one of these. Between forest and town, chicleros built a new social hierarchy that was simultaneously rigid and volatile. They described forest life as dangerously thrilling.

Documenting the lives of elderly chicleros, Ponce Jiménez decries industry conditions but admits that tapping offered many an improved standard of living. Chicle workers of the 1920s were mainly Mayans, experimenting with freedom from peninsular haciendas. An elderly woman recalled conditions on the estates: "When someone wanted to leave the estate . . ., they had to ask permission. Sometimes, they gave you permission, but first they spit and, when you returned, if their saliva had already dried up, they gave you two whippings. . . . They chose our husbands for us, and if you didn't want to marry, . . . they gave you twenty-five lashings and salted you as if you were a deer" (ibid.:41).[2] On the plantations, future chicleros farmed corn and produced sisal rope. In return, workers might receive food rations and two changes of clothes each year. Workers described conditions of permanent food scarcity, and those who found an abundance of game meat in Calakmul's forests would remember this, as well as the pleasure of travel, as chicle's main attractions (ibid.).

Although Mexico's revolution of 1910 legally ended slavery, hacienda rule on the peninsula was slow to change (Knight 1986). As one chiclero recalled: "People heard there was a revolution and that people were free beginning around 1915 . . . [but] nobody distributed lands. That was later with Don Lázaro [Cardenas, president in the 1930s]. They gave the [workers] their freedom, but the patrons didn't lose their estates. When campesinos gained their freedom . . . they went to cut chicle" (Ponce Jiménez 1990:39). Another respondent recalled chicle as the only opportunity for people living where isolation, and, likely, a postwar recession (Knight

1986) inhibited agricultural markets: "I went to cut chicle because there wasn't any work. Some people had land but there wasn't anyone here to buy corn" (Ponce Jiménez 1990:44).

As Mayans traded plantations for distant forests, many still worked for their former overseers. Plantation owners repackaged themselves as contractors to U.S. companies. A former contractor remembered: "They moved from the hacienda to chicle because that was how you earned money. Chicle was good business. I started without a cent and thank God it went well for me. I have a house, a ranch, I raised 4 children, and they all have a professional career" (Ponce Jiménez 1990:43). This story was offered by a Mestizo from Mexico's state of Tabasco. Opportunities for advancement were unlikely for Mayans, whose slave ties took on new shape in the form of debt peonage.

Contractors deducted from chicleros' pay the cost of meals, tapping equipment, and support to a man's family while he was in the forest. Contractors used this debt to cheat tappers, but tappers resisted the fraud. Chicleros in northern Guatemala recall the industry as rife with *engaño* or deceit. People assumed everyone was cheating others out of money whenever possible (Schwartz 1990).

Like oppressed people elsewhere (Tsing 1993), chicleros recast abuses and dangers into a source of pride. Malaria, venereal disease, and leishmaniasis (a mosquito-born disease akin to leprosy) were ever-present ailments in chicle camps. Former chicleros, in the 1990s, remembered most the threat of snake bites. With an air of bravado, one described how the only hope for a person bit by the venomous fer-de-lance required slicing the skin so rushing blood would carry the poison out of the body. Calakmul's chiclero families still keep in mind men who made pacts with forest spirits to increase their harvest, ant eaters who dared men to test their strength in an arm wrestling contest, and jaguar who, placing their paws in a man's own footsteps, silently followed chicleros through the forest. These mystical associations operated as a subtext in Calakmul, as scientific ideas of the environment dominated in public realms (see also Haenn 1999).

Hidden beliefs and resistances are even less accessible in historical records. In stressing the industry's exploitation, Ponce Jiménez says little about people's creative reactions to those conditions. Nonetheless, the interviewees hint that chicleros were establishing a new social world in Calakmul by transforming gender relations and creating a new ethnic dynamic.

In the camps, Mayan chicleros helped build a multiethnic society, dominated by men. Although connection is not causality, the principles of ethnic and gender difference established in these sites resonate with how these issues played out later in Calakmul. Peninsular haciendas tended to be ethnically homogeneous, and tapping represented many Mayans' first contact with distinct ethnic groups who shared their social class. They met men from the counties of Tuxpan and Balancan in the states of Veracruz and Tabasco, respectively. Chicle collection first began in these states. Experienced Tuxpeños and Balancanos, as they were called, taught their craft to Mayan recruits (Ponce Jiménez 1990:74). By the 1990s, when migrant points of departure had multiplied, state-of-origin replaced county-based identities. New migrants from Tuxpan and Balancan would adopt and be ascribed the monikers Veracruzano and Tabasqueño.

Like earlier municipio-based identities, state-of-origin operated as an ethnic marker. Ethnic differences were structured partly around physical aggression, where isolated forests stood as both metaphors and sites of asocial behavior. "The Tuxpeños were really bad," a Maya chiclero recalled, "all machete wielding. . . . Life in the forest was difficult, really tough. . . . The law of the jungle ruled. Now, whenever there's a place with a lot of men and just one or two women, there are problems. But, a place without women is terrible" (ibid.:54). Below, I return to questions of violence in Calakmul's history. A prominent point in this commentary is the way people built gender differences around notions of aggression.

Women, sometimes accompanying chiclero husbands, worked as cooks and launderers. Socially, women also were assigned the impracticable task of reigning in men's violent and sexual energies. The task was impracticable because male aggression was defined as innate. Nonetheless, the scarcity of women in the camps also gave them a limited authority. A tapper described how some "men . . . signed on according to who would be cooking in the camp. . . . The female element in the kitchen was basic. . . . To put it another way, a good cook controlled the chicleros" (ibid.:56).

In campesino communities, this advantage to women's status would be lost, while men continued to hold women responsible for men's transgressions. The gender dynamics that arise in the following chapters mark this phenomenon. Women's enduringly defensive position may have roots in chicle camps, where women were beholden to the same men who would harm them. A former cook shows the ambivalence arising from this contradiction: "The chicleros weren't crude, only if you started to play with them. Me? I entered my kitchen and if some son of a bitch came to screw me over (chingar), I grabbed my machete and I went after him" (ibid.:69–70).

Schwartz believes chicleros' violent reputations were exaggerated and, instead, reflected industry conditions (Schwartz 1990). Tappers operated under a captain who could not supervise people scattered in the forest. The very fact of autonomy incited in contractors images of unruliness, which contractors then used to rationalize their abuses. Tappers might participate in this fabrication and use their reputation to draw a line on overseers' power (ibid.:184). Exaggerated or not, the chicle industry created an atmosphere of fear and violence linked to concrete acts. Possibly, this was a transformation of hacienda norms with the difference that all social groups now held out the possibility of violence. The impunity of hacienda owners then became a more general impunity.

This discussion expands our understanding of what it meant for campesinos and government agents alike that, in the 1990s, Calakmul still had a reputation for autonomy and rebelliousness. Learning just what this reputation meant could be difficult, as expectations of violence often were shrouded in silence. This silence related to people's impotence in containing violence, but also to the way that violence was so common as to go without saying. When people did discuss violence, they employed practical and mythical concerns that reflected how, until the late 1990s, campesinos at Calakmul had to rely on vigilante justice. An indigenous man's description of early-twentieth-century justice in his home state of Chiapas could apply to Calakmul in the 1990s. Justice, he said, was "one's own strength (La justicia entre ellos era la propia fuerza). Justice was, if someone rubs me the wrong way, he dies right there." Vigilantism had its own dangers, and many campesinos moved to Calakmul precisely because they did not have the wherewithal to defend themselves under these terms (see chap. 4). At the same time, people's cosmological beliefs distinguished between individual crimes and a more general atmosphere of lawlessness.

While individual crimes could be addressed, people noted the existence of cycles of violence that lie outside human control. These cycles were rooted in particular locales. Along with Calakmul's Mestizos, the man noted above believed an unnatural death—an accident as well as a violent death—poisons the place where the death occurred: "Evil takes hold in the earth, and, as they say, it has to look for food to sustain it. And, while evil reigns, it has to do bad (tiene que hacer mal)." Campesinos living in ejidos free of unnatural deaths took comfort in this knowledge. They noted how, elsewhere, a car crash or a murder had resulted in additional deaths in that same locale. Was there some way to cleanse a place of this stain? Through roadside shrines and home altars, campesinos could incorporate the departed into their ritual lives, but they had no means to counter the larger forces of evil.

This is not to say the contexts surrounding violence remained the same throughout the twentieth century. During Calakmul's chicle era, violence was framed by industry hierarchies and new concepts of agency arising from the demise of Yucatán's slave economy. Agricultural colonization (see below) appears to have intensified the use of violence while adding to it an agrarianism built on patron-client ties. While I have depicted violence as intra-chiclero and intra-campesino phenomena, reconsideration of the state in Calakmul shows government authorities were always complicit in these acts.

Comparing chiclero accounts with Calakmul's official history, we find that one of the most marked differences is the former's depiction of an enduring state presence. The industry's foundation in the hacienda system and U.S. colonialism affirm that local chicle managers acted as extensions of government interests. To a certain extent, for chicleros, contractors were the government, the principal authority governing their lives through debt and violence. I also draw this conclusion from interviews with one of Calakmul's few remaining sawmill managers. He remembered his constant visits to authorities in the Campeche capital. Timber companies collaborated with authorities on issues such as expanding state, as opposed to federal, land holdings in Calakmul. In the 1950s, timber managers housed and formed fictive kin ties with military officers on maneuver near Mexico's border with Guatemala. When chicle markets collapsed, timber companies inherited the clout left by the weakened industry. The two regimes continued to coexist in Calakmul, but their managers had no formal dealings. Chicle collection remained in the hands of the cooperatives, while timber companies became the main arbiters connecting Campeche to U.S. markets. Chicleros fell outside the timber companies' discriminating social visions, such that even while the industries' low-skilled workers might blur their boundaries, the industries appeared distinct from elite perspectives.

An Intertwined Timber and Farming Economy

Here, I describe the management and public relations practices of Caobas Mexicanas, a timber company that dominated Calakmul from the 1940s through the 1980s. Chicle and timber industries continued to share logistical features, such as camps and reliance on air transportation.

Caobas, however, differed from any chicle company or contractor in its self-promotion. Caobas succeeded in making itself, rather than logging, the primary symbol of its enterprise. Caobas was also unique in drawing on paternalistic U.S. corporate practices and self-consciously establishing a new social dominion in Calakmul. In particular, Caobas built a showcase town of Zoh Laguna. There, Caobas fashioned an atmosphere of grandeur overseen by a new middle class. Always dependent on U.S. markets, Caobas nonetheless effectively portrayed itself as an independent power. For the bottom-rung laborers on which the industry depended, Caobas's symbolic strength affected a relatively weak identity construction. The chicle industry produced pronounced chiclero identities that find little counterpart in logging. Where themes of violence indicated the challenge chicleros posed to their managers, challenges to timber would come from outside the industry. As Calakmul's farm population grew, these residents would use their identity as campesinos to oppose Caobas.

No detailed history of Caobas exists, but visitors to Calakmul encounter the company's legacy in Zoh Laguna, a town of 1,000 people (INEGI 2001a). Throughout the 1990s, Zoh Laguna served as a base for nearly all research conducted on the region. Zoh Laguna also housed the offices of the Calakmul Biosphere Reserve and Calakmul's four nongovernmental groups working in conservation-development. In Zoh Laguna's conservation klatch, newcomers learned of the town's former glory. In its heyday, Caobas sponsored a pharmacy and a Catholic church (see chap. 1). The company delivered electricity and piped water. Although environmentalists decried Caobas's exploitative practices, I sensed that environmental managers would adopt Caobas's stature and envied the company's ability to force environmental outcomes.

Those outcomes were billed as triumphs by Caobas's founder, Alfredo Medina. Medina's biography informs both manager's reminiscences and a 1951 *Reader's Digest* feature, both of which suggest a man who deftly wove U.S.-style capitalism with the personality politics of Mexican patron-client ties. A resident of Yucatán state, the young Medina held an engineering degree from New York's Rensselaer Polytechnic and began his career with financing from his family's sisal plantation. In the *Digest* article, Medina acts with the ease and foresight of an enlightened executive. In the course of five pages, he convinces skeptical bankers to finance his 2,100,000-acre logging concession in Yucatán state, courts U.S. furniture makers, forsakes upper-class dandyism by engaging in manual labor, and passes over the "vagabonds and fugitives" found in chicle camps to hire better quality workers at elevated salaries (Benjamin 1951). By the time

Medina began a new "conquest" in Zoh Laguna, he had opened offices in Mexico City and signed on a U.S. forester to manage his operations (ibid.:24).

A manager for Caobas, Don Adolfo, remembered how this activism, as applied to Zoh Laguna, drew on policies of U.S. companies. In building a company town, Medina regulated everything from housing design (modeled after houses he saw in Texas) to farm animals. This approach would have been congruent with Medina's hacienda experience, and Medina's real innovation may have lain in the way he mapped the hacienda model onto a capitalist enterprise.

Medina was also different in the extent of his national connections. He worked in Calakmul just when nationalization of forested lands was dealing a blow to logging operations elsewhere in Mexico (Collier 1994). Just how Medina thrived in this setting is unclear, but evidence of his success lies in Zoh Laguna's construction. In the late 1940s, Medina used his connections to recruit a group of WWII Polish refugees then living in northern Mexico. As Zoh Laguna's original social core, these men provided an instant set of services as bakers, cobblers, and carpenters. The Polish contingent lasted only a few years. Don Adolfo remembered the men as "turned inside out by the war," and they left for other destinations. By the time of their departure, the Poles had carved Zoh Laguna out of surrounding forests, and Caobas was exporting mahogany and Spanish cedar to U.S. markets.

Demystifying Medina's personal claims, three factors hinted at thus far appear critical to Caobas's success: Medina's use of local hierarchical norms, technological innovations that allowed access to Campeche's forests, and Caobas's close ties with U.S. markets. I take each point in turn.

In addition to his connections, Medina was a native of Mérida city in Yucatán state, a fact that would have impinged on his work in Campeche. First as a colonial-era capital and later as the peninsula's economic capital, Mérida has long held the advantage in its rivalry with Campeche city. Medina's Campeche conquest, and comparisons between timber and chicle regimes, should be considered in light of Yucatán's assumption of privilege toward its neighbor. Medina largely recruited people like Don Adolfo and Doña Belén and her family from his home state. Traveling constantly between the Campeche capital, Zoh Laguna, and Caobas's camp- sites, Don Adolfo earned the nickname "The Duke." The royal analogy was apt. Don Adolfo's reminiscences are catalogs of governors and powerful people with whom he closely identifies. His neighbors, who maintain close ties to Yucatán, still consider themselves a kind of cultural establishment.

Technologically, Calakmul's conquest depended on motorized vehicles and road construction. Relative to other parts of tropical Mexico, logging in Campeche was delayed by more than half a century. Logging in neighboring Chiapas and Tabasco saw its augur in the nineteenth century, when loggers used waterways to transport timber to coastal cities (de Vos 1996). Calakmul's lack of streams hindered timber harvests until the invention of planes and automobiles. As director of Medina's construction company, Don Adolfo oversaw road work that included the 250-kilometer paved segment that still connects Calakmul to the nearest port. While road construction was under way, Caobas relied on airplanes to transport materials. *Reader's Digest* described Zoh Laguna as "literally created out of thin air" (Benjamin 1951:124). According to Don Adolfo, U.S. companies facilitated this creation by paying for timber in diesel fuel.

Although none of Medina's companies were subsidiaries of U.S. enterprises, Medina's connection to U.S. ventures could hardly be closer. Until the early 1960s, most timber leaving Zoh Laguna traveled via Cuba to Jacksonville, Florida. Throughout 1946–47, U.S. buyers posted staffers to Zoh Laguna to ensure the milled three-ply met their specifications. Caobas continued to host potential U.S. buyers into the 1960s, on one occasion flying in a mariachi band to entertain U.S. guitar manufacturers.

Don Adolfo cites Medina's death in the early 1980s as causing the company's decline, but I wonder at the effects of changing ecological and political landscapes. Beginning in the 1960s, Caobas incorporated Calakmul's growing farm population into its work. Most of these people were Mayan, originally recruited to work in logging. Managers allowed farming on lands adjacent to mill towns, a scheme they likely found advantageous. Local food production aided an industry otherwise dependent on imports. Subsistence farmers also supplied a reserve of contingent workers. The first wave of ejidal formation took place during the 1960s in these same mill towns, where Caobas continued its managerial role by appointing ejidal authorities. People occupying former camps also recalled being pressured by state agrarian officers to sell timber to Caobas, ostensibly to recoup monies paid to process ejidal claims. Campesinos resented this arrangement, but wherever possible, Caobas controlled tensions by backing ejidal strongmen or *caciques*.

Although *cacique* can have many meanings, for the moment, Sabloff's definition is useful (see also chap. 4). She describes a cacique as someone who "with the help of a small group of followers, controls the economic, political, and sometimes even the social activity of the members of that community. He gains and maintains control through various means—patronage, coercion, co-optation, [and] violence" (Sabloff 1981:1). Caciques usually have close ties to the state. At Calakmul, caciques' power rested partly on monopolizing timber sales. Timber was one of the few local sources of cash. Timber was so crucial to migrants' survival of periodic droughts, a campesino opponent of Caobas still insisted in 1995: "Timber is what maintains life here. You have to sell wood in order to plant crops, to keep on living."

Disputes between campesinos and Caobas were most acute in Zoh Laguna, and understandings of local history are shaded by the way Zoh Laguna acts as an entry for research. Zoh Laguna's peasants agitated for nationalization of the land they farmed and even the mill itself, a battle that ended only in 1996. Campesinos who led this struggle emphasized local, rather than international, connections in narratives that depict timber agents and campesinos in sharp contrast. These generic notions of frontier hardship, however, obscure the way campesinos held different positions in respect to Caobas. An exploration of these positions suggests colonization was an uneven process. On the one hand restricted by environmental and economic conditions, colonization was facilitated by social structures built on violence and exploitation of the area's newest arrivals.

Diverse Strands of Colonization

As with other sites on Mexico's southern frontier (Gates 1993), some people in Calakmul were directed to the area by agrarian offices in their home states. At the same time, three local strands of colonization fostered a more expansive migration into the area. The first strand entailed those farmers who worked in mill towns. These families moved into logging and chicle camps, converting these into permanent settlements. The second strand consisted of Mayans from Campeche state, sent to the area by Campeche authorities. Arriving in the late 1960s and early 1970s, these migrants formed a second wave of ejidal establishment initiated at the state (rather than federal) level. The third strand included a series of local caciques who encouraged a colonization that bolstered their power and wealth. In this section, I focus on these latter two. Altogether, these strands opened the way for the majority of Calakmul's people who describe themselves as arriving on the advice of family and friends already living in the region.

Although researchers describe Mexico's agricultural frontier as driven by land pressures in the country's populous north (Arizpe et al. 1996), campesinos in Calakmul mainly originate from southern Mexico,

with colonization initiated partly by issues internal to Campeche. Historically, Campeche's population has clustered along the Gulf of Mexico coast.
In the early 1970s, these communities were stressed by economic stagna-
tion and land scarcity. Some towns responded by applying to the state for
an *ampliación*, an extension to an ejido's existing lands. Although such
extensions belonged to the ejido as a whole, people listed on the petition
were expected to occupy the new site. My analysis here draws on research
in three Calakmul communities founded as extensions to towns located
hundreds of miles away. In the legalization process, these extensions were
reclassified as independent ejidos. Nonetheless, the notion of an extension
affected the commitment with which coastal migrants approached their
new homes.[3]

The ejido of Eden typified these hesitant resettlements that generally
foundered on ecological constraints. Eden was occupied in the late 1960s
by twenty-four men from the town of Calkiní, while paperwork legalizing
their situation was still in process. The group included a network of relatives, many of whose wives remained in Calkiní. These relations became
the community's lifeline when Eden experienced a three-year drought.
Town wives supported their families by selling hammocks and foodstuffs.
As the drought continued, an increasing number of men abandoned the
colonization effort. By the late 1970s, Calkiní's economic situation was
improved, and government work programs in town attracted all but one
of the original settlers, Don Gerardo.

Although extensions generally failed as settlement schemes, their
initiators reacted differently to this failure, spawning diverse trajectories
thereafter. In another extension reduced to four of its original 229 colonists, the Mayans were approached by fifteen Tabasco migrants who requested residence in the ejido. Fearing the newcomers would politically
displace them, the Mayans decided to create a multiethnic ejido, where no
single state-of-origin would gain majority. Don Gerardo's situation contrasted in important ways. Eden's legalization was nearing completion just
when the community had disbanded. Determined not to lose ten years of
work, Don Gerardo urgently searched for a solution as an abandoned
Eden caught the attention of land hungry migrants. Men from the state of
Zacatecas offered to buy his land. Don Gerardo refused, but the Zacate-
cans insisted and came armed with shotguns to press their point. Fearing he would be killed whether he sold the land or not, Don Gerardo
contrived for Eden's immediate recolonization. He invited nearby Ch'ol
Maya to relocate to Eden. Ch'ol and Yucatec Maya are both indigenous
groups, but they speak distinct languages and have different histories.

Don Gerardo believed that this common indigenous status would be enough to build bonds. In the space of a month, the Ch'ol brought kin from their home state of Chiapas, and these newcomers dominated Eden's ejidal assembly.

Any goodwill evaporated as the Ch'ol resisted Don Gerardo's cacique postures, including his brokerage role with Caobas. When I spoke with him in 2001, Gerardo resented that his land battles had not translated into power within his ejido. In aspiring to be a cacique, however, Don Gerardo argued Mayans were distinct from Ch'ol in their peaceful ways: "Mayans lost the tradition of doing evil." Here, Don Gerardo used the word *maldad*, which also translates as witchcraft. Ch'ol people, he asserted, harbored resentments toward the state and did not know how to partake in peaceful dialogue. These allegations closely related to government presumptions that Ch'ol were Zapatista sympathizers. Don Gerardo contrasted Mayans with Ch'ol saying, "We are not people of war. We are people of peace." If Don Gerardo indeed rejected violence, he may have been unusual in this regard. Calakmul's caciques often used physical force to shape their communities.

Throughout the 1970s and 1980s, various men (rarely a woman) built personal fiefs in Calakmul, by inviting family, friends, and acquaintances to settle former camps. Achieving a population mass was necessary to the ejido granting process. These men, however, had no interest in the ejido's democratic aspects. The son of one of these men explained his father first sought to convert a camp into his private ranch. But, agrarian authorities requested a bribe the family could not afford. The family then sought settlers whose names and financial help they used to request an ejido grant. After an ejido's founding, these men overpowered their neighbors as they brokered the sale of ejidal timber (some had worked for Caobas), sold abandoned homes to new arrivals, and otherwise sought to transform their neighbors into a source of revenue. Taking a cue from the chicle industry, caciques might own stores in isolated areas. Some colonists thus depended on caciques for access to consumer goods and the jobs to pay for such items.

As an expedient way to legalize settlements, the ejido also connected people to development aid and state patronage. Campesino activists in the 1990s condemned government inattention, but documents kept by ejidos show that officials had a focused presence in Calakmul. As early as 1975, campesinos received state credits for corn production. These funds appear so important that one ejido's archives for the early 1980s are silent on all policies other than loan amounts. Caciques benefited disproportionately from state programs. For example, ejidal documents show a 1985 community credit designated for ten beneficiaries was divided such that two men, the cacique and his son, received 82 percent of the funds. As elsewhere in Mexico (DeWalt 1979; Lomnitz-Adler 1992; Sabloff 1981), state agents ruled through Calakmul's caciques. These men are still careful to mention their ties to elected politicians and the PRI machinery. Although their fortunes vary, at a minimum, caciques enjoy a security in food and land tenure not shared by their neighbors.

Caciques intimidated their neighbors into silence (Parra Mora and Hernández Díaz 1994), and people willing to recall their reign habitually found they had no words. Instead, they made a fist to describe cacique rule. Caciques often led coalitions of family and friends who tolerated financial excesses in return for a share in the spoils and protection from social volatility. In places like San Lorenzo, this structure included measures of consensus and accountability. People there were able to build a fairly harmonious community life. In the worst of cases, caciques sponsored campaigns of terror (Haenn 2002).

Prior to the 1990s, this intravillage violence added to Calakmul's inhospitable farming conditions and poor job opportunities to drive a constant population turnover. Between 1980 and 1995, Calakmul saw a population growth of 400 percent, from 6,800 inhabitants to 24,000 people (Ericson et al. 1999). At the same time, research in the late 1980s found it not uncommon that ejidal communities might be settled three times over in response to repeated out-migrations (Boege and Murguía 1989). In this tenuous setting, campesinos drew heavily on the ejido as a minimum point of commonality. At this point, I want to examine the ejido in greater depth as its structure helps explain much of what follows in subsequent chapters.

The Ejido in Calakmul

In 1995, campesinos in Calakmul controlled their lands through two institutions: the ejido and the Regional Council. The organizations were related. Membership in the Regional Council first required membership in an ejido.

In its current form, the ejido has its roots in Mexico's revolution of 1910. Broadly speaking, peasant armies fought the war to counter land concentration (Haber 1996; Hart 1987; Nugent 1993). Alan Knight writes, "The Mexican revolution . . . was fundamentally . . . popular, rural, and agrarian in character, and heavily dependent on peasant participation" (Knight 1998:27). Events relating to the war and its outcome varied throughout Mexico (Otero 1999). At a national level, however, negotiations to end the fighting had to respond to peasant demands for land. The Mexican Constitution of 1917 thus included Article 27 in which peasants and land reform (in the form of ejidos) became a foundation for building the new state. In subsequent decades, Mexican authorities equivocated on their promises to the peasantry. Most significant, in 1991, state agents altered Article 27, ceased their promises of land distribution, and opened the way for ejidal privatization. (I discuss these changes further in chap. 5). Even with these modifications, state agents have been unable to escape the notion that, for many of Mexico's rural dwellers (perhaps 25 percent of Mexico's total population),[4] revolutionary ideals justify the state's very existence (Collier 1994). This is why the ideals and practices surrounding Article 27 had such an impact on conservation programming.

Via the original Article 27, the state gave a defined group of people (usually men) the right to utilize an extension of land, while the state retained actual ownership. For example, in Orozco, residents retained legal papers that declared twenty-eight *ejidatarios* (people with vested rights in a particular ejido) had the right to work the 2,603 hectares of land comprising their community. The documentation outlined the ejido's geographic coordinates and stipulated that each ejidatario have access to 50 hectares of land. Orozcans had divided their lands so that each ejidatario independently managed 50 hectares of contiguous land, what they called their *parcelas* or farm parcels. After division, the ejido had a surplus of 1,203 hectares of common land, known as *el común*.[5] Between common lands and unfarmed bits of parcelas, the ejido placed significant amounts of forested land in campesino hands.

Because the state retained ultimate authority over ejido lands, the ejido acted as a bridge between its members and Mexican rulers. At Calakmul, this bridge was noticeable in the two names assigned to many communities, one a camp name and the other an ejidal name, usually related to state history. When Icaiché was recognized as an ejido, the town became "Josefa Ortiz de Domínguez" (a protagonist in Mexico's war for independence). As an ejido, Zoh Laguna became "General Álvaro Obregón" (a figure in Mexico's revolutionary war). Camp names expressed people's aspirations and the obstacles they found to realizing their dreams: Scorpions, Muddy Waters, Sacrifice, The Refuge, New Life. Ejidal names aimed to incorporate places into a national mythology. The persistence of dual names underscored the tension between these state efforts and an order arising sui generis out of local experiences.

Authorities created ejidos at Calakmul over the course of forty years, when changing ideas about how campesinos might support themselves resulted in radically different land bases. These difference would result in communities' distinct positions vis-à-vis natural resource management and Reserve-Council programming. Like Orozco, San Lorenzo was considered small because it had just 1,750 hectares for twenty-four ejidatarios, each of whom had rights to 20-hectare parcels. Large ejidos may house more than a hundred ejidatarios, each with access to 150 hectares of farmland, in addition to a reserve of some 20,000 hectares designated for forestry activities. These *eijdos forestales* or forestry ejidos formed only a handful of Calakmul communities, and members of these ejidos combined farming with work in forestry. Most campesinos lived in small ejidos where their size and forest quality made extractive activities largely unworkable.

Within this framework, resources available to individual ejidal members varied further still. Rather than think of the prescribed ejidatario/land ratio as fixed, most ejidal members used these numbers as a point of departure. Ejidal members regularly accepted more ejidatarios than was legal. Accordingly, the amount of land they held in parcels and in common was changeable. Also, state documentation belied the fact that neither ejidal nor parcel boundaries were known with precision. People commonly worried neighbors might manipulate boundaries to usurp land. Campesinos lived with a keen awareness that land distribution as outlined in ejidal documentation rarely matched land distribution on the ground (a tension between policy and practice that would apply to conservation). And, even though these differences were often the result of decisions agreed upon by ejidal members themselves, in disputes over who should have which land and how much of it, campesinos never forsook the ejido's documentation as basic material for asserting land claims.

These kinds of arguments usually took place in the context of the assembly of ejidatarios, described legally as the "maximum organization" in the ejido (Procuraduría Agraria 1993). Assemblies were critical sites of governance within the ejido. Ejidal assemblies ruled on questions ranging from road repair to participation in development schemes to who qualified to farm ejido lands. Many land use decisions rest on how the decision might affect neighborly relations. Assemblies were supposed to be based on democratic norms, but in practice, ejidos often operated through factional politics or cacique rule, both of which could be affected by state policies. Ejidatarios' control was never perfect, but they insisted on the prerogative to order their communities. In this regard, the law stipulated a specific governing structure, one that proved onerous for small ejidos.

Ejidatarios voted thirteen office holders and another thirteen men to act as stand-ins for these positions. Ejidal offices were divided into three committees. In Calakmul's ejidos, the Ejidal Commission (Comisariado Ejidal) held the most authority. The Commission's president, sometimes referred to as the ejido's president, was often the most powerful man in the community. He presided over assemblies and relations between the ejido and extra-ejidal bodies. The Commission's treasurer controlled ejidal funds (scarce as they were). The ejido's second most powerful officer was president of the Oversight Council (Consejo de Vigilancia). This committee acted as a check against the first to ensure that it followed legal procedure. Otherwise, the president of the Oversight Committee was charged with keeping track of who had rights to what land. Finally, the Muncipal Committee (Agente Municipal) oversaw internal ejidal affairs. The president of this committee dealt with crimes perpetrated by ejidal members against one another. All committees included a president, secretary, and treasurer (some of whose duties were essentially nonexistent), but the Municipal Committee also included three police officers. In both San Lorenzo and Orozco, young men were pressed into serving as low-prestige policemen. Their main job entailed notifying ejidal members of an impending assembly.

Ejidatarios struggled to fill this list of offices, even as the ejido structure was replicated in Calakmul's conservation-development agenda. The Reserve-Council required that each project in an ejido include a supervisory committee composed of a president, treasurer, secretary, and oversight council. To give a sense of how much work these offices entailed, Orozco, which had room for twenty-eight ejidatarios, housed only nineteen men eligible for ejidal offices. This paucity of candidates meant that finding people willing and competent to carry out committee duties was difficult. This fact opened the way for ambitious men who generally focused on two crucial offices, the presidents of the Ejidal and Oversight Commissions.[6] As with the Reserve-Council committees, ejidal power holders rotated through these offices or controlled them from behind the scenes. Many officers acted as delegates to the Regional Council. In this way, ejidal officers transformed power within the ejido into a platform for cultivating outside contacts.

Despite this elaborate governing mechanism, ejidatarios were less able to control their lands when faced with state directives. Throughout Mexico, the ejido has served as a tool of political control as much as land management (compare Gupta 1998). Not unusually, state agents might negate the legality of assembly decisions (de Janvry et al. 1997). Gerardo

Otero explains how state agents have decreed what ejidatarios could plant, how much fertilizer ejidatarios should apply to crops, and other farming details (Otero 1999). Poor ejidatarios could be forced to follow state directives because, often, they were indebted to the state for subsidizing their farming. Ejidatario bondage has been such that Otero found, in some places, the state's Ejido Bank referred to ejidatarios working outside its programs as "free ejidatarios" (ibid.:86). This level of interference was not present at Calakmul, although people had cause to watch for its possibility. State subsidies made up a large share of household incomes (see chap. 6), and people were wary of what would be asked of them in return.

Despite these fears, Calakmul's campesinos continually lobbied for state aid. Not only was aid an economic necessity, but campesinos viewed aid as an appropriate (if troubled) form of state attention. The practice also imputed legitimacy to state agents who, through aid, appeared to care for campesinos. Calakmul's conservation-development agenda fell under this rubric. For many campesinos, conservation-development was the fruition of a decades-long battle for state support.

Campesino Organizing and Conservation

Throughout the 1970s and 1980s, campesinos pressed for a place upstream in the logging industry. In considering the history of campesino organizing in Calakmul, these paragraphs finish outlining the background to local conservation efforts. For decades, campesinos sought government help to exploit their natural resources. When state agents finally committed to a campesino-based economy, they did so within the unanticipated framework of conservation. This change forced a renegotiation of campesino-state relations, one in which conservation became mapped onto development.

Campesinos' first victory in gaining a foothold in logging came in the 1970s, when the Union of Forested Ejidos successfully petitioned Campeche authorities for small, mobile saws. Located in a few ejidos, the saws briefly allowed campesinos to compete directly with Caobas. Speaking in 1995, Alejandro, a Union activist, recalled that within a few years, the saws fell into disrepair. Campesinos wanted the machinery fixed, but reminiscent of ejidal land tenures, felt they could not touch the saws. Although campesinos had usufruct rights to the machinery, the saws belonged to the government. In the early 1980s, Alejandro moved to legalize the saws as ejidal property. Remembering these endeavors, he claimed the support of Campeche's governor, federal environmental authorities (SARH), and the state's rural bank (Banrural). This backing reportedly angered Calakmul's timber companies. Alejandro caricatured how industry representatives lobbied the governor to stop campesinos: "Those bastards in the Union are against you. In a little while, they'll be overthrowing the state." Industry representatives pressured the state to repeal campesino logging permits and began to label Union members "communists."

Logging companies also struck at Union membership by offering to delimit ejidal boundaries for those communities that dropped their Union affiliation. Recall that boundary maintenance is a persistent worry in Calakmul. Many ejidal leaders took this bait, and the Union saw its membership halve. Remaining affiliates, Alejandro asserted, searched for new ways to "sell our timber at a just price" and prevent the logging companies from "finishing off the forest."

Campesino fortunes again changed around the time the Biosphere Reserve was formed in 1989. Declaration of the Reserve came just when campesinos had made renewed gains in logging. Alejandro remembered the Union was receiving better prices for its timber. Perhaps not coincidentally, about this time, a campesino-based forestry program in neighboring Quintana Roo state was receiving acclaim, and state support, for sustainable harvests (Bray et al. 1993). The political winds were shifting, again, when Calakmul's Reserve posed questions campesinos thought were already settled. Because many ejidos were accidentally included inside the Reserve, campesino access to land was now in doubt. Campesinos who had been working to insert themselves in the timber industry suddenly had to backtrack to protect their land claims. Where campesinos were not always unified in their timber interests, they easily rallied around defense of their land.

I revisit Calakmul's campesino organizations along with the cycling of state attention to the same in chapter 8. Foreshadowing those discussions, I note the resonance of this history with George Collier's work on the cyclical quality of state support for rural peoples. As successive administrations supported first one campesino organization then another, rural people were left to jockey for position as the next favored group (Collier 1987). Although state agents at Calakmul shifted between promoting campesino and promoting logging interests, campesinos, nonetheless, could count on sporadic support. The inevitability of the state's eventual attention (even within an unknown time frame) placed campesinos in the anxious place of figuring out what it would take to procure that attention in the present. In this sense, the Reserve aided campesino claims on the state. Because it was such an egregious betrayal of Article 27, the Reserve gave campesinos a bargaining wedge to hold authorities responsible for their promises. Campesinos were able to force state agents—formerly hidden behind chicle and logging companies—to step forward. As this forcing took place simultaneously with efforts to convert campesinos to PRI voters, it also proved an opportunity for the state. Even more than an ecological crisis, Calakmul's conservation-development agenda provided a momentary response to the crisis of a state and a constituency seeking alternate forms of governance.

History Making

All history making at Calakmul, including my own, takes place within the larger project of creating, sustaining, and comprehending a regional culture in Calakmul (Lomnitz Adler 1992). A common history provides common ground upon which Calakmul's diverse people might communicate. A common history also explains the Reserve and county's geographic boundaries while rationalizing the environment's central, if disputed, role in local governance. In reading across historical sources, I found the official history's inevitable incorporation of Calakmul into global political economies contradicted by the way people have long argued over area forests. I also found the solidity of the official history contrasted with the fluidity of people and boundaries in practice.

Calakmul continues to be imagined differently by distinct people. My history might offer alternative lessons had I taken the perspective, say, of a Campeche city elite. Urbanites compared Calakmul to the United States' "Wild West" of the nineteenth century. They characterized campesinos in Calakmul as fierce (*bravo*) and dangerous (*peligroso*). Calakmul was culturally different in ways distasteful to some Campeche elites. Where Campechens claim a common Maya heritage, Calakmul's ethnic diversity presented problems to the state's cultural unity. Identity is a common political concern on the peninsula, where Campeche's neighbor, Quintana Roo, recently promoted a state slogan aimed at its immigrant population, "Unidos por una misma identidad (United around a single identity)." The creation of the municipio of Calakmul effectively territorialized the problem of an immigrant population by placing colonists within a single governmental frame, where before they were divided between municipios dominated by people of Mayan heritage.

Calakmul's forest-centered history likely helped Campechens incorporate Calakmul's migrants into the state's mythology, even as forest concerns appeared small in comparison to other economic matters. In the 1990s, Campeche's cosmopolitans worried that their state failed to benefit from oil pumped from Campeche Sound (75 percent of national production; *Diario de Yucatán* April 9, 1997). They looked enviously at how tourism has made Quintana Roo (home to Cancún and other mega-resorts) one of Mexico's fastest growing states. In contrast, Mexico's professional classes found Campeche City so lacking in style and services that universities and businesses had difficulty recruiting staff to a place largely perceived as a backwater.

Calakmul's official history makes a nod to these development desires. However, in portending a strong, state-directed economy—one arising out of the conservation-development agenda—the history stumbles on the question of deforestation. Does Calakmul's future necessarily entail deforestation and peasant subjugation to state authorities? What material exists for imagining alternative futures at Calakmul? The answers to these questions lie partly in Calakmul's people themselves, their aspirations, and the material they have to realize those hopes.

4

The Migrant's Journey

In many ways, people in Calakmul are unlike other migrants. At a time when millions of rural Mexicans responded to worsening economic conditions by moving to the United States or to Mexico's cities, people in Calakmul chose to stay in the countryside. Conventional wisdom emphasized that people come to Calakmul in search of land. When I scratched below the surface of this truism, a more complicated story came to light. Although 24,000 people live in Calakmul, at least that number are likely to have left the region after a stay of months or years. Calakmul's appeal and disenchantment speaks to the hopes and pressures facing rural Mexicans. The situation at Calakmul is not unlike other areas where rural residence places people on the fringe of the ideas, symbols, financial structures, and power relationships currently formulated in globally connected cities (see Appadurai 1996). Yet, as the media savvy Zapatistas have shown, this fringe position can provide an effective public platform. Rural dwellers have creatively employed their supposed difference to reshape their relationship to urban centers (Tsing 1993, 1999).

Here, I consider how stories of journeys leading to Calakmul demonstrate both diverse and common experiences of state and environment. Although most campesinos arrived from other rural areas in Mexico, I approach these stories from a postcolonial concern for transnationalism, a position that views distinct places as connected through social relations. As I discuss in the chapter's final section, transnationalism offers a way to think about how experiences of many places contribute to people's diverse constructions of Calakmul. Government-farmer relations at Calakmul form one point within a web of intertwined spatial commitments and identities (Gupta and Ferguson 1997). Migratory journeys show how that web is built partly around the patterned ways government authority acts, and is absent, in people's lives. In light of this absence, immediate social relations take on considerable import, influencing people's access to land and their environmental practices. People readily shared their migration stories with me, although, as I will explain, they also edited their accounts. I first describe how I collected migration histories and, then, move on to explore three migratory journeys in greater depth. I conclude by considering what these stories contribute to postcolonial environmental understandings.

Collecting Migration Stories

Although campesinos talk about their past, they rarely catalog events in the way I report here. These particular stories are the result of semi-structured questioning with twenty-nine households in Orozco and San Lorenzo. I asked the date people arrived at Calakmul, the location of their last four residences (some had moved more than four times, some less), what kinds of jobs they formerly held, whether they previously had access to land and, if so, how much land they held. Finally, I asked why people left their former homes. Although the survey imposed an artificial structure on people's stories, critically, it showed that, despite differences of identity, gender, and work experience, people's shared experiences of strife had left them deeply wary of their neighbors and government authority.

Campesinos in Calakmul came from throughout Mexico, although an overwhelming number originated from the states of Chiapas, Veracruz, and Tabasco (see fig. 1.1). The people of Orozco and San Lorenzo shared this tendency. Nearly all Orozcans and San Lorenzans grew up in rural areas as the children of farmers. For a variety of reasons, these families sought to make a living elsewhere than their home communities. Before arriving to Calakmul, they moved on average 1.5 times. For almost all the families, residence in Calakmul was a secondary choice.

Families tended to arrive to Calakmul when husbands and wives were in their late thirties. Many Orozcans and San Lorenzans came to Calakmul with their extended family, including brothers and sisters who moved together as adults, after establishing separate households. In addition to material aid, family members provided the good neighborly relations that are key to long-term survival in Calakmul's ejidos. People might move to join their family ("We never get used to being alone," one man explained); they also followed family forced to move because of violence or village factionalism.

A decision to move evolved in the context of a couple's own particular dynamics. In some cases, a husband's or wife's decision was definitive: "We came here because my wife didn't like the other place. I have to respect her word." More commonly, a couple negotiated a move over time, during which men held more say in final decisions. In San Lorenzo, Doña Luisa's family had done well, but their first years in the ejido were grueling. She winced recalling what she had to endure when the family arrived in 1984. The nearest store, where the family sold their crops, was a three-mile walk away. "I had never suffered like that before," she professed. "There were days when we had absolutely nothing to eat. And the mosquitoes! I had to sit my children under mosquito netting, so they could eat their dinner. My daughter was eleven years old, and she couldn't handle it. She said, 'Mommy, I want to go live with my grandmother.' She left, but my husband said, 'Sit tight; later it's going to be different.'" Like other migrants from Veracruz, her husband, Don Esteban, said he came to Calakmul "fleeing wage labor (huyendo el jornal)" and determined to be his own boss. Over time, he achieved these goals.

Esteban believed his success was due to his upright character and his opposition to scoundrels. Like all of Calakmul's ejidos, San Lorenzo had seen a flow of migrants over the years. Don Esteban's explanation of why those people moved on condensed issues of ejidal factionalism, failed prospects, and Esteban's own refusal to tolerate challenges to his authority: "People left because of problems in the ejido. They wanted to become powerful. In all the ejidos, people are like that. They're never at peace. Some come with visions of doing great things without having to work. Some bring crafty ideas, and some are just lazy." In fact, people did come to Calakmul for all kinds of reasons, and they encountered varying degrees of welcome in their new homes. The following three profiles reflect people's association with Calakmul's forest economy, the effects of the Zapatista uprising, and people's experiences of enduring agrarian strife.

The Chicle Life

In the ejido of Orozco, I sat down with Don Venancio and Doña Ana to collect their migration history, when Don Venancio began to laugh. He said their many moves would never fit into my questionnaire. In the mid-1970s, Don Venancio and Doña Ana met in a chicle camp when he was fifteen years old, and she was thirteen. They had exchanged only a few words when Don Venancio, accompanied by his father, asked Ana's parents formal permission to date the girl. Her father's response was gruff: "I don't want to see this boy running out of my home with his pants around his ankles. If he wants to date her, he'll have to marry her!" So, they married. Given these inauspicious beginnings, Don Venancio and Doña Ana knew they were lucky. After twenty-one years, they continued to share a warm confidence.

Both Doña Ana and Don Venancio came from chicle families. The women worked as camp cooks, while the men tapped trees. The couple said they left chicle work only because a growing family (nine children in all) made it difficult to travel. Don Venancio always had ambitions beyond chicle. As a boy, Don Venancio enjoyed school, but his father pulled him out of classes and put him to work. Don Venancio regretted not having a better education. With mixed success, he worked for his own sons' continued schooling. Doña Ana had never been to school and could not read or write. This fact mattered only on the occasions the couple thought of opening a store in their home. Doña Ana did not trust herself to handle the accounts. Instead, the greatest difficulty Doña Ana had faced was the life she shared with her in-laws. Typical of this patrilocal society, the couple lived with his parents during the first eleven years of their marriage. Her mother-in-law, she said, berated her for sloppy housework. Doña Ana's father-in-law occasionally hit her. Because of this, Doña Ana was strict with her own daughters' housekeeping in the hopes that they would have an easier time with their in-laws.

Before arriving in Orozco, Don Venancio described himself as a "vagabond." Always with his father, he combined chicle work with logging and construction, while occasionally farming alongside his brother who had settled in Calakmul. In the first year of their marriage, Venancio and Ana moved to Campeche city, where he worked in a factory freezing fish. The pay was good, but, because of the job's long hours, he never saw his family. Besides, city life was not to their liking. Don Venancio believed his children were healthier living in the country. Doña Ana described city life as especially hard on the financially strapped. There, the children "are always asking you to buy the things they see. In the countryside, the children see nothing and ask for nothing." Don Venancio left the factory, and the family again followed itinerant jobs before settling in Acán, an ejido in Calakmul.

Life in Acán gave the family an opportunity to become founding ejidatarios in an ejido just seeking legalization, but certain costs outweighed this significant benefit. At this time, in the late 1970s, Acán had no services. After four years, the family left Acán because of "a lack of communication. It had no road, no doctor or school." Later, when I knew the couple better, Don Venancio and Doña Ana described another reason for departing Acán. I was getting ready to leave Orozco and live in San Lorenzo, located *más adentro*, or further inside, the forest. They wanted to warn me about the dangers of living más adentro. Don Venancio advised I have a dependable car to escape the bandits who patrolled interior roads (luckily, I never met one). In fact, he and Doña Ana had been unsettled by recent reports that a man, nicknamed "The Millionaire," had been robbed and murdered in his cornfield. I heard different versions of The Millionaire's fate as news of his death sent a chill throughout Calakmul. For Don Venancio and Doña Ana, the death reminded them of their stay in Acán. At that time, Doña Ana was often alone with their small children, when Don Venancio walked to the nearest store in a distant ejido. In order to fit the trip into one day, he would leave home at 2 a.m. and not return until 11 at night. The couple felt unsafe with this arrangement and said it was one of the reasons they moved. Rather than discount their original explanation, I wondered how often people's complaints about a lack of services also indicated concern for their physical safety.

After leaving Acán, Don Venancio met the chicle contractor Don Mauricio, who invited the family to settle in Orozco. Venancio and Ana moved to Orozco in the mid-1980s, one year after Don Mauricio succeeded in having the village declared an ejido. Like other caciques of the time, Mauricio reigned in Orozco. In 1995, Don Venancio continued to hold a grudge against the man. Venancio remained bitter that Mauricio forced him to wait seven years before allowing him to become an ejidatario who could control his own plot of land. In the meantime, Don Venancio worked national lands adjacent to the ejido while Mauricio logged the ejido's timber. Don Venancio's bitterness was not softened by the fact that Mauricio occasionally supported his neighbors in crucial ways. For example, he once used his connections to free an Orozcan from jail after he instigated a machete fight. Orozco's historical records showed that, in the fight, Mauricio sided with a fellow Mestizo against a young Ch'ol man. The Ch'ol family, along with their extended kin, fled the community. Without Mauricio's support, the family would be vulnerable to future assault.

Orozcans hinted that Mauricio's control extended to profiting from ejidal funds. Nearly every community in Calakmul had stories of people who stole a public purse. In Mauricio's case, researchers often refer to such men as caciques (women rarely attain this kind of power). People in Calakmul, however, hesitated to use this term. Instead, they preferred descriptors such as "pirate" (un pirata) and "corrupt" (un corrupto). Even more commonly, people used phrases that emphasized power as the product of ongoing actions. They described powerful individuals as "él es quien manda (he is the one who runs things)" Additionally, they said, "Por profesión quiere hacer político, quiere hacer cacique [sic] (by profession he wants to make politics; he wants to be a cacique)." He "greases his palm (se echa manteca en la mano)" and "grabs things up (lo tiene agarrado)." Powerful individuals proved themselves repeatedly through performance. In a recent analysis of caciques, de Vries argues these performances can include elements of enjoyment, as these "uncanny characters" invoke a sense of "special powers" when they negotiate with the state (2002:906). At a regional level, the pleasurable aspects of cacique performance, in the work of the Reserve Director, lent excitement to Calakmul's conservation-development agenda (see chap. 7). At the ejidal level, this spectacle tended to be more ambiguous. Each cacique aspirant must undergo the test of local conflicts, and the momentary quality of performances meant that sons did not necessarily inherit a father's position as cacique. In Orozco, people remembered the precise encounter when Don Venancio stopped Mauricio's son from logging at will in the ejido. By tempering the influence of a cacique's son, Don Venancio proved himself a man to be reckoned with.

In 1995, Don Venancio was powerful in his own right, but one might question why he and Doña Ana tolerated Don Mauricio for so long. Only two families that entered Orozco in the 1980s still resided in the ejido in 1995. Compared with a 1995 population of 230, nearly 265 people had come and gone from the village. Why not move on like the rest? An array of factors contributed to this decision summed up in Don Venancio's assertion "aquí me hallé (here is where I found myself)." Given the couple's earlier fears of random violence, Don Mauricio's forceful character clearly provided protection as much as it served as a point of complaint. Later, I explore this feature of cacique rule in more depth. Additionally, by the 1980s, the chicle industry had declined to a point where it could not provide a family's principal income. For Venancio and Ana, a return to the chicle life was impossible. Besides, they had to consider their children's future. They wanted to stake a claim in an ejido where their sons might gain a plot of land. Sons may inherit land from their fathers, but (until the late 1990s) they could also request land from the ejidal assembly. Don Venancio would need enough influence in an assembly to ensure his five sons received land.

After eleven years in Orozco, Don Venancio's strategy had paid off. As an old timer, he had authority over new arrivals. Don Venancio, along with a few others, managed the development projects once monopolized by Mauricio. Meanwhile, he and Doña Ana counted on continued prominence within the ejido. The couple brought members of their extended families to live in Orozco. Although not nearly as powerful as Don Mauricio, Don Venancio might now be the one to intimidate his neighbors into silence.

The Refugees' Plight

Throughout my stay in Orzoco, Venancio and his fellow ejidatarios were preoccupied by two issues: participation in conservation-development programs and disagreements over the ejido's newest arrivals. In 1994, Orozco's ejidatarios accepted a group of refugees from Chiapas.

Overnight, the number of people living in the ejido doubled. Official estimates do not exist, but policy makers believed 200 Chiapan families (perhaps 1,000 people) entered Calakmul to escape the uprising's violence.[1] Nearly all these families belonged to an indigenous group. The new arrivals in Orozco spoke Ch'ol. They sought entrance to Orozco from the ejido's president, a man who was also ethnically Ch'ol. He accepted the refugees and, along with Orozco's other Ch'ol ejidatarios—whose numbers equaled their Mestizo counterparts—insisted the ejido had enough land to support the newcomers. Mestizos such as Don Venancio were more doubtful. They resisted the newcomers' permanent integration into the ejido.

Orozco's ethnic situation was a microcosm of Calakmul's larger identity politics, one reorganized by the Zaptista movement. Ch'ol speakers constituted between 25 percent and 40 percent of Calakmul's population (Stedman-Edwards 2000). Ch'ol have migrated steadily to Calakmul since about 1980. Two larger migration waves took place in the early 1980s (when eruption of a volcano in Chiapas ruined much farmland) and in the 1990s after the Zapatista uprising. These moves were ones of desperation, and Ch'ol migrants tended to be poorer than their neighbors. They moved into existing ejidos where, as in Venancio's case, newcomers occupied subordinate positions. Since the Zapatista uprising, Ch'ol have lived under an additional burden. Because nearly all originated from Chiapas and because many supported Mexico's PRD party, PRI government agents suspected Ch'ol of sedition. At best Ch'ol were characterized by authorities as "closed" and unfriendly toward outsiders. At worst, authorities viewed Ch'ol as guerilla supporters. Some Ch'ol families had been forced to leave Calakmul under pressure from the military.

The Ch'ol families I met failed to fit their popular descriptions. They were cautious in getting to know me, but once I learned their stories, this caution seemed more than advisable. Typically, Ch'ol spoke little Spanish. According to state estimates, roughly one-third of the 114,000 people who speak Ch'ol are monolingual (INEGI 1993). And, as my Ch'ol assistant Arnoldo described his own foreign language skills, "there is always a doubt" about how well one manages in Spanish. At the same time, Arnoldo's uncle gave a telling commentary on Ch'ol-Mestizo relations when he said, "We understand what they say, but they cannot understand us." Even monolingual Ch'ol often had a working comprehension of Spanish. The same was generally not true of Spanish speakers, although some Mestizos in Orozco knew more Ch'ol than they were willing to admit.

Breaking this language barrier proved an important way for me to gain the confidence of my Ch'ol neighbors. I studied the language for about three months. Although I never learned enough to be conversant, Ch'ol who could speak Spanish warmed to me when I showed interest in their language. Later, I discovered that my short-term failure to learn Ch'ol was a benefit in disguise. I found the prejudice between Ch'ol and Mestizos was strong enough that had I identified myself too closely with Ch'ol, my Mestizo neighbors probably would have distanced themselves from me. My Ch'ol friend Don Timoteo alerted me to this dynamic. He was especially shrewd about the ethnic and ejidal politics surrounding him. His family's journey to Calakmul shows how the Chiapas uprising reverberates in the individual and collective lives of people in Calakmul.

Don Timoteo and his wife, Doña Nancy, were the proverbial outsiders in their own community whose insight anthropology students are advised to seek. Years earlier, the couple had been one of the few families in a Catholic village to convert to Protestantism. Doña Nancy converted first, and, after many years, Don Timoteo accepted her faith. He stopped drinking alcohol, and their family life became centered on their faith. Profoundly religious, they were also thoughtful and reflective. Once, Don Timoteo recalled a man who helped the family in a difficult time, a man who did not believe in God. Don Timoteo wondered about this man as he sorted through ideas of good and evil. Where was the seat of this man's goodness, he asked, if not in God?

I almost did not speak with Timoteo and Nancy about their journey to Calakmul. I had already interviewed his brother and sister, as well as her aunt. They had lived all in the same village in Chiapas and moved with their families at the same time. They continued to claim their land in Chiapas, suggesting they were only waiting for the situation to calm before returning home. I knew Timoteo's brother Don Dionicio was especially homesick. He had made a recent trip to Chiapas to see if a return was possible. After listening to Timoteo and Nancy, I saw how dim were their prospects for return.

Don Timoteo began his story with his and Nancy's arrival in the early 1970s to Sierra, a newly forming ejido on an agricultural frontier in eastern Chiapas. Similar to the descriptions other Ch'ol gave of their teenage years, Timoteo's parents moved temporarily to Sierra to help their children establish a new farm. Ejidatarios are unlikely to accept an unsupervised youth. Thus, a father's duty in finding his sons land extended to helping sons build the networks necessary to access land. In this sense, Timoteo's father was enormously successful. Three of his children settled in Sierra, where his sons and son-in-law grew to occupy ejidal offices. Don Timoteo had traveled to Mexico City as an ejidal official and briefly worked for a federal agency, the National Indigenous Institute. Don Dionicio prospered enough to send his eldest sons to secondary school in a distant city. Don Dionicio remained nostalgic for his home in Chiapas, while Timoteo quickly reckoned with the idea of his exile. Don Timoteo's description of his last days in Chiapas explained this resignation:

> When we arrived in Sierra twenty-five years ago, all the people were from different places. It was a happy place. We played marimba, and we danced. I got married at seventeen, and we celebrated with fireworks. We celebrated the Virgin Mary by cooking together. In the evenings, everyone was home eating, very tranquil. I never thought I would see that village change. Now, we can't go there. About five years ago, things began to change. First, people came to do good things. A teacher arrived named Francisca. We gave her the nickname Pancha. She ran a school, she taught the women to sew, and everything was going well. I was the one who represented the people, I was ejidal president. But, then things turned bad. . . . In 1994, people armed themselves. The first of January they took out the radio at Ocosingo. The war began. In Sierra, all those who weren't in agreement with the war met to see if we should leave. Then three men died; they disappeared. They went to their parcels and never returned. When we left Sierra, they were ready to kill me next. They wanted me, because I said it shouldn't be like this. People should organize, but to work. [Here, I asked who was doing the killing, and he responded that his neighbors were the culprits.] Now, it's worse. I left my house with a sewing machine. I left dishes, mattresses, a garden with many fruit trees. They took it all, and now other people live there. Dionicio went to visit, but they threw rocks at his house at night. They can't stand to see him anymore, *ya no lo pueden ver*.

Later, I learned that life in Sierra was more complicated than Don Timoteo described. Founded in the early 1970s, the ejido was overcrowded by the late 1980s. A number of people were forced to work national lands adjacent to the ejido. This group wanted their situation legalized and were frustrated with what they saw as the ejidal hierarchy's slow action. Such conflicts are common in Mexico, but divisions in Sierra became exacerbated by the Zapatista uprising. Landless and land poor families effectively used the uprising and its rhetoric of fighting the rich to expel relatively wealthy ejidatarios.

Don Timoteo and his family were unsupportive of the Zapatistas, rooting their understanding of the war and its aftermath in their religious beliefs. The refugee group included Catholics and Protestants of different denominations. All of these people first saw the war as evidence of a biblical apocalypse. Later, Don Timoteo placed the blame for the violence squarely on the Catholics (see Harvey 1998 for connections between the Zapatista movement and the Catholic church). Dionicio's continued Catholicism and his work as a Catholic catechist became a sore point in the brothers' relationship. Dionicio defended his faith, but when I visited Calakmul in 1999, I found Dionicio had converted to Timoteo's church. Don Dionicio declined to comment on his conversion, but Timoteo asserted his brother "se dio cuenta (he realized)." Usually, people speak of conversion in terms of "accepting" a doctrine. Don Timoteo suggested his brother had realized the social and political ramifications of his religion.

By 1999, many individuals in Calakmul had begun to use religion to signal their position within the ongoing tensions associated with Zapatismo. A certain religious fervor had taken hold in Calakmul, and religious conversions were common events. While families like Timoteo and Nancy's displayed forceful adherence to particular faiths, it was hard to tell how much recent converts felt the urge toward orthodoxy. People seemed to appreciate any preacher who put on a good show. What was clear was that people sought in religion a stabilizing force. People who saw the Zapatista movement as destabilizing might choose Protestantism as a way to voice their intentions toward their neighbors. One woman's description of her conversion to Protestantism drew these issues sharply: "Having God in your heart, you also have your neighbor in your heart. Catholics fight among themselves. They're confrontational, and they even kill each other." Many campesinos in Calakmul supported the Zapatista movement, but, in 1995, my personal networks chanced to lead me in the other direction.[2] Among both Zapatista supporters and detractors, migrant networks between Chiapas and Calakmul imported and transformed the discourses, issues, and identities at play in Chiapas in ways that would alter conservation programming.

Persistent Tremors of Violence

If the Chiapas uprising underscored problems of violence in Mexico's countryside, it was not the only thread of violence in Calakmul. Staff with the Reserve and Council murmured that Calakmul's people included criminals escaping prosecution for past misdeeds. Verifying such beliefs was impossible, as people were not likely to admit their own transgressions. However, they would speak about other people's misdeeds. Don Timoteo, for example, asserted that a man he believed to have committed murder in Sierra came to Calakmul to visit relatives. Don Timoteo refused to lodge an accusation against the man. He feared the police would be ineffective, and his actions would place him in further danger. The man's presence was a potent reminder of all Timoteo and Nancy had lost as well as the threats they endured.

Listening to migration histories, I was struck by the way violence and village strife could force families to leave situations in which they had a relative wealth of land. Of the twenty-nine households interviewed in San Lorenzo and Orozco, twenty-one reported they had been ejidatarios at some point prior to moving to the area. In our 2001 survey, we found 94 of 151 respondents had held ejidatario status sometime before arriving in Calakmul. Theoretically, the ejido's common property characteristics bind individuals to a place because access to land depends on carefully built social relations (Ostrom 1990). Re-creating similar connections in another ejido takes time and expense. In the 2001 survey, however, twenty-three individuals had gone so far as to twice leave ejidatario positions. Campesino willingness to abandon ejidatario status suggests our understanding of what attaches people to a particular place requires reconsideration. These moves occurred even when the family's landholdings went beyond that of most ejidatarios. Individuals from the 2001 survey who had held ejidatario status had an average of 83 hectares per person. This compares with a national average of 9.44 hectares per ejidal parcel (DeWalt and Rees 1994). When I asked why people would leave apparently secure situations, they complained that the poor quality of land was insufficient to support a family. Just as commonly, they said they fled situations of violence and "problems with the neighbors."

The situation of Don Carlos demonstrated the intertwined quality of farming and political issues. Don Carlos traced his migratory journey to agrarian problems dating to his boyhood. In San Lorenzo, he and his wife, Doña Fatima, had built a relatively secure position surrounded by family and harbored by Don Esteban's forceful personality (see above). When I first went to inquire about the family's migration history, I found Doña Fatima and her mother-in-law working in the kitchen. I did not know the women as well as I knew Don Carlos, whose farm work impressed me as very near to self-sufficient in a place where most families openly depended on aid programs. The women shared a familiar story of various moves, each precipitated by a failed crop, a desire for land, or a family illness. As I was typing up my notes from the interview, I found a small gap in their story and returned for the missing information. This time, I found Don Carlos at home. His story differed significantly.

Don Carlos described growing up in a Tabasco town that, in the 1960s, became part of an enormous government development initiative known as the Plan Chontalpa. As part of the plan, large tracks of Tabasco's wetlands were drained and channeled to open the area for cattle ranching. The program entailed a reorganization of village geographies and membership. People's access to land and the new development programs became dependent on participation in government controlled cooperatives (see also García et al. 1989). Don Carlos described his father as resolutely opposed to working for the government. When Don Carlos was twelve years old, the family moved to neighboring Veracruz state, where they farmed for two years.

Don Carlos described their home in Veracruz as "an ejido, but it didn't suit us because it included some land that rich people had fixed." The family was actually squatting on what they thought was unoccupied land. Don Carlos's father was ejidal president, and, when he went to formalize their situation, the Agrarian Reform office explained the area was already owned. Don Carlos said the owners lived in Mexico City and did not utilize the lands in any way. At this point, Carlos's father decided it was best to move. When I asked what happened to those who stayed, Don Carlos responded that they were forcibly removed.

The family then traveled to another site in Veracruz, the ejido of San Marcos. They would stay in San Marcos for twelve years. Don Carlos, his father, and brothers all became ejidatarios. Each controlled a parcel of twenty-four hectares, while the extended family held a total of ten parcels. In San Marcos, Carlos and Fatima began their own family. Unfortunately, in the early 1980s, Don Carlos's father fell ill, and the family left San Marcos to seek medical help. They sought out a doctor in Tabasco and remained in that state for six months. Don Carlos's father never recovered from the illness. After his father's death, Don Carlos, his mother, and his brothers returned to San Marcos with some trepidation. They worried their lands would be threatened after such a sustained absence from the ejido. In fact, their parcels had been taken over by neighbors. In the ensuing disagreement, one of Don Carlos's brothers was murdered. As Don Carlos remembered, the remaining siblings decided it was better to leave than "start spraying blood." They returned to Tabasco, where they spent the following two years working as day laborers. During that time, they learned about land availability in Calakmul through a friend.

Don Carlos, his brother, sister, and their families arrived at San

Lorenzo in 1985 when the ejido was recolonizing after considerable up-
heaval. In the previous year, San Lorenzo's cacique was shot at point-blank
range in his store. Don Carlos believed this was the work of *mafia*, or drug
traffickers. His neighbor, Doña Virginia, was not so sure. The man had
many enemies, she asserted, any of whom might have sought vengeance.
Doña Virginia had been living in San Lorenzo at the time when the cacique
began to make life difficult for her family. He refused to sell them anything
from his shop. She added that he stole people's crops by pushing families
out of the ejido just when he saw they were about to take in a plentiful
harvest. In any case, upon his death, the cacique's family fled San Lorenzo.
They left the ejidal seal and legal documentation with friends in a neighboring village. It is not clear how many people were living in San Lorenzo
at the time. Current residents report that, when the remaining families
could not get control of the ejidal seal—necessary for all correspondence
with external authorities—they too left. At the time of Don Carlos's arrival,
people from the states of Veracruz and Tabasco were repopulating San
Lorenzo, and the village was, again, an ejido in formation.

By the mid-1990s, Don Carlos and others who came to San Lorenzo
in the 1980s had built strong, sociable relations centered on Don Esteban
and a dense network formed by their children's intermarriage.[3] Most af-
ternoons, Don Esteban sat under the awning in front of his home. There,
he watched his grandchildren at play and chatted with his wife, Doña
Luisa, and their children. In the evenings, the men of San Lorenzo returned from their fields and drifted to Don Esteban's home for a game of
volleyball or checkers and, finally, to watch the evening soap operas. These
were times of camaraderie and consensus building.

Don Esteban used these hours to catch up on gossip, but also to
communicate his power. He condemned the government as liars, saying
he had no interest in listening to promises that would go unfulfilled.
Esteban also criticized his nemesis in town, Don Tomás. The two men had
argued over the ejido's political direction when Tomás was ejidal president. Esteban effectively forced Tomás out of office, and the two men were
not on speaking terms. It is difficult to convey in writing the force of will
that Don Esteban brought to these relationships. He displayed an immov-
able strength and browbeat his opponents who could not match Esteban's
tenacity or grit.

Behind Don Esteban, people like Don Carlos and Doña Fatima took
shelter. They affirmed his antigovernment stance even as they participated
in government aid programs. Don Esteban saw his relationship to govern-

ment agents as mutually exploitative, and his followers approved of his tactic of beating the government at its own game. Don Esteban's relationship to his followers was hierarchical but consensual. For example, Don Esteban and his children were among the few in San Lorenzo to have a cement (rather than dirt) floor in their home. One of Esteban's detractors accused him of skimming cement off a government project that built household water tanks. If Don Esteban received the first fruits of the ejido's economic activity, he ensured that his followers also benefited. Opponents like Don Tomás were shut out of the jobs and material benefits that projects offered. Under Don Esteban's direction, San Lorenzo's ejidatarios organized to enforce their own social order. They pressured one another to keep out of marijuana cultivation, an activity that brought other ejidos problems with government fines and military surveillance. Within this organization, Don Carlos and Doña Fatima found stability to raise their family. The couple's achievements included building a solid agricultural base, seeing two of their daughters marry locally, and sending two of their sons to secondary school.

Fractured Lives, Patterned Experiences

Like their counterparts who cross international borders, campesinos in Calakmul grappled with changed meanings of citizenship, social contracts, and the creation of ritual spaces to work through these changes (see Appadurai 1996). As they wove migration into their broader lives (Cliggett 2000), Calakmul's people incorporated migration into social performances. People used suggestions that they might move to give voice to the pressures in their lives and to test their neighbors' desire to have them stay. In talking about moving, people talked about their aspirations and indicated the various openings and closings that shaped those aspirations in practice.

Unlike their transnational counterparts, campesinos undertook these performances and reinventions under paradoxical circumstances. Where theorists of transnationalism view international migration as a challenge to the nation-state's authority (Glick Schiller et al. 1992), people in Calakmul were reinventing Mexico within the confines of Mexican territory. Their migratory journeys were part of a *continuous* experience of the Mexican state. In many cases, migration represented people's efforts to rework the state, to find a place where state structures supported their life desires or, in the least, did not threaten their ability to survive. Not everyone left behind the experiences or ties to their former homes. Instead, life in Calakmul sat in tension with what campesinos knew to be happening elsewhere in Mexico. As events in Chiapas, Veracruz, and Tabasco continued on separate courses, the touchstones against which people evaluated events in Calakmul also remained distinct.

Migration stories counter these differences by showing patterned experiences of government authority, both its presence and its absence. Migrants' relationship to land—gaining it and losing it—stood as milestones in their travels. The space where land and the state converged (in the person of a cacique or in ejidal land tenures) was tumultuous, a point that people handled in different ways. Men like Don Venancio and Don Esteban might work to enforce their own personal political order upon this space. People such as Don Timoteo and Doña Nancy might search for a religiously based, moral framework with which to order this space. Finally, people like Don Carlos and Doña Fatima might do their best to avoid the state altogether. In their reliance on Don Esteban, the couple worked with a man who sometimes appeared as a state official (when he negotiated with governors and development agents) and sometimes appeared as the state's opposition. People like Don Esteban embodied the state's mercurial qualities. These men alternately collaborated with the state and reappropriated state programs, while otherwise establishing a domain beyond government mandates.

Disconcertingly, people showed how government agents consistently failed as a refuge for those in fear for their safety. Mexican authorities admit that, historically, only 10 percent of reported crimes receive any kind of punishment. "Impunity has become a historical constant," declared a president of Mexico City's Human Rights Commission (Posada García 1996). Given that government agents were often at the center of land disputes, campesinos felt keenly that those most responsible for their protection were also those most free to act without fear of reprisal. Whether opposing the Zapatistas, carrying out the Plan Chontalpa, or acting on behalf of wealthy landowners, government agents were protagonists in major events that campesinos found threatening. This was the case even for people supportive of government authority. Government advocates secured relatively few benefits for their allegiance. Instead, such benefits were reserved for people like Don Mauricio and Don Esteban, rewarded for their close ties to state patronage regardless of their political beliefs.

In their migration stories, both government supporters and detractors reported that the benefits of working with government agents rest largely on development aid. For example, another Tabasqueño man whose family, like Don Carlos's, opted out of the Plan Chontalpa questioned his father's decision. People in his former home now have paved roads and trucks. "If I had stayed, I would probably have the same, but my father didn't teach us these possibilities. People complained the cooperatives were a kind of government communism, and all we saw were problems." Given how migration histories show the state's role in creating disorder, it is revealing that financial linkages are a constant, if qualified, benefit in people's relations to government authority.

Campesinos invariably arrived in Calakmul through family and friends. These networks directed migrants to ejidos whose residents worked, whenever possible, to share kinship ties, the same state of origin, and the same ethnicity. These identities formed a potent social structure in Calakmul. Because its effects will reverberate in later chapters, it is worth exploring here how people transformed their state of origin into a quasi-ethnicity.

Even though people from Chiapas, Veracruz, and Tabasco shared common experiences, they viewed the fact that they were from distinct states as creating irreconcilable differences. People used state of origin as shorthand for a host of presumptions about personality traits, lifestyle choices, and how groups interact with one another. They said that living in an ejido with their *paisanos*, people who shared a state of origin, and marrying within one's group helped avoid conflicts. Tellingly, each group accused the others of undue violence. Researchers often discuss rural violence in Mexico as resulting from structural causes, such as agrarian problems (Greenberg 1989). Although some people in Calakmul might take this approach, campesinos also emphasized that violent acts were committed by *people* against other people. They evaluated one another, not land distribution, for the potential for violence.

Within these divisions, some ethnic groups did tend to get along with each other more than others. A young man from Tabasco once lectured me for an hour on why marriage to a Tabasqueña woman was the only way for him to secure a happy home life. This Mestizo found the indigenous women of Chiapas and Yucatán fit for a brief flirtation or affair but not a respectable marriage. To the extent people viewed ethnic divisions as flexible, Calakmul's residents were more likely to build on common Mestizo or indigenous identities rather than bridge an indigenous/Mestizo divide. These ethnic ideals affected not only community life, but also Calakmul's conservation-development agenda, where Mestizo managers ignored indigenous people's demands for recognition.

Postcolonial Migratory Environments

My account departs from what ejidal members generally asserted about migration. When asked casually why they came to Calakmul, they almost always said "for the land." When asked why past residents left the area, people invariably responded, "They left because of the water," meaning the lack thereof. I do not aim to displace these truisms. Instead, I hope the information found in the previous pages places environmental concerns in context and demonstrates how nature itself lies in the thick of these issues. As a subsistence base, as a touchstone for identity differences, as a force around which people built class differences, as an entity worth killing over and motivating large-scale social movements, as a site of government action and inaction, the natural environment was viewed by people (sometimes simultaneously) through a variety of lenses.

Rather than reconcile these perspectives, I note how these tensions persisted as people's identities positioned them differently within the land-power matrix. For example, women like Doña Ana could describe a cacique's excesses because, where men had to work together in ejidal management, women's purported confinement to the private sphere provided a buffer against the public humiliation caciques wrought. At the same time, women suffered the most during Calakmul's droughts, when household water for washing clothes, dishes, and children was in short supply. Women's complaints about water were central to conversations among Orozco's refugees regarding whether the families should leave the ejido.

Condensing complex frontier experiences into notions of land and water scarcity was socially acceptable for a few reasons. The two points acted as a minimal area of agreement. Also, the issues invoked in listeners real anxieties regarding subsistence concerns. In the case of water, people were struggling with drought in 1995, and by noting the detrimental effects of past droughts, they underscored that water scarcity remained an unresolved issue. Moving as these pleas were, they could obscure significant contradictions. People recalled droughts where water was so scarce they purchased soda pop for their children to drink. A place without water, nonetheless, had soda pop. In the late 1980s, residents of Orozco moved their village site to access electricity, but in doing so they left behind both a pond and a cistern they had built to collect rainwater. Orozcans were willing to forsake water for electricity.

These kinds of trade-offs appear curious, but make sense if one thinks of development as both a necessary and ambivalent undertaking, weakly informed by a detailed plan of action. This point connects to land cover. Rather than a purposeful encounter with local ecology, local land use also reflects neglect, serendipity, errors in judgment, luck, carelessness, and outright ignorance (Dove 1993; García et al. 1989). This is not to say that campesinos forsook attempts to steer their personal, community, and ecological futures. The migration histories speak to people's persistence in shaping their future, despite considerable odds. The following chapters will show how ejidal assemblies and farm practices similarly showcased campesinos' attempts to influence events and their neighbors.

5

The Fractured Ejido, the Fractured State

The ejido was basic to both managing the environment and structuring notions of poverty. Nearly all campesinos in Calakmul lived in an ejido. Although people complained that "in ejidos, there are always problems," there were no alternative models for agrarian village life. As with Don Carlos (chap. 4), people implemented the ejido's structure even in squatter settlements, where they were under no legal obligation to do so. The ejido was virtually synonymous with community life, and it framed people's imaginations, as one thirteen-year-old girl, inquiring about the United States, asked me what life was like in my ejido.

From a legal perspective, life in an ejido meant compliance with Mexico's agrarian law (see chap. 3). As we saw, historically the state has used the ejido to influence community affairs, although in Calakmul this tendency has been less pronounced. Instead, people emphasized that ejido life meant their neighbors had considerable impact on their quality of life. Ejidal members were collectively responsible for building schools, maintaining roads, ensuring their water supply, and implementing conservation-development programs. Feelings of collective responsibility could weigh heavily. With a weak regional police force, ejidatarios described feeling "encerrados" (shut inside) when they took on the work of jury to instances of theft or violence.

In this chapter, I explore this combination of isolation and permeability as a central contradiction in ejidal political life and, by extension, people's environmental management. Although in their assemblies, ejidatarios formed a state institution, ejidatarios often saw themselves in opposition to the state. This opposition arose, in part, from the exploitation and extortion campesinos experienced at the hands of government agents. The ejido's distinction from other government bodies also arose from the way ejidal governance never fully conformed to the law. Ejidal members often operated as they saw fit. This fact meant that ejidal practices included highly localized features, peculiar to Calakmul (compare Leyva Solano's 2001 description of ejidos in frontier Chiapas). Ejidal autonomy furthermore left powerful individuals space to assert themselves. The ejido, alternately independent and permeated by outside policies, partly democratic and partly demagogic, "quasi-communal" (Nigh 2002), stood as people's most immediate experience of a fractured, contradictory state. Critically, these fractures and contradictions coincided in the place where campesinos worked to create an environmental order consonant with their subsistence needs.

I follow these experiences first through the lens of ejidal isolation, as ejidatarios negotiate new migrants to their ejidos; second, through the lens of ejidal permeability, in the context of state farm programs; and finally through legal changes in ejidal structures. For most of the chapter, I focus on assemblies, meetings in which men and women worked through ejidal policy and convened with state representatives. Assemblies were ongoing sites of public gathering. Other sites included church events, evening soap operas and soccer games, and, in Orozco, the *jagüey*, an artificial pond where women washed clothes and everyone stopped for a bath on the way home from their fields. At assemblies, people commented on the social relations taking place across these sites. Notably, ejidal members did not draw on notions of ecological management to negotiate these relations. This was the case even as they densely wove agricultural issues into their everyday relations.

Because I spent more time in Orzoco, most of the material is from that community, with brief comparisons to San Lorenzo. The two ejidos were very different. People in Orozco admitted an enduring distrust of one another. Social life in Orozco contained deep silences. San Lorenzans gregariously voiced their disagreements and had an active, public community life. Orozcans confronted a less congenial farming environment and their financial situation was much more precarious (see chap. 6). Orozcans appear to have compensated for their poor ecology by accepting migrants in ways I describe below. This meant that Orozcans were often neighbors to people about whom they knew little and toward whom their intentions were not always salutary.

By focusing on disputes, I explore an area that affected people's place in Calakmul's conservation-development agenda. Reserve and Council staff gauged communities according to a perceived level of factionalism. Ingenieros believed programs foundered on internal ejidal arguments, even as staffers refused to address such disagreements.[1] Technical staff warned me away from San Lorenzo, worrying I would be caught in arguments over control of development programs. Staffers viewed Orozco as relatively calm. As it turned out, Orozcans maintained a veneer of equality that masked profound divisions. San Lorenzans did promote their irascible characters, but their argument also provided a measure of order. Throughout my stay in Orozco, ejidal members were most divided on what to do with Don Timoteo, Doña Nancy, and the refugees newly arrived that year. Following explication of this particular conflict, one that arises throughout the chapter, I turn to the assemblies and other considerations of ejidal political life.

Arriving at Calakmul's Ejidos

From the moment a family requested permission to live in an ejido, they had to contend with ejidal hierarchies. Ejidatarios voted on accepting or, less frequently, expelling members. People therefore had to earn their neighbors' support to access farmland. Before moving to Calakmul, Don Timoteo and his family sent an advance team to the area to investigate farming possibilities. Family members living in Calakmul introduced the group to Don Guillermo, Orozco's president. Like the Chiapans, Guillermo spoke Ch'ol, a point that later created conflicts with Guillermo's Mestizo neighbors. Guillermo and some Orozco residents took pity on the Chiapans: "They came fleeing the guerillas. They were completely screwed (vinieron jodidos en plano). They didn't have anywhere to stay." As it turned out, Orozco's residents had different reasons for accepting the group, not all of which were altruistic.

Calakmul's ejidos had a standard acceptance process, which Don Timoteo and the others followed. They first spoke with Orozco's ejidatarios. The ejidatarios required a letter from Chiapas authorities certifying the supplicants had no criminal record. Orozco's ejidatarios then charged an entrance fee (una entrada) of $300 per man.[2] (All prices are in pesos. San Lorenzo's entrance fee was set at $500.) Because wage labor paid $20 a day and often as little as $15 a day, Orozco's entrance fee equaled somewhere between 15 and 20 days of work. The refugees put money toward this debt with promises to complete payments in the future. In all, twenty-three men signed on with the expectation that, at some point, they would be given their own parcels of land. Orozco's ejidatarios later disputed whether they actually promised the group land.

In the meantime, ejidatarios assigned the newcomers the status of *poblador* or *avecindado*. My preference for poblador reflects its common usage in Calakmul. Pobladores were men awaiting land distribution and included the sons of ejidatarios.[3] Like ejidatarios, pobladores were required to partake in communal work projects (*faenas*), attend assemblies, and pay for village costs. But, a crucial difference separated the two groups. Pobladores could not speak or vote in the assemblies that decided ejidal matters. Pobladores were entirely dependent on ejidatarios, who lent newcomers land or sent them to work the common lands that ejidatarios had found undesirable.[4] In Orozco, ejidatarios argued that such beneficence did not extend to development aid, and they denied pobladores access to Calakmul's sustainable-development programs.

Orozco's ejidatario/poblador hierarchy was a microcosm of the points structuring ejidal politics. Although a legal distinction limited pobladores' self-determination, ejidatarios could effectively restrict one another in similar ways. In these struggles, identity and individual force of will provided material for people to counter their neighbors' bellicose tendencies. Reports from assembly meetings demonstrate these points in practice.

Ethnicity and Assembly Politics

"He's going to have problems in the assembly," people said about men who ran counter to their neighbors. Assemblies were stages on which ejidatarios worked through or sublimated community issues. Occasionally, ejidal assemblies were explosive affairs, as long-simmering issues boiled to the surface. More often, the debates were one phase in an ongoing discussion. Even firm decisions could quickly become irrelevant if ejidatarios changed their minds. Assemblies could be difficult to follow because participants often drew on unspoken subtexts, events, and relationships outside the anthropologist's purview. Assemblies could also tax the energies of the most patient observer. Important assemblies lasted between four and eight hours. Ejidatarios moved among topics, revisited questions, and held repeated votes on the same issue. The votes were not so much decisive as a means to an end. Through votes, ejidatarios judged whether the group had reached a consensus and whether dissenters had been sufficiently appeased.

The excerpt below derives from an assembly in which Orozco's simmering question of ejidatario and poblador relations broke into the open. Some background to these events is necessary. For months prior to the assembly, Mestizo ejidatarios had been impatient with the newcomers. I wondered to what extent ejidatarios feared the pobladores' strength, as the refugees doubled the ejido's size and left the fractious Mestizos a minority. Mestizo ejidatarios were especially keen that people pay their entrance fees. But, they also worried the pobladores might, instead, take advantage of *them*. Ejidatarios argued, "We support newcomers, but they take our help and then leave. That's why we're so distrusting." In the excerpt, ejidatarios refer to another group of pobladores who acquired government agricultural loans and later "left under cover of night." Ejidatarios worried they would be saddled with the debt.

Ejidatarios feared that, while they sought to use pobladores to boost their economic position, poblador demands for land and aid might have a countereffect. Thus, underlying this debate were persistent anxieties about poverty. Poverty played out in different ways. Ejidatarios asserted a shared poverty with pobladores—when they said "we're all screwed"—that was clearly not in evidence. Many pobladores were launching tenuous farm operations while living ten people in a one-room house. In voicing questions of poverty, Orozco's ejidatarios skirted the extent to which poblador poverty might contribute to ejidatarios' survival.

This debate also had ethnic nuances, as Mestizo and Ch'ol ejidatarios differed over whether the ejido had enough land for the pobladores. The ethnic dimension was not always straightforward. The two Ch'ol office holders sought to support the newcomers without alienating Mestizo neighbors. Ch'ol ejidatarios, who stood outside the ejido's governing committees, had their opinions, but they had long since ceded the ejido's governance. As a small group vied for control of Orozco, Ch'ol ejidatarios implied the constant turf battles were not worth the effort.

Orozco's ethnic conflict ran deep, but it rarely entered the public domain. In their homes, Mestiza women complained that Ch'ol used witchcraft and did not know how to behave as *compadres*, the fictive kin ties that bind families together. Ch'ol pobladores responded to Mestizo ejidatarios by saying, "It seems their heart does not know God." This doubt about one another's morality was seldom seen in public, except on one occasion. A drunken Ch'ol man ranted on the ejido's square, in Spanish, that the Spanish-speaking people (Españoles, or Mestizos) were few and the "neighbors" (vecinos, or Ch'ol) were many. The vecinos should advance their own candidates and take over the ejido. The Spanish-speaking people, he said, "pay no attention to us." His audience of Ch'ol men shifted uncomfortably and quietly drifted away. Not everyone accepted this politicized ethnic consciousness. The implications of such a position were hugely problematic.[5] The ejido, designed to subordinate communities to the state, had little means to deal with this scale of conflict. At the same time, the ejido wove households together in a web of interdependence. A few families included marriages of mixed ethnicities. This ethnic subtext further complicated the ideals of ejidal governance that arise in the following excerpt.

The Isolated Ejidal Assembly

Orozco's assembly to deal with overdue entrance fees began at 6 p.m. on an April evening and continued for three hours. Ejidatarios called on each poblador to explain why, after a year and a half, he had not paid his fee.[6] The electricity was out that night, so the meeting continued by candlelight. The air in the one-room building, with its laminated cardboard roof, felt close. The ejido's men crowded in attendance, while women listened from outside the door. As a point of background, the meeting took place following a drought year, when many failed to harvest corn, but some effectively harvested jalapeño chile peppers, the region's cash crop. Dionicio spoke first as the pobladores' senior man:

> DIONICIO: I haven't been able to pay, but not because I don't want to. There's no work, and although we have corn, it isn't enough. Life is difficult. We're screwed (estamos jodidos). But, we'll see if in May we can earn a little money. We'll see if we have a better harvest this time and pay during the chile season. We're living here, our families are here, and we'll continue to work in faenas.
>
> GUILLERMO (ejidal president): Well, Dionicio spoke, and he spoke well. As long as there isn't a problem, there won't be an argument. But I was talking to Sergio [a chile buyer] in Xpujil. He said he has a problem with someone here in the ejido. I don't know who, but someone seems to have borrowed seeds and chemicals from Sergio and not delivered his harvest. He sold it to another buyer. This person is starting a serious argument, and it's not fair. I said to Sergio, "Why didn't you tell me before, so I could bring it up in an assembly?" If one person does this, the whole ejido could be affected.
>
> LUCIANO (speaks in Ch'ol, Guillermo translates): I wanted to pay my entrance fee and fulfill my promise. I live here, I eat here, I have to pay. But, my family is big. There isn't enough money, but if you'll accept $60 now, I will finish paying.
>
> GERARDO (Ch'ol ejidal committee member): In this case it's okay. Luciano didn't sell any chile this year. People should try to pay little by little, because it's embarrassing (da pena) for us to have to ask. The problem is when people don't want to pay anything at all. There are people who sold chile and didn't pay anything.
>
> VENANCIO (Mestizo ejidal committee member): Who on the list received PROCAMPO? [PROCAMPO is a subsidy that pays cash for planting corn, among other crops; see below and chap. 6]?
>
> LUCIANO: I didn't receive any. I didn't sign up because I didn't plant any corn.
>
> VENANCIO: What about your son? Didn't he receive PROCAMPO?

The ejidatarios discussed Luciano's son, who received a small PRO-CAMPO payment and returned to Chiapas. Don Guillermo reminded the newcomers that other ejidos did not even allow their pobladores access to PROCAMPO. The ejidatarios agreed to erase Luciano's son from the list of pobladores. At a later assembly, they debated who should occupy the young man's place in PROCAMPO. Luciano protested the erasure: "He didn't say he was leaving permanently. What if he returns tomorrow?" The ejidatarios decided he could stay as a visitor but not as a poblador.

The ejidatarios then turned to the prickly situation of Alonso. Alonso was the son-in-law of a poblador, Romero. Alonso had begun farming in the ejido in the previous month. The ejidatarios disagreed whether Alonso received permission to work ejidal lands. For those who opposed his presence, Alonso betrayed ejidatarios' vulnerability in controlling their land. In the exchange, they pressured Romero and the ejidatario who originally lent Romero land. Guillermo translates for Alonso, who asks if the ejidatarios will allow him to pay his entrance fee in the future, when he has the money.

GUILLERMO: Now, Alonso is not yet on the list of pobladores. He's working, but he says there isn't enough money to take care of his family. He's even buying corn.

VENANCIO (angrily): I don't know how this can be! When did we accept this man?! Nobody has said anything to him, so I don't know who accepted him!

GUILLERMO: Alonso spoke in the last assembly and said when he gets money he'll pay us. We are just as humble as the pobladores.

PACO (Mestizo president of vigilance council, the office that oversees where people plant): I wasn't at that assembly, but he came to my house. He said he was going to pay. I told him that all the houses in the ejido were occupied, and when he asked where he might plant, I told him he would have to wait for the next assembly. But, I hear he's planting anyway. I don't know who showed him where to go. I think it was Romero.

VENANCIO (now livid): This is bad! How can a poblador give someone the authority to work here?! Eusebio, didn't you lend Romero land?

EUSEBIO: I did, but I don't know who's working there.

GERARDO: Venancio is right. Pobladores can't just lend land to whomever. An ejidatario doesn't even have the right to tell someone to work in the common lands.

PACO: There it is Romero. You have a problem.

GERARDO: Look, we need to finish with the business of the entrance fees. Let's get back to this later.

Other ejidatarios agreed and made noises about the fine they would levy against Romero. But, the situation was never resolved. When the issue of the fine came up, Romero argued that "the land is there to support everyone." Paco responded, "That's not the point. The point is to respect the ejidal authorities." Ch'ol ejidatarios gently defended Romero and Alonso. Mestizo ejidatarios countered, if they accept Alonso, "When will the problem end?" Ejidatarios worried Alonso might be felling older growth forest, for which authorities would hold them all responsible. In reality, ejidatarios could not prevent Alonso from working with his family and having failed to preempt his own farming concern, they would have to sabotage Alonso's fields to enforce their ruling.

Finally, the ejidatarios moved on to Ignacio. All pobladores doubted the ejidatarios would give them land. Many held off paying their entrance fees as they sized up the situation. Ignacio, however, was the most vocal in this complaint. He, also, had made a few trips to Chiapas to look for land there.

GUILLERMO: I think now we need to talk seriously with Ignacio, to learn more about his situation.

VENANCIO: If we give him land, of course, it's to his advantage to pay. If not, he doesn't want to help out the ejido.

GERARDO: He had land to work. I supported him with two hectares, and he had PROCAMPO. I think he didn't want to pay because he doesn't want to stay. If he didn't pay when he had the money, how's he going to pay now?

GUILLERMO: When PROCAMPO pays again, he better not do the same or we'll get him in the assembly (lo jalamos en la asamblea).

VENANCIO: The same thing is going to happen again. Ignacio likes his drink. We all like it, but we won't see his money.

GERARDO: That's right, and then it will be like that group who took their loans and left under the cover of night. The ejido was left with that debt.

PACO (speaking to other ejidatarios): When these people came, we told them we weren't going to give them land, but they would have to pay their entrance fees. That way they could take advantage of ejidal services, like water. They haven't been without water, and we've known times the children went eight days without being able to take a bath. We're not demanding they stay with us.

The ejidatarios discussed how much chile Ignacio harvested and at what price he sold it. They debated how much corn he sold and whether he planned to sell his house. Ignacio was quiet as ejidatarios talked about his expulsion. This is the harshest punishment ejidatarios could mete, one that touched on a common insecurity. Both Orozco and San Lorenzo were home to people once forced out of an ejido. Such a momentous decision required consensus, for which ejidal officers pressed those who had thus far been silent.

> VENANCIO: What does everyone else say? Because, the majority aren't speaking. Later, you'll say the committee doesn't listen to you. You'll say we're mean, but this is embarrassing (da pena) for us, too. We're all screwed (estamos jodidos).
> PACO: Eusebio, what do you say? You're an ejidatario. Say something! You can speak in Ch'ol.
> GUILLERMO: I don't want the committee to look bad. People should speak up. I'll write up whatever decision the assembly approves.
> VENANCIO: Since when does the majority ever speak? Let's move on.

The majority never did speak, but the officers read the ejidatarios' response in their silence. Ignacio remained in the ejido, and the meeting continued. The conflicts raised at the meeting persisted for years. Orozco's frustrated pobladores eventually moved to an abandoned village inside the Calakmul Biosphere Reserve. Only in the year 2000 did pobladores who stayed in Orozco receive land.

Certainly not all ejidal relations were this contentious. In San Lorenzo, the same dynamics supported more felicitous events—such as organizing sport teams and providing financial aid for widows. I chose to share this material because it demonstrates both the political tools at hand and the pressure people can bring to bear on one another. People in an ejido may interfere in someone's personal business dealings (as in the case of the chile sales), and they may come between an individual and government or nongovernmental farm programs. People can also interfere in one another's agricultural activities. Orozco's ejidatarios later threatened to confiscate the crops of people who failed to pay their entrance fees. Anticipating such problems, pobladores cultivated an appearance of poverty with which they sought ejidatario aid. In these aspects, poblador-ejidatario relations mirrored the campesino-government relations described later.

In Calakmul's ejidos, people wed agrarian concerns to an emotional intensity built on a precarious subsistence and the closeness of small-town life. A San Lorenzan described the anxiety levels ejidal members could inflict in these exchanges: "They talk and talk and talk. You don't know how hard it can be when they start talking!" If dramatic performance shaped involvement in an argument, the engagement itself was made possible by ejidal members' interdependence. Performative aspects of disputes further allowed people in Calakmul to draw on ideals of personal willpower in ways that countered these group dynamics.

Personal Acumen in Ejidal Disputes

The example of Josué demonstrates this notion of personal acumen. Josué eagerly described his response to ejidal challenges, convinced as he was that his superior intelligence and willpower would cause him to win out over his rivals. His case is relevant because, in disputes and ejidal assemblies, people carefully measured how a person might react to challenges. Should a widow inherit her husband's land? Ejidatarios said it depended on how she presented herself to the ejido's assembly. How should a petty thief be punished? Ejidatarios responded by examining what demands a victim could enforce. In Josué's case, he wove ideas of environmentalism into his quest to become an ejidatario. This inclusion was partly for my benefit, since my introduction to San Lorenzo through the Regional Council labeled me an environmentalist. As one of San Lorenzo's few pobladores, Josué believed he was denied land and ejidatario status as part of a campaign to run him out of the village. I had arrived at Josué's home seeking his migration history. He responded by describing the ejido's factionalism and, implicitly, asked that I take his side in matters. Notice how, in his argument, Josué moves between notions of individual autonomy and appeals to state agents and ties both these points to questions of subsistence:

[The ejidatarios] don't want someone to bring more strength. Since I arrived here I haven't bought corn. They don't work because they're always wandering around hunting in the woods. The first day they give me problems, I'm going to denounce them to the wildlife authorities. The same people who throw around trouble are the same ones who don't work and shoot wildlife.

. . . The ejidatarios gave land even to minors and conveniently put me aside. They thought that would finish me off, but if they want me out, I won't be going. They want to see me working for them, begging at their houses, but my heart is stronger than that. The people here lack ideas. "How is it that the foreigners (fuereños) have so many crops?" they ask. . . . Well, if a person has an idea, but he doesn't like to get sunburned, he won't put it into action. [I asked for clarification on the word *foreigner*.] Don't you see that they're all from the same state? That's how they see someone else as strange (extraño).

Although Josué touches on themes resonant with Orozco's assembly, his decisiveness contrasts with the ambivalence of Orozco's ejidatarios. There, the emotional intensity appeared to fall flat when ejidatarios refused to fine Romero or expel Ignacio. Jane Collier writes that ejidal members always have to juggle wanting to get their way with the need to work out a compromise that lets them live together in these close settings (Collier 1973). Because of this, ejidatarios generally opted for momentary fixes that avoided more damaging ruptures. At the same time, ejidatarios and pobladores alike kept in play the possibility of ending relations, of moving on, or of forcing someone out of the ejido. For ejidatarios, a definitive break with an opponent would decrease their influence in a larger way (Warman 1980:295). However, the threat of a break—one that placed an opponent and his family's subsistence in crisis—proved effective in forcing antagonists into a dispute.

The gendered and ethnic quality of these arguments should not go unnoticed. Men created powerful personas through aggressive performances, while Mestizos and Ch'ol differed in the value they placed on these performances. Ch'ol complained Mestizos took aggression too far. Ch'ol rules for handling disputes entailed "using pretty words" and giving an opponent the chance to save face. Ch'ol ejidos were not free from conflict, but Ch'ol and Mestizo norms for arguing differed markedly. At the same time, both groups agreed that aggression was men's work, not women's, even though women's ideas and actions could be central to disputes (see below). Performances were necessary to men's power but not sufficient. Over time, a man's willingness to back his words with deeds would undergo testing. Josué, for example, attempted to poison an opponent's dog that kept eating his chickens (the rival had refused to restrain the dog). Below, I discuss a fist fight between Orozco's president and his principal rival.

Aggressive protagonists calculated their success based on the ejido's insularity. They estimated reprisals could be confined to the small set of ejidal relations managed in their everyday lives. Indeed, despite Josué's assertions, people hesitated to seek recourse outside the ejido, because external authorities were undependable. (Josué himself occasionally joined in the camaraderie of the same hunting parties he reproved.) A failed appeal to police or agrarian officials could cause a complainant even more trouble inside the ejido. What might happen if outside state agents did intervene in a dispute? Following closer consideration of women's roles in ejidos, I consider such everyday interactions between ejidal members and state agents.

The Women's Ejido

Where men's influence was readily visible, understanding women's influence in ejidos required attention to informal structures. Even though women could vote in presidential, gubernatorial, and other elections, they could not vote for the men who represented their ejido. Because of this, women asserted their influence in ways not always clear to outsiders. Women did hold assemblies exclusive of men, but these lacked any power to rule on ejidal policy. The assemblies were linked to government initiatives, such as the Women's Agro-Industrial Unity (Unidad Agro-Industrial de la Mujer, or UAIM). Where men were ejidatarios, women were members of the UAIM (pronounced why-eem). UAIM meetings reflected the different shapes of men's and women's political realms in the two ejidos. In San Lorenzo, the UAIM meetings were festive. Women who spent most of their time at home took the chance to gossip and joke with neighbors. Women whose husbands barely spoke to one another could, at least, put on a jovial face. In Orozco, the UAIM meetings were quiet affairs. Without fail, women sat close to relatives, or, lacking relations in the ejido, they sat alone. In contrast to Orozco's fluid men's assemblies, one could chart Orozco's factionalism in the women's seating arrangement.

Through the UAIM, women accessed agricultural loans and other projects that almost always demanded men's participation. Agricultural loans required women to plant crops, work that often demanded men's help. Some programs required women to travel, for which a wife would need her husband's permission. A San Lorenzo program that offered women roofing material included a copayment, which women would likely have to collect from their husbands. Only women who could count on their husbands' support were able to take advantage of UAIM incentives, and, purposefully or not, these programs reinforced women's dependence on men.

UAIM structures touched on the point that a woman's power was framed by her relationship with her husband. In this sense, women defended their rights within their marriages and extended families just as men defended their rights within the assembly. At the same time, a marriage's emotional content made the relationship entirely unlike men's associations. A woman and a man's public relationship resulted from the complex inner workings of their marriage. Couples offered glimpses into these processes, but, at Calakmul, gathering information on marital dynamics presented special difficulties. Marital norms required that wives never publicly contradict their husbands on ejidal policies. Wives might complain about a husband's drinking, his violence, or his personality quirks. In ejidal matters, however, wives were their husband's allies.

This is not to say that women worked only through their husbands. Women were creative agents within ejidos, even if they were denied a formal voice. Women did not openly contribute to assemblies, but information discussed at the meetings was seen by all parties as affecting men and women alike. Following assemblies, men typically returned home and discussed the meeting with their wives. In these private exchanges (which I did not witness), couples debated issues and formulated a common response.

Women's power spilled out from the house as they contributed to public opinion through the vox populi and their influence on family members. I had the opportunity to see this influence translate into women's roles as peace makers in a dispute that impinged on the ejido's position in Calakmul's conservation-development agenda. After a weekend in Zoh Laguna, I returned to Orozco to find a drunken fistfight had broken out between Don Guillermo and his Mestizo rival for Orozco's presidency. The rival reportedly chastised Guillermo for thinking his job made him important. Working at the Regional Council, Guillermo was the only Orozcan with a secure salary. The rival also questioned Guillermo's masculinity by noting that Guillermo had no sons. Women separated the fighting men and monitored the ensuing tensions. For days, the men continued their liquored posturing on the public square. Wives and daughters watched warily, ready to steer their men home should things get out of hand. Privately, the women hurled ethnic and familial insults as they blamed the chaos on their opponents.

Development practitioners often portrayed Calakmul's women as strongly oppressed because of their lack of formal power. It is true that women stood outside the most important areas of ejidal decision making, and this fact restricted their power within and beyond the ejido. It is also true that within a marriage, men's decisions were expected to prevail. As I got to know women, however, I saw how such blanket statements glossed over women's informal power and failed to do justice to women's struggles. Calakmul's technical staff learned of the Orozco fistfight and speculated whether Guillermo's black eye marked his fall from power. Ingenieros had little notion of women's role in shaping the lines of cleavage that impinged on Orozco's relationship to conservation-development programmers. Women's power was not always visible in a place where men, operating within male-dominated power structures, assumed a male prerogative. Even Calakmul's conservation-development managers could

be ambivalent about this public erasure as they reinforced a male hegemony (see chap. 7). Nonetheless, women's power was palpable within
Calakmul's ejidos even as women were marginalized in regional environmental management.

The Ejidal-State Archipelago

Thus far, I have depicted the ejido as an isolated island to emphasize
the immediacy of intra-ejidal relations. No ejido, however, is entirely
detached. In fact, some researchers have described Mexico's ejidos as permeated by the state (de Janvry et al. 1997; Otero 1999). At Calakmul, people
were furthermore aware of events taking place in area ejidos. Gossip networks converged on Xpujil's shops, street corners, and cantinas, where
people evaluated events throughout the region. These connections require
careful contextualization. Apart from border issues, other ejidos had no
jurisdiction over Orozco and San Lorenzo's internal workings. At the
same time, Orozcans and San Lorenzans worried gossip might affect their
ejidos' reputations, especially as ejidos competed for state programs. Government aid deeply affected ejidal members and their relationships with
one another. The state, nonetheless, stopped short of *determining* these
relations and often reinforced ejidal members' independence in dealing
with one another.

The two programs I describe here show the combined inability and
unwillingness of state agents to follow through on regulating an ejido's
internal affairs. The programs also demonstrate spaces where ejidal members could resist state actions. The examples draw on different perspectives. In the first case, state officers described how they should regulate
ejidos and how impossible this mandate was to carry out in practice. In
the second case, Orozco's women sought to resolve interpersonal arguments through a state development project. In each example, Calakmul's
ejidos and state offices appear as a series of islands. Standing on the shores
of these islands, people regarded one another and considered the implications of each other's presence. But, the bridges connecting the islands were
often flimsy.

Earlier, Orozco's ejidatarios raised the issue of PROCAMPO payments.
PROCAMPO served as a useful tool in forcing poblador compliance because, in 1995, PROCAMPO was the largest subsidy in Calakmul (see chap.
6). The program paid campesinos a fixed sum for each hectare of land
planted in pasture or subsistence crops, including corn, beans, and rice.
Authorities devised PROCAMPO in response to the 1994 North American
Free Trade Agreement (NAFTA). NAFTA threatened to bring cheap U.S. and

Canadian corn onto the Mexican market. Correctly, as it turned out, policy makers worried that low corn prices would further impoverish subsistence producers. PROCAMPO payments aimed to offset losses to campesinos unwittingly forced into this free trade relationship. People in Calakmul, however, knew little of these policy debates. Instead, they described PROCAMPO, as they did all government aid, as "a help."

To get the program off the ground, campesinos first needed to volunteer how many hectares of land they would inscribe in the program. PROCAMPO ingenieros held ejido assemblies to conduct this census. (Women's participation was left to the ingenieros' discretion. An officer in Orozco required women to participate, but San Lorenzo's women were not given this opportunity.) Officials feared that if people knew of the impending subsidy, they would inflate the amount they farmed. Thus, at the time, even PROCAMPO staff were uninformed of the program's contents. Many campesinos underreported their farming, fearing the state would use the census to impose a tax. One ingeniero congratulated himself on overcoming such skepticism in an ejido that now receives the highest PROCAMPO payments in Calakmul. He exhorted ejidatarios, "We don't know what's coming, but if it's a tax, we'll pay it. If it's a benefit, we'll benefit from all the work we do." With all its confusions, this census turned out to be a critical count. Throughout the program's fifteen-year duration, people received payments based on the amount agreed to in the original census. Failure to plant the noted hectareage could lead to expulsion from the program. PROCAMPO staff monitored compliance by requiring that ejidal members appoint a liaison to report anyone who failed to sow his or her allotted amount.

Despite assertions of some common "we," staffers' relations with the liaisons betrayed a divide between ingenieros and campesinos. The ingenieros admitted they usually doubted the truth of liaison denunciations, concluding the reports were vendettas motivated by internal ejidal conflicts. To avoid being caught in this factionalism, ingenieros asked accusers to evidence their claim with signed statements from the ejido's authorities. This demand required that liaisons rally the ejido around their accusation, a difficult proposition if ejidal authorities wanted to keep peace. In general, the three staffers noted that, given their responsibility for more than seventy ejidos, they did not have the personnel to investigate denunciations. Their supervisors, in any case, were not that concerned with compliance in Calakmul. From a larger perspective, local payments for 1 to 20 hectares appeared insignificant in comparison to payments for 200 hectares taking place elsewhere. State monitoring was concentrated in these places of larger payments. In Calakmul, PROCAMPO demanded ejidatarios monitor one another and supplied a new element in intra-ejidal disputes, even though PROCAMPO staff admitted little need for such oversight. This policy allowed ejidal members to use PROCAMPO to regulate one another, while simultaneously disallowing state enforcement of such regulations.

Orozcans and San Lorenzans viewed this quixotic behavior as typical. They were never sure what might result when their disputes entered the larger state framework. Would authorities act? With what force? Conventional wisdom asserted the bribes demanded by state bureaucrats made it futile to seek state aid. Still, ejidal members regularly threatened recourse to higher authorities precisely because the doubtful quality of government involvement held a sway of its own. Often enough, fear of the unknown, rather than assurances of justice, connected families to one another vis-à-vis government agents.

Other researchers have remarked on rural Mexicans' desire to keep the state at bay (Nader 1990). Sometimes, however, this was not possible. Emergencies, such as droughts, and even less dramatic problems were sometimes beyond an ejido's or an individual's slim resources. Orozco's women called on county managers of a cattle project to help them resolve a dispute that threatened the project's existence. Of all the projects entering Orozco, people arguably lent the most importance to this one. Campesinos viewed cattle as the key to wealth. Orozcans frequently asked that I take portraits of them standing alongside their cows, much like people in the United States might display cars or homes in photographs. Although large herds usually begin with the help of urban investors,[7] Orozcans hoped to use this project to start independent cattle ventures.

County officials sponsored the project by providing loans to Orozco's UAIM. The women used the funds to purchase their cows. The UAIM also borrowed collectively to buy a bull that would build the women's individual herds. In addition to creating income, the project had an environmental slant. Policy makers worried that clearing for pasture contributed to deforestation. The project thus required women to feed the cattle. Cattle owners spent at least one hour a day collecting edible leaves in nearby forests to feed the animals.

Problems arose when the women tried to share this work to maintain the bull. Doña Paula, the UAIM's exasperated Mestiza president, had to pick up the slack when other women reneged on their obligations. Paula asked a project manager to visit and pressure everyone into doing their share to feed the bull. Meanwhile, the UAIM officers were in a state of disarray, and Paula was having trouble finding anyone willing to help out.

The UAIM secretary had renounced her position. Publicly, she said she was unqualified because she was illiterate. Privately, she said the women complained that her husband interfered in UAIM affairs. The UAIM delegate to the Regional Council also had quit her post. She cited her pregnancy and her husband's unwillingness to let her travel. Privately, she said, some of the women questioned her participation because she was a poblador. This Mestizo family was able to use kin ties to access development programs. As with the men's assembly, the UAIM meeting demonstrated tensions surrounding ethnicity and poblador/ejidatario status.

The women convened on a sunny afternoon. The ingeniero began with a brief speech. This was his first visit to Orozco, and he did his best to build rapport. He declared that the program was designed to help women "work together, so there aren't any divisions. . . . I want to know what is the problem and help to find a solution. Here everyone has a voice and a vote."

Paula explained the problems began when Chencha's cow died. "Was the cow insured?" the ingeniero interjected. Paula answered in the negative. At the project's start, only six women gave money for insurance, and since this was not a majority, they did not qualify for insurance. Insurance would have covered the loss of the cow whose cost contributed to the argument. The ingeniero responded they did not actually need a majority to qualify for insurance, and whoever explained the program gave incorrect information. Paula continued reporting that, since the cow died, Chencha did not want to help maintain the bull: "We said that the obligation to the bull was separate, so that even if a woman's cow died, she should continue providing food for the bull." Chencha spoke in Ch'ol to say she had paid for the deceased cow, so she owed nothing to the group.

The ingeniero responded that Chencha should support the bull. By refusing, she absented herself from the group. She could not simply leave and reenter the UAIM at will. Paula expressed some doubt about whether the cow was really paid in full, implying the UAIM would be responsible for the debt. At this point, Chencha ran home to collect receipts that proved her payments.

In the intervening moments, the ingeniero urged the women to unite: "I'm from an ejido. I grew up under a thatched roof. I want you to unite." Paula took advantage of the break to assert that Elsa, a Ch'ol UAIM officer, improperly maintained the list of who should give food to the bull. Elsa's sister, a capable Spanish speaker, came to her defense. She corrected Paula for not advising people when to feed the bull. Meanwhile, Chencha had returned. The ingeniero noted the family made final payment on the cow just the previous day. "Since her husband works for the Regional Council, they have money," Paula explained.

As the meeting descended into finger pointing, the manager tried to restore some feeling of goodwill. "We're all human beings here. We all have problems, but we can find solutions to our problems. Chencha should continue supporting the bull, so the group doesn't disintegrate. Soon the rains will be on us, and there will be pasture everywhere. This problem will pass. Is everyone in agreement?"

Paula agreed, but complained that "as soon you leave, everyone pulls back. In other meetings, it's been the same. As soon as the ingeniero leaves, some of the women threaten to sell their cows." The ingeniero emphasized that each woman had an obligation to the group, regardless of the cows: "I repeat, I'm from the country. I don't like to fool people. I won't just walk away from this meeting and leave it at that. My office is the one that lent you the money, and we want you to take advantage of the program. If the bull dies, who will pay us our money? If this program succeeds, I will have the honor of seeing you all continue to work. I will come visit more often to make sure the project is succeeding. Are there other problems?" Paula responded that when she sent her son to remind women to feed the bull, "they answer the boy with rude words." The ingeniero refused to address the issue, saying the matter was an internal problem.

The ingeniero never did return to oversee the fragile project, and the following year, most of Orozco's women sold their cows. The project failed for a combination of technical and interpersonal issues. As Orozco's women pressed on with the details of snubs and hurt feelings, it became clear that project ideals of harmonious cooperation clashed with the reality of ejidal divisions. Even when ingenieros recognized ethnic and hierarchical politics, they regularly refrained from addressing such problems, citing them as internal ejidal matters. This refusal left a broad gap between the kinds of justice people sought from government agents and the kinds of justice agents were willing or able to deliver.

In this particular case, the women were using state offices to work out the latest episode in long-standing disagreements. The argument's extension from the bull to questions of who was employed, and who got along with whom indicated that the subtext may have been more relevant than the original complaint. Jane Collier notes that, in Chiapas, local judges addressing such arguments looked beyond current grievances in search of a problem's source (Collier 1973). By addressing this history of relating, judges developed what they hoped would be a more enduring compromise. Despite this project manager's assertions of his own rural identity, this wider aspect of the dispute was lost on him. Even if he were able to ascertain what Orozco's women were asking of him, the passing quality of his position meant his effect on ejidal relations was cursory.

In the end, the cattle project raised many of the problems the ingeniero hesitated to resolve. The project required that the women work together, but project managers could not affect the *way* women worked together. The project required women to take on debt, when few women had access to income. Orozco's women were able to pay only a part of their cattle debts with funds from a separate government credit scheme. One might note with irony the ingeniero's anti-environmental solution of putting the cattle out to pasture. In general, the project's work requirements were as much a problem as the women's inability to organize. Families strained under the labor of collecting forage. Chencha's cow had died of hunger, because the family was unable to feed it sufficiently. These technical problems never arose in the meeting. Instead, Orozco's women bristled against forced cooperation and, implicitly, bristled against this reproduction of the ejido's organization.

Who were these ingenieros who comprised such a critical component of state formation at Calakmul? Typically, ingenieros were sons of campesinos (only three of the dozens of ingenieros working in Calakmul were women) who, upon graduating from university, took up jobs providing advice and services. Calakmul's ingenieros were as engaging and complex as the campesinos with whom they worked. The majority came from northern Mexico; a second group originated from the Yucatán peninsula. Only one area ingeniero had grown up in Calakmul. With roots in both campesino and middle-class society, ingenieros' motivations included social activism, economic advancement, and the excitement they found in Calakmul's social and ecological wildness. While some ingenieros differentiated themselves from campesinos, others worked to bridge the divide they otherwise depended upon for their livelihood.

When state-employed ingenieros visited San Lorenzo and Orozco, they staged assemblies where an ejidal space briefly transformed into a national space, one brokered by the ingeniero. The paternalism characteristic of this space is evident from the above. Less evident, but equally salient, is the extent this paternalism was based on ingenieros as educated, salaried people in the know and campesinos as overly emotional, difficult individuals who failed to see reason (Champagne 2002; Liebow 2002). These characterizations allowed ingenieros to obscure the way they might resort to emotional blackmail to enforce their projects (Julia Murphy, personal communication) or persist with projects that were ecologically and/or economically unsound (Champagne 2002). The dichotomy was useful in an additional way. It reinforced an ingeniero prerogative to comment on and influence ejidal workings without the need for inge-nieros to take responsibility for ejidal affairs. This point will become especially important in discussing the limits to Calakmul's conservation-development agenda.

Adding to these complications, during the early 1990s, the ejido itself was undergoing transformations such that its governing structure was in doubt. We already saw how the ejido acted as a performative stage for creating power, a site of subordination, a welcoming home, a site of con-flict, an economic entity, and an environmental entity (see also Goldring 1998). Ejido reforms did little to streamline the ejido's multiple and con-flicting meanings. Instead, the modifications further wove environmental policies into familiar ejidal contradictions.

Agrarian Changes, Community Changes?

During the 1990s, Orozcans and San Lorenzans took part in a social experiment, initiated when federal authorities changed the content of Article 27. This change in land tenure could potentially alter the fabric of ejidal members' land management and their everyday friendships and animosities. Perhaps doubts about these implications are the main reason that, nationally, ejidatarios have largely declined privatization (Cornelius and Myhre 1998; Jones 2000). At Calakmul, environmental concerns fur-ther inhibited the reforms, known locally by the acronym PROCEDE (Pro-gram for the Certification of Ejido Land Rights and the Titling of Urban House Plots). In these paragraphs, I explore the effects of PROCEDE, shift-ing again between campesino and ingeniero perspectives. Then, I follow the reforms to Orozco, San Lorenzo, and Calakmul more broadly, where, years after their implementation, ejidatarios continued to decipher the reforms' content and implications. In this brief space, it would be impos-sible to cover this topic comprehensively (see Haenn forthcoming). Here, I concentrate on areas that relate the program's ambivalence: ingenieros' diverse interpretations of the program as well as the program's parallel reinforcement of common and private property norms.

In 1995, PROCEDE staff in Xpujil outlined the national program to me before describing its altered implementation in Calakmul. PROCEDE's veterinarian-trained staffer described the program as an end to the "pa-ternalism" and "deceit" in government-farmer relations. Government agents, he said, had deceived people by promising land when none was available. Additionally, state officers used ejidal tenures to interfere in ejidal affairs. Before the reforms, state officers of all stripes offered development programs with an attitude of "participate or we won't help you at all." "Before," the veterinarian declared, "it was chaos. Campesinos did not know if the land belonged to the nation, the ejido, or individual ejidatarios. The changes clarify that land belongs to the ejido."

As our conversation continued, however, it became clear that PRO-CEDE at Calakmul would maintain the former chaos. At a national level, PROCEDE offered ejidatarios three possible land titles: to house plots, farm plots (or parcels), and a percentage of the value of common goods (including common lands). In Calakmul, ejidatarios would be allowed to privatize their house plots and receive a certificate to a certain percentage of community goods/land. Crucially, the program would not permit titling of agricultural lands. As with former ejidal tenures, the certificates associated with common lands signified usufruct rights, and relations between ejidal members would remain largely unchanged. The ingeniero hesitated to admit these contradictions but finally explained that privatization of parcels had been forbidden due to area forests. The reforms treated forests differently from agricultural lands.[8] Forested lands could not be broken up into privatized parcels (Zabin 1998:412). Legally, state environmental officers were supposed to study ejidatario parcels and map out standing forests. Forests could then be removed from the titling process, and ejidatarios would receive a certificate to land they cultivated. At Calakmul, this narrow option was rejected by ejidatarios, who saw it as a loss of land. The ingeniero specified the connection between the ejido and state environmental regimes: "If they [ejidatarios] have private property, the government cannot affect their actions (el gobierno no puede meterse)." Furthermore, the staffer hinted at continued paternalism. In his personal opinion, campesinos lacked the training to administer private property ("no son capacitados"). He compared local people with residents of a distant ejido who counted agronomists among their members. That group handled computers, photocopiers, and a truck. By implication, campesinos' lack of formal education and scant economic resources meant they were too immature to manage their own affairs (cf. Escobar 1995; Pigg 1992).

In 1995, Calakmul's ejidos were in the early stages of participating in PROCEDE, and only by 2001 were the program's effects apparent. The slow pace of implementation (only two PROCEDE staffers were responsible for the Calakmul region) gave people plenty of time to think about its implications. Some Orozcans saw the program as providing more secure land rights: "With the new law a person will always be an ejidatario.

Nobody can take away someone's land." Another Orozcan viewed PRO-CEDE as a way to profit on his land. He expected to title his parcel, sell the deed, and continue working on Orozco's common lands. Ejidal autonomy and control were also important issues. People interpreted the changes as strengthening ejidatario decisions in respect to external state agencies. Over time, San Lorenzans and Orozcans used PROCEDE's environmental aims to shore up land claims and reinforce this autonomy.

Ejidatarios, in 2001, reported that, since PROCEDE, they were "closed" to new migrants. They meant that PROCEDE had capped the number of ejidatarios the ejido could house. In the past, ejidatarios assigned their sons and new arrivals ejidatario status whenever they found it convenient. Following PROCEDE, they said, a person could become an ejidatario only if he or she purchased someone's ejidal rights or if an existing ejidatario died, thereby leaving a spot to fill. Both Orozco and San Lorenzo continued to house pobladores. Under these restrictive conditions, these people now had little chance of becoming ejidatarios.

This interpretation of PROCEDE was not technically correct, but its widespread adoption in Calakmul was intriguing.[9] Did ejidatarios rework PROCEDE, or did ingenieros send out confused messages? The two inge-nieros working with PROCEDE in 2001 (distinct from that above) gave two different answers to the question of whether PROCEDE "closed" ejidos. One ingeniero answered a strong negative, but he also noted that he was aware of only one ejido in Campeche that chose to adopt PROCEDE in a way that would allow them to create new ejidatarios. The second ingeniero hedged his response. He claimed the bureaucratic process by which ejidatarios could name individuals to their ranks was not recommended "because people confuse this process with a land sale." This ingeniero did not connect his hesitancy to Calakmul's environmental setting.

This conflation of land sales with the sale of ejidal rights and the hesitation to commodify farmland more generally was notable. At a na-tional level, PROCEDE's private property aspect included a move toward commodified ejido lands. Ingenieros, who might reflexively side with Mexico's tradition of barring ejidal land sales or who recognized the bu-reaucratic failings of their own institution, could effectively subvert na-tional aims and open a space for local reinterpretations. In the case of Calakmul, however, this repackaging ultimately coincided with national agendas. "Closed" ejidos circumscribe the number of ejidatarios and, consequently, government obligations to a newly delimited sector.

My excursion into the hotly debated question of ejidal land tenure will surely prove too brief for those anxious for answers to questions regarding Article 27 and its changes. However, for my purposes, the above description of PROCEDE communicates two lessons. The first is the persistent contradictions in state policies toward this critical component of people's agrarian lives and, by extension, their land management. The second lesson is ejidal members' creative reworkings of these inconsistencies.

With this description, the chapter completes a path from the ejido to the ejido/state space to national ejidal policies. Now I return to the ejido to complicate this narrative. I do so because the ejido played such a critical role in conservation-development programming. Top-down planners assumed a relatively open course that their strategies might follow into ejidal members' lives. International conservation and development specialists often had little understanding of the ejido's structure, although the ejido's collective aspects appealed to some outsiders' romantic notions of political solidarity. The ejido thus provided an air of populism to Calakmul's conservation-development projects. It would be impossible to unravel these complications. Instead, I offer my own changing awareness of these issues as a lesson. In particular, I add to questions of open/closed and autonomous/dependent ejidos the issues of public and private realms and where these might be located.

The Public Ejido, the Private Ejido

When I first arrived in Calakmul, ejidal life seemed like those Hollywood movies that depict small towns as peopled by intriguing characters whose social life is dense with secrets and emotions, including animosities that, at first glance, obscure a profound interdependence. But, as with the wilderness depictions found in rain forest protection campaigns, I began to question what these feelings of the exotic might mean. Romanticizations often signal cultural differences (Lutz and Collins 1993). As the romance wore thin under the weight of growing familiarity, I questioned whether there were cultural explanations for what I felt and whether my intrigue might shade my understanding of conservation-development.

A first step in responding to this dilemma is to note how surprised I was at the access I had to people's lives. I knew this access was not provided out of benevolence. All of Calakmul's ejidos worried about their public image, and accepting me was part of their strategy to appear as good working partners to development agents. Maintaining a public image, however, was much more difficult with an anthropologist in residence than it was during the ingenieros' sporadic visits.

Over time, I realized my fascination in collecting data on people's lives arose from a few points. One was that I had retained certain messages about tropical conservation circulating in the U.S. public sphere. In U.S. media, rain forests appear commonly under attack, and rain forest dwellers appear commonly trapped (culturally and economically) in environmental destruction. Part of my excitement lay in getting beyond this facile story. Another point was the easy access I had to Calakmul's ejidos, especially in comparison to the difficulty of anthropological access to middle- and upper-class representatives. As a U.S. member of those classes, I trust my privacy can be protected through such things as laws, gated communities, ideals of individualism, and a relatively secure financial base. Thus, living in Orozco and San Lorenzo, I was breaking my own cultural norms. All the while, my presence indicated campesinos' vulnerability to outsiders. I believe it worth questioning whether access to Calakmul's ejidos isn't too easy, while access to the middle and upper classes isn't too difficult. Can a research emphasis on the poor reinforce the way responsibility for environmental change is shared unevenly across social classes?

Lastly, my excitement rested on an encounter with new concepts of *public* and *private*. Sometimes, I was excited by learning what felt like the inside skinny on people's lives, but this turned out to be a cultural confusion. Orozcans and San Lorenzans constructed private and public differently, not only by drawing different lines between the two, but also by constructing each sphere in distinct ways. Questions of private and public complicate attempts to standardize human-environment interactions, so the definitions of each sector demand some explanation.

Researchers Kay Warren and Ann Twinam have examined public/private distinctions in Latin America from different perspectives. Reporting on indigenous people in Guatemala, Warren relays the tale of a shape-shifting spouse to explore the maxim "cada cabeza es un mundo (each mind is a world unto its own)." Warren concludes the refrain signifies an understanding of the self as essentially unstable (Warren 1998). At Calakmul, people additionally used the saying to indicate a private sphere located in people's thoughts and emotions. The unknowable quality of this sphere was captured in another saying, "cara se ve, corazón se desconoce," literally, "one can see a person's face, but one cannot know a person's heart." In Calakmul, the phrase signaled social dangers, especially to people fearful that a neighbor was secretly a criminal, having arrived in Calakmul to escape some felony. While these phrases point to the delineation between private and public, Twinam's writing, on Hispanic colonial-era elites, is provocative in noting these distinctions might be so strong that "individuals could have different status in their private and public worlds" (Twinam 1999:29). Twinam describes how people created distinct realities, one relevant to his or her most private realm of family and intimates and one relevant to a public world. While colonial-era comparisons have limited applicability to Calakmul, Twinam's writing adds to Warren's idea a notion of layered intimacies and areas where outsiders might encounter the opaque in a person's character—in his or her personal history, in the gap between how a person relates with intimates and with others, and in a person's confidential thoughts and emotions. These private realms persisted even though the closeness of ejidal life meant that most aspects of a person's life were public knowledge.

Ejidal members struggled with this opaqueness and, sometimes, a deeply held belief that they had discovered another's private reality and found it wanting. People were said to reveal themselves in particular sites, for example when they managed funds and encountered powerful temptations to steal. Isolated forests and fields were especially suspect, and people were hesitant to accompany strangers to these places. Ejidal members recounted pivotal moments they believed provided evidence of another's inner reality. This reality was usually duplicitous, a point relating to Calakmul's history. Much of the subtext undergirding assemblies, for example, drew on ejidal members' assumptions regarding each others' motives and anxieties that people's overt actions aimed at deflecting attention from hidden agendas.

Ejidal members applied these sentiments broadly, especially to relations marked by power differences. This fact affected their stance on environmental policies. Canadian aid, for example, was believed to be a land grab; as one Orozcan asserted, "Canada owns the Calakmul Biosphere Reserve." A transcontinental off-road car race was believed to be looting archaeological ruins. Presumed duplicity had a basis in fact often enough to suggest to people that a generalized cynicism was their best protection. Theft of shoes, machetes, and foodstuffs from people's fields was common, and, given ejidal geographies, some thefts could have been committed only by people's neighbors. Similarly, although unadvertised, when people acceded to PROCEDE, the program was used to levy a tax.

These persistent doubts about motives made the ejido resistant to environmental policies. People presumed state policies held ulterior motives, and they saw their transformation of state programs as a necessary form of self-defense. Meanwhile, contradictory state practices reinforced campesinos' belief that nothing was quite as it seems.

Postcolonial Ejidal Environments

This chapter demonstrates how tricky land management decisions emanating from ejidal assemblies could be. The ejido was designed to connect rural people to the state and to one another in personalized power dynamics built on and about land. Natural resource management was secondary. Ronald Nigh places the failure of ejidos in this regard at the feet of government authority: "It is clear the generally poor showing of the ejido . . . as a common-pool resource manager is primarily due to the hostile institutional environment created by the authoritarian, paternalistic, and corporatist . . . policies of the Mexican state" (Nigh 2002:454). This chapter outlined part of that institutional environment along with additional challenges. A lack of trust, common identity, commitment to community norms, and depth of history all conspired against collective efforts (Ostrom 1990).

I do not mean to imply the answer to governance and environmental issues lie in private property (see Gibson et al. 2000). The ejido as a cultural ideal was so strong in Calakmul as to open the question of how private property institutions in the region might operate in practice. The 2001 survey examined two such communities and found that, rather than offering an alternative model, these places looked more like poorly functioning ejidos (Haenn forthcoming). Also, the state itself appeared unsure of how to work with private property governance. Throughout Calakmul, state ingenieros and Reserve managers reproduced ejidal norms as a central idiom through which they communicated with campesinos. Even in private property communities, ingenieros demanded collective participation in state development projects.

In the ejido, agrarianism became conflated with environmental management and poverty concerns. Thus, studies of environmental issues in Calakmul must take into account these accompanying issues. In the following chapter, I follow these concerns to Orozcans' and San Lorenzans' farming and economic lives. Building on themes already salient in this chapter, I turn to a consideration of "poverty" as both a cultural construction and a concept linked to specific economic practices.

El Señor de Calakmul. In the late 1990s, a jade mask found at the Calakmul archaeological site became a mascot and marketing gimmick aimed at selling the region to tourists and campesinos alike. The mask's likeness was reproduced on state buildings, in public parks, and on taxis.

A resident of Orozco laughs as I take her snapshot. When water supplies were scarce, villagers gathered once or twice a week to fill jugs from water trucked to the community.

During a drought year, Calakmul's ponds can become so dirty as to stain white clothing. A night of solid rainfall eventually filled this pond and provided clear water.

Calakmul is home to charismatic species living in close contact with people. This man found a jaguar cub in his cornfield. When the cat became too large to keep safely at home, he donated the jaguar to the local zoo.

This is the home of a relatively wealthy individual. Ornamental plants are courtesy of the Reserve-Council.

This boy plays with a homemade toy in front of the house his parents had built just the previous year. As refugees from Chiapas, this family counted among those with the least resources.

Clearing land is arduous work that campesinos fear can be punished legally. These men are clearing a cornfield. The density of the weeds shows how aggressively forests in Calakmul grow. The forest in the background is considered older growth and is illegal to fell.

Because of poor farming conditions, many Calakmul families rely on aid for survival. This photo shows food aid entering an area where hurricane floods had cut off road transportation.

Calakmul's aid programs are overseen by technical outreach staff. Posed in front of a Reserve truck with a snake found dead on the road are three staffers who all grew up in northern Mexico, where they earned their university degrees.

Doña Belén and her husband, Don Antonio, pose in front of the conservation-inspired mural at their Zoh Laguna restaurant, a meeting ground for just about anybody interested in conservation. People joked that a person could study regional programs without ever leaving the eatery.

6

"Toying with Survival"

Compared to pobladores, visitors to Calakmul—associates of conservation, development, and academic agencies—received a very different introduction to the area. Visitors usually toured two or three ejidos, where they dropped in on a few homes, maybe a farm parcel. They talked to campesinos about their lack of water, health care, and farming needs. To some, Calakmul impressed with its penury. The houses appeared ramshackle. In 1995, no home I visited had running water and hardly any had a gas stove. People looked overworked, especially in the drought season, when a bleak landscape mirrored people's worries about crop loss. As I gained a more specific understanding of the local economy, this uniform appearance of poverty was lost to me. I was reminded of it by visitors' remarks, as when a U.S. biologist used a photo of my Orozco house to warn students of the conditions awaiting them in Calakmul. In previous decades, Calakmul's chicle and timber had connected the area to global networks. By the 1990s, this linkage included campesino poverty. For conservation and development practitioners alike, poverty was an entrenched problem, threatening forests and campesinos' quality of life. Even though poverty is a relative construction measured against various definitions of wealth, within these paired concepts, visitors never viewed wealth as a potential problem.

If poverty was the main issue in Calakmul, who should eradicate it? At the Reserve-Council, people held either campesinos or government agents responsible for this work. Neither party saw foreigners as germane to the debate. Rather, discussions centered on campesino farm practices and "campesino" as an identity that made people the object of development aid.

In addition to exploring these two issues, here, I depict how campesino households juggled a series of state development programs. The programs never effectively resolved people's economic frustrations. In fact, I will show how some programs effectively *reinforced* qualities that were otherwise thought by state agents to contribute to poverty. As one of Calakmul's ingenieros put it, the contrary pressures development programs placed on Calakmul's families mounted to gambling with people's subsistence or, as the ingeniero said, "toying with survival."

Conservation-development programs figure in this chapter in a minor way. Although conservation-development was the most visible aspect of Calakmul's development setting, these programs provided relatively few financial benefits. By noting how conservation-development entered households already immersed in aid, readers can begin to identify the trade-offs conservation-development required and people's ulterior motives for participation.

It is worth mentioning that clandestine activities were also a part of Calakmul's economy. People might cultivate marijuana, ship drugs, sell timber and wildlife, or smuggle Central American migrants on their way to the United States. The scale of these activities, as well as their ecological impacts, was unknown. Their financial quality, however, was widely acknowledged. In 2001, a campesino reportedly could sell a kilo of marijuana for $1,000, while prices for a kilo of jalapeño chiles, the area's principal cash crop, hovered around $3 (again, all prices are in pesos, unless otherwise noted).

A minority of people participated in this illicit economy. Nonetheless, through no fault of their own, nearly all of Calakmul's swidden farmers were implicated in illegal activities. Mexico's federal forestry law (Ley Forestal) prohibited alteration of broadly defined forests without prior government approval.[1] The ruling led campesinos to fear state agents might find fault with almost any kind of forest clearing. (Various people have been jailed for clearing older growth forest.) Because of this felonious tinge, campesinos approached farm work with a mixture of apprehension and resentment toward authorities. I first outline that work along with idealized discussions of slash-and-burn agriculture before discussing how this farming related to campesino identities and the programs campesinos received in 1995.

Slash-and-Burn Farming and Self-Sufficiency

Slash-and-burn, or swidden, agriculture has been cited as an inefficient farm method and a principal cause of tropical forest loss (see discussion in Sponsel et al. 1996). The phrase "slash-and-burn" has even entered everyday speech to connote reckless destruction. Countering these generalizations, researchers have long recognized a diversity of swidden practices that, especially under conditions of low population density, can be sustainable (Netting 1993). Felling and burning vegetation before planting crops can be adaptive where burning releases nutrients that sustain farming. In many regions, farmers find fertilization endures for a few years, when they must occupy new fields. Because swidden farmers move around the landscape, they can decrease forest cover. An important counter to deforestation is that people usually return to former fields, and many swidden agriculturists cultivate forests to improve their future farming. Today, people largely associate slash-and-burn practices with tropical ecosystems, but the method is practical in many climates (Myllyntaus et al. 2002).

A discussion of swidden farming is necessary because the authors of Calakmul's conservation-development agenda had conflicting attitudes toward the practice. To a certain extent, they shared sentiments with those who considered slash-and-burn farming inherently destructive. For example, the management plan for Calakmul's neighboring protected area in Guatemala describes "incompatible farming" as a threat to biodiversity, raising the question, what counts as compatible farming? (See CONAP 2001.) Is slash-and-burn farming destructive by definition, or is farming for market purposes the culprit? (See Atran 1999.) As they explored these questions, Calakmul's Reserve director and nongovernmental groups were committed to a campesino empowerment in which slash-and-burn farming was a necessary component. Tensions regarding the possible destructiveness of subsistence and market-oriented farming remained unresolved. In a way, noncampesinos found these discussions unsolvable. Arguments among researchers and development practitioners about slash-and-burn farming often worked as proxies to concerns over the environmental effects of market economies more generally and our own compromised place within those economies.

In the meantime, one environmentalist circulated a book by Silvia Terán and Christian Rasmussen as indicative of what sustainable, self-sufficient, slash-and-burn farming might look like (Terán and Rasmussen 1994). Reserve and Council staff rarely spent their time reading, so the book had little impact. I relate the authors' findings because they are highly suggestive. The conservation-development programs alternately emphasized subsistence work and market-driven farming. These positions contrasted with campesino ideas of three economic realms: market, subsistence, and state driven. Bringing Terán and Rasmussen to these discussions, we see the possibilities for subsistence work in these configurations as well as the gap between those possibilities and Calakmul's economy.

Terán and Rasmussen show that slash-and-burn agriculture supported relatively large populations during the fifteenth century in northern Yucatán. The area's rocky soils prohibited the construction of terraces and other modifications that supported Mayan cities elsewhere (including Calakmul; Turner II et al. 2003). In the mid-1500s, however, at least

800,000 people lived from swidden farming in what are now Yucatán, Campeche, and Quintana Roo states (Terán and Rasmussen 1994:47).

Pre-Columbian peoples used swidden farming to make *milpa*; the word can refer simply to a cornfield but also indexes complex agricultural systems. Pre-Columbians working milpa had no metal tools, and Terán and Rasmussen find this lack meant, at the felling stage, people likely left standing larger trees. Intensive tree pruning allowed sunlight to reach crops, while the trees acted as a seed bank for future forests. At the burning stage, pre-Columbians built firebreaks to control burns that might damage dense settlements. While the size of cultivated fields is unclear, a single household could have fields spread out in as many as five places. Through this dispersion, people took advantage of soil and rainfall variability.

Pre-Columbian milpas included additional features to hedge against crop loss. Within any single field, people sowed as many as sixteen distinct plants. This intercropping included plants with different water requirements and maturation rates. Intercropping helped ward off insects, rodents, and other pests. In general, people were aware of the threats to the crops, but they could not predict exactly where or when damage might occur. Pre-Columbian peoples thus countered stochastic threats with variability in crop type and growth requirements. Variability provided a hedge against total loss, as no single stressor, such as a single month without rain, would affect all crops in the same way (ibid.:45–69).

Despite these precautions, crop loss was regular enough that added steps were needed. Terán and Rasmussen note that centralized storage and distribution centers could house surpluses in years of bumper crops. Yucatán's ruling class likely operated such a system. Individual families, additionally, used forests intensively to replace farmed foods. Terán and Rasmussen's novel findings show the extent to which forest products formed an integral part of pre-Columbian milpas. Wild foods always supplemented people's diets, but forested areas gained in importance when crops failed. Terán and Rasmussen argue that forest fruits, leaves, and roots were so crucial to survival that people worked an intensive agroforestry (ibid.:79). In brief, self-sufficient swiddening entailed intensive management of an array of farmed and wild resources with the pointed, but not heavy-handed, intervention of state authorities (see also Alcorn 1981; Clay 1988; and Posey 2002 for discussions of cultivated forests).

As I explore in more detail below, agriculture in Calakmul differed from Terán and Rasmussen's formulation in critical ways. While all of Calakmul's farmers followed the general outlines of slash-and-burn farming, their specific practices ranged widely. People continuously tested agricultural possibilities while taking into consideration the area's financial setting. Perhaps most important, campesinos differed from pre-Columbian farmers in environmental knowledge and planning for harvest loss. As newcomers to the area, campesinos were still learning about their environment. People generally ruled out farming on rocky terrains, clay soils that flooded in the wet season (*bajos*), and soils in which gypsum and *saskab* (a calcium carbonate) predominated. Other areas remained open for consideration. The proof of soil quality, they said, ultimately lies in the harvest. Testing under erratic weather conditions increased the likelihood of harvest loss. Throughout 1994, 1995, and 1996, weather conditions did force people to rely on aid for corn supplies. In times of crop failure, people counted on government help and used the subsidy programs described below as food aid, regardless of their original intent.

With this foreshadowing, I should note how descriptions of slash-and-burn farming can be misleading. Emphasizing as they do techniques, such portrayals suggest farming is just a series of tasks. At Calakmul, people brought together farm practices and notions of social class to define themselves as campesinos. They emphasized the relational quality of this identity. That is, people compared themselves to others who did not farm or who occupied other social strata. In this defining, people in Calakmul took subsistence farming as a point of departure rather than, as did those who tried to direct campesino work, an end point.

Enduring Agrarian Identities

The word *campesino* is used throughout Mexico to denote someone engaged in subsistence agriculture, but generic definitions obscure regional differences. Writing on northern Mexico, Nugent describes *campesino* as a derogatory word (Nugent 1993). At Calakmul people used the term to supersede other identity differences of indigenous/nonindigenous and state of origin. They described being a campesino as a point of both pride and vulnerability.

As people explained, one of the most important qualities of a campesino in Calakmul was that he or she did not receive a regular salary. Some suggested this fact provided campesinos independence. For example, a politically leftist young man who worked odd jobs in Xpujil explained how "campesinos tienen control (have control)," because, in their subsistence work, they are boss of their own time. He believed that when campesinos entered the marketplace, either as day laborers or cash croppers, they lost some measure of control. Only by abandoning subsistence farming entirely, he maintained, did campesinos lose command of their lives. Although clearly interested in being his own boss, this young man did not undertake farming. Instead, he sought to open a photocopy store.

People working in agriculture were more unsure about the connection between subsistence farming and personal power. At the end of a day in his fields, David reclined in a hammock as he described a campesino as someone who "lives by his hands, eats because of his pure strength. When there is no money, a campesino looks for work to buy food, soap." David outlined "three classes of campesinos: There's the middle-class campesino who knows how to save money, has cattle and a car, produces corn and chile. Another class of campesinos is more advanced. They no longer work, but pay other people. They continue to be campesinos, because even though they pay people, before they suffered. Finally, there's the campesino who is simply screwed (está simplemente jodido). They don't have any more than a house and ten children." Could someone cease to be a campesino? "Someone might look for a job in the city, but this is a different level of life. Those people principally manage money to live."

As we spoke in Spanish, David's sister sat tending her baby when she interrupted to ask, in Ch'ol, whether he wasn't embarrassed to participate in this conversation. In his translation of *embarrassed*, David used the word *pena*. Embarrassment, in its connection to humiliation and having less, were common themes in campesino conversation. People talked about the humiliation of needing financial help by saying, "da pena pedir (it is embarrassing to ask)." Poblador women in Orozco complained about the ejido's water shortage, "Here you have to ask and ask and ask, and asking is embarrassing." Recall in chapter 5 that ejidatarios asserted it was embarrassing to force pobladores to pay their entrance fees. Ejidatarios tried to soften the way fees breached ideals of equality by calling on feelings common to campesino experiences. As a medium of control or resistance, pena was a salient theme, because campesinos constantly negotiated social encounters that placed them in subordinate and disregarded positions. As campesinos, people in Calakmul were fregados, jodidos, or "screwed," an appellation government agents applied to them as well.

As a metaphor for exploitation (Lomnitz-Adler 1992:125), "jodido" and "fregado" indicated the identity of underdevelopment campesinos ascribed to the intersection of farming and social class. Shifting between the verbs *ser* ("to be" in an absolute sense) and *estar* ("to be" in a transient sense), campesinos were ambivalent about whether jodido was a permanent state or not. Understanding the fixity of these feelings was complicated by the fact that many campesinos spoke Spanish as a second language, and monolingual speakers spoke dialects that educated Mexicans recognized as grammatically flawed. Jerónimo, a Ch'ol speaker, defended his failure to pay his entrance fee by saying "estamos jodidos, no hay como (we're screwed, there's no way we can pay)." A left-leaning Mestizo from the Regional Council similarly expressed his belief that campesinos needed to do more than just receive development aid; they needed to organize politically: "si el dinero resolviera problemas, no estaríamos jodidos (if money resolved problems, we wouldn't be screwed)." However, a monolingual Spanish speaker was not out of place when he complained about pobladores not paying their entrance fees: "I thought they came here to live without war or conflict and that they came screwed, as we all are, all the time (que vinieron jodidos come somos todos siempre)." He echoed a campesino speaking at a conference organized by an international environmental group: "si estamos pobres del suelo somos jodidos por que nosotros como campesinos trabajamos los suelos (if our soils are poor, we're screwed, because as campesinos we work our soils)."

Perhaps a more appropriate interpretation of this dissonance is that by employing *ser*, as well as the grammatically correct *estar*, campesinos gave voice to the obstacles they faced in achieving social dignity and personal advancement. As David mentioned above, campesinos saw these obstacles as structural in character, a series of classes through which one could move. At the same time, many campesinos saw these structures as personified (in the form of caciques) and closed to outsiders. One of Calakmul's campesino organizers succinctly related the personal/structural, transient/permanent quality of being screwed in recollecting his search for opportunity. He described his former home in Yucatán state: "Allá hay bastante ganado y él que tiene, tiene. Él que no, está fregado, nunca va tener (There's quite a bit of cattle in that area, and whoever has cattle, has something. Whoever doesn't have cattle is screwed. He's never going to have anything)." Escape from these strictures required moving to Calakmul.

Campesino identities of poverty and being "screwed" were closely tied to the nation-state. Where the nation offered a positive source of identity, the state often worked to the contrary. Thus, a man drunk on the proceeds of his PROCAMPO check harangued a soldier conducting a routine search on a bus: "Article 27 says a campesino has the right to decide his life for himself. Nobody can manipulate him." This opposition between campesino society and the state held certain consequences for conservation-development.

Campesinos involved in state-campesino relations found themselves in a charged and suspect position. At the Regional Council, people questioned whether the campesino aspects of managers' identities would prevail. Or, would managers be seduced by their salaries and state ties to work at campesinos' expense? Regional Council managers maintained their authority as authentic campesinos by appearing to work on their families' farms. Even though commitments allowed them only supervisory input, these appearances were crucial to countering managers' critics. When evidence of treachery was lacking, accusers used inattention to farm duties to charge managers of no longer being campesinos, of entering a domain where self-interest could not be tempered by poverty's equalizing effects.

This scrutiny accompanied a growing state and academic surveillance of farm activities and household incomes in Calakmul throughout the 1990s. Through research, environmental groups learned the extent families were reliant on the programs described below. The amount of subsidies would lead some NGO agents to argue that campesino claims that their subsistence required burning forests were a farce. Interestingly, environmentalists were silent about payments to ejidatarios, living at a distance from Calakmul, to hold off on exploiting their chicle and timber concessions inside the Reserve. Decrying state subsidies in Calakmul, state and private sector environmentalists worried that if people in Calakmul learned of these separate payments, campesino demands that they be paid not to cut forest would be tremendous.

My consideration of campesino identities should demonstrate the futility of thinking of farming as an ingredient one can simply add to or subtract from a family's livelihood. Rural livelihoods sit within a matrix of material and social relationships (see Bebbington 1999). An environmentalist who demanded campesinos cease subsistence farming found the authority to make such an assertion in his or her class position, a position that hinged on *not* farming. From campesino perspectives, it appeared ridiculous that upper- and middle-class representatives would call for elimination of the same work upon which their power rested. More immediately, such calls threatened families' ability to feed themselves. Even though people in Calakmul enjoyed certain subsidies, these inputs never fully covered a family's consumption needs. Families still relied on farming for their food. In this regard, Calakmul offered a range of possibilities, as farming conditions varied significantly.

Farming Conditions in Orozco and San Lorenzo

My discussion of farming conditions focuses on corn. People in Calakmul remarked that, without corn, the family enterprise falls apart. Corn tortillas composed or accompanied every meal. Transformed into feed for chickens and pigs, corn offered long-term savings. To say a household was buying corn, or was without corn, was to say a family had crossed the threshold into hard times.

Corn production in Orozco and San Lorenzo demonstrated the diverse agrarian opportunities in Calakmul. Campesinos in neither ejido irrigated or artificially fertilized their cornfields, while the two ejidos experienced strongly different soils and rainfall. Orozco sat on the meseta baja de Zoh Laguna, home to relatively poor tsek'el soils (see chap. 1). Farmers on the meseta reported 1994 corn harvests ranging from 330 kl to 840 kl per hectare (Ericson 1996). Government officials estimated the meseta offered on average 300–400 kl per hectare (Julia Murphy, personal communication). Even in 1998–99, a year of neither excessive rain nor drought, municipal corn harvests averaged 727 kl per hectare. Comparatively, throughout Campeche state, cornfields tend to produce 1,200 kl per hectare, and national yields may reach 1,900 kl per hectare (INEGI 2001b; Lambert 1996).

Moving off the meseta to the east, where San Lorenzo lies, Calakmul offered kan-kab and ya'ax-hom soils, both characterized as deep, fertile soils (Gates 1993). Yucatec Maya agronomists described San Lorenzo's land base as "truly agricultural." Yields in San Lorenzo neared 1,200 kl per hectare, at least 50 percent more than Orozco's soils and, perhaps, four times the amount offered by Calakmul's least productive lands.

San Lorenzo and Orozco also had different humidity levels and different rainfall patterns. A nuanced study of rainfall variation in Calakmul did not exist, but San Lorenzans were able to plant a second, dry-season crop that supplied corn more continuously throughout the year. Orozcans declared that rain scarcity made such work pointless.

People in Orozco and San Lorenzo estimated they needed between 2,000 and 3,000 kl of corn each year for their households.[2] Based on this, San Lorenzans, who reported harvesting nearly 4 hectares of corn, might surpass household needs by reaping 4,800 kl of corn. Ejidatarios in Orozco, who harvested an average of 3.2 hectares of corn, would attain self-sufficiency only if their yields reached 700 kl per hectare. Orozco's pobladores found their work constrained as they adjusted to their new home. They harvested just 1.75 hectares of corn, an amount that would leave them short of corn even in the best years. (See table 6.1 for comparison of corn and cash cropping, in which ejidatario and poblador data are combined for Orozco.)

Might people compensate for poor soils by planting additional fields? This question raises two issues: labor and the extent to which forest cover

Table 6.1 Area Planted and Estimated Harvests for Cash and Subsistence Crops (includes wet and dry season crops)

	Orozco (25 households)	San Lorenzo (33 households)
Average number of hectares in corn per household	2.54	3.9
Estimated corn harvests under optimal conditions (compare with minimum household requirement of 2,000 kl)	2,032	4,680
Average number of hectares in chile per household	1.2	0.45
Estimated chile harvests per hectare in kl (1994–95 price approx. $1.4/kl)*	4,884	1,831
Average number of hectares in chihua per household	0.7	1.86
Estimated chihua harvests (1994–95 price approx. $3.5/kl)	N/A	N/A

Sources: Keys 2002; INEGI 2001b
*Figures based on average harvests of 4,070 kl per swidden hectare as determined by Keys 2002. Average municipal harvests are 5300 kl (INEGI 2001b), a number boosted by mechanized fields which average 6,564 kl/hec, again as determined by Keys.

can replenish soil fertility. Because families contained a limited number of workers (Calakmul families averaged five people per household), and a person could stand only so much physical exertion, expanding farm operations was not always possible. In such a setting, people wanted to gain the most they could from available land. The quality of forest cover at the time of burning adds to soil fertility, and in this case, farmers were hampered both legally and logistically. Legally, campesinos could burn only *acahual*, secondary forests that may be as old as ten or fifteen years. Analyses of the quality of leaf litter at Calakmul suggest a forest twelve to twenty-five years old may provide peak litter fall (Turner II et al. 2003). Even if people could legally work older forests (i.e., their entire farm parcels), the San Lorenzan who planted about 6 hectares, and moved those 6 hectares every two years throughout his 20-hectare parcel, would find himself limited to a three-year rotation cycle. San Lorenzans would need to plant the same field four years in a row to position themselves within the eleven- to twenty-five-year framework. An Orozcan who planted 4.4 hectares and planted the same field two years in a row would approach the twenty-five-year benchmark.

In the 2001 survey of Calakmul households, we found broader agreement on how many years people worked the same field than on how long farmers left their fields in fallow (see figs. 6.1 and 6.2). Only 32 households reported planting the same fields continuously for three or four years. Another 76 percent of the sample, or 113 households, reported planting the same field two years or less. The amount of time farmers left fields to rest was more varied. Six respondents practiced something close to sedentarized agriculture, while on average men reported leaving fields to rest 3.5 years. All but one household reported fallow periods short of eleven years. (For those citing a range of years, I rounded up to reflect the longest a person might farm or leave a field in fallow.) Readers should consider data on field rotations in light of the three economic realms in Calakmul—subsistence, government directed, and market. Differences in fallow preferences might reflect how different campesinos approached opportunities in these realms.

While the structure of this chapter implies it is possible to compare across these realms, I want to warn readers that such comparison can be hazardous. In particular, researchers, environmentalists, and state officers often use peso amounts to compare the relative value of each realm. Social activists argue against this practice and assert we should not put a price on subsistence corn farming. Doing so suggests that subsistence work and

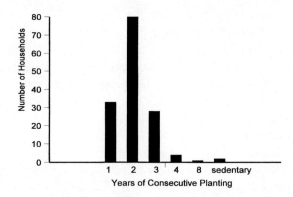

Fig. 6.1. Field rotation chart showing the years of consecutive planting of fields for 148 households.

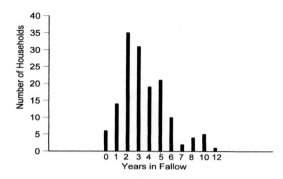

Fig. 6.2. Field rotation chart showing the years in fallow for 148 households.

wage labor can somehow substitute for one another. However, subsistence farming provides at least a limited food security while wage labor is often erratic and temporary (Collier 1994). Temporary labor cannot compensate for what is priceless, the ability to feed one's family. In any case, the value of corn in Mexico has dropped to such an extent that few campesinos viewed it as a source of cash. In this regard, the situation at Calakmul was similar to that of subsistence producers throughout Mexico (de Janvry et al. 1994). The crop that was critical to campesino survival held little remunerative worth in the marketplace.

Instead, farming for jalapeño chile peppers and *chihua* (pronounced chee-wah), a squash grown for its pumpkinlike seeds, formed a central part of any household's economic profile. Even families who did not extensively farm chile and chihua benefited from these crops during the harvest when high-paying jobs became widely available. Job opportunities were particularly scarce for women, but many took on work during harvest season. Of the two cash crops, people believed chile peppers the more profitable, although I doubt these conclusions below. Given its higher costs and work requirements, chile production tended to benefit most people who could afford its risks. In his analysis of chile farming, Keys found that "chile farmers cultivate more land across the board—in corn and other crops—because they can" (personal communication).

"Crazy for Chile" and Chihua

Chiles' risks sat alongside the prospect of great bonanzas. Stories abounded of people who bought a truck from the profits of a single harvest or who earned more than twice the amount of a year's worth of wage labor. Chile production required expensive labor and chemical inputs, costs people could lose to drought or flood. Despite these draw-backs, people in San Lorenzo emphasized chihua production only because the roads connecting chile buyers to the ejido were poorly maintained. Perishable fresh peppers would not survive the trip to shipping points. People in Orozco espoused a typical opinion when they described them-selves as "crazy for chile."

Chile planting took place in May and June, with the harvest in November and December. As with corn production, farmers prepared their chile fields by felling and burning forest. Given the crop's potential, campesinos often chose the more fertile, secondary forests for their chile fields. Chile thus had a terrible reputation among environmentalists for deforestation. Campesinos, however, may convert as much as 50 percent of their chile fields into milpa in the following planting season, while 24 percent of fields remain in chile (Keys 2002).

After planting, chile plants need ongoing attention. Campesinos ap-plied insecticides and fungicides to the crop two to three times; fields required weeding the same number of times. These processes could be expensive and often required that farmers hire extra hands. A middle-range producer in Orozco spent $1,740 on a field that netted him $1,842, the equivalent of ninety-two days of wage labor. Five years later, average earn-ings from swidden chile fields equaled eighty days of wage labor (ibid.).

The most expensive part of chile production came at harvest season. The same plants could be harvested three and four times over as new chiles grew to maturation. Given the cost of inputs, campesinos might begin to see profits only on the third or fourth harvest. Buyers delivered special sacks to hold the chiles and arranged for a pickup time. The field's owner then invited family and friends to join the harvest. Work began at dawn, and harvesters spent the day doubled over the knee-high plants. Harvest-ers were paid for each sack they filled, so fast workers did well. If people were not hired on their ejido's own farms, they traveled to industrialized fields in the nearby ejido of Hot Springs. (The economics of industrialized chile production differed significantly from that of swiddeners; see Keys 2002.) Anxious men abandoned ejidal assemblies and the nightly soap operas when a contractor from Hot Springs arrived to sign up workers. Nearly all of Orozco's men, women, and children boarded the pickup trucks that took them to the fields.

By asking six Orozco families to help me record their spending, earning, and work activities, I learned that people earned the lion's share of their yearly wage-labor in Hot Springs' chile fields. For Orozco's pobla-dores, this work proved vital. An assiduous worker earned up to $80 a day, four times the standard daily wage of $15 to $20 a day for other wage labor. Household incomes during 1994's harvest rose, incredibly, to $1,000 a week over a six-week period. Poorer families were able to afford basic items, and shoes appeared on children's feet. Wealthier families splurged on a horse saddle or roofing material. Grim faces turned giggly, as the influx of cash temporarily relieved financial worries.

Chile was a boon to people who worked the harvest, but, given its costs, how did campesinos afford to plant the crop? Depending on their timing, government subsidies supported chile fields. Also, chile seeds were so valuable, they acted as currency. Other chile products included dried red peppers and a chile paste. These durable products created income long after the harvest. More commonly, campesinos contracted with a chile buyer, sometimes a local planter who combined financing small plots with his own mechanized operations. Known as *chileros*, these men delivered agro-chemicals on guarantee that the crop would be sold to them (see chap. 5). The costs of the chemicals were then deducted at the time of harvest. The relationship between campesinos and chile buyers could be exploitative. But, Calakmul's respected buyers offset this exploitation by acting as patrons, offering connected families jobs and emergency aid during the off-season.

Calakmul's other cash crop, chihua, had neither chile's show quality nor its intense social relations. Chihua lacked excitement, partly because it did not have the reputation for great earnings and partly because chihua blended with corn production. People planted chihua in their milpas and applied fewer agrochemicals to the crop. Green chihua are edible, and early harvest samples added variety to people's dinners. Most of the squash, however, was left in the field to mature.

In comparison to the frenzy surrounding chile, chihua harvests appeared leisurely. Chihua tended to be a family affair, and few people traveled outside their ejido to harvest. Chihua seeds do not spoil easily. This gave people a larger window of time to harvest, during which one or two people moved through the milpa piling squash and splitting them with a machete. Other workers sat around the piles extracting the seeds. Some people fed the remaining chihua to their cattle. Most left the mature squash to rot. Chihua seeds dried on tarps outside homes until they were ready to be bagged and sold. Because of their durability, families might store the seeds a week or two as they speculated about price changes. As with chile, people sold chihua seeds to buyers visiting the ejido or to another villager who acted as middleman.

Chile's reputation for dramatic reward contradicted the fact that chihua and chile had similar net earnings, and chile production had a calamitous downside. During 1994–95, chile prices ranged from $1 to $1.4 per kilo. A few years earlier, campesinos remembered a price of just $0.30 per kilo. Buyers monopolized information about chile prices in the country's central exchanges near Mexico City. As with timber in earlier times, campesinos found it difficult to receive a fair price for their crop. In order to break the buyers' monopoly, the Regional Council's earliest work in Calakmul included an attempt to bypass chile's local marketing structure. The group tried to ship the peppers to the central markets for direct sale. The Council bought chiles with promises of higher prices, amounts the Council would have difficulty paying once the project failed. Reportedly, the Council's venture collapsed for two reasons. Council leadership was unfamiliar with details of the marketing process. Poor timing left tons of chiles rotting on the Council's doorstep. The Council also found itself shut out of central markets. In alliance with local contractors, national buyers refused to work with the Regional Council, thereby colluding to depress payments to campesinos.

The Regional Council intervened in chile because even environmentalists had to reckon with its importance to Calakmul's economy. Apart from PROCAMPO, jalapeño production was often a household's single most important source of income. Given chile's high-profile role in Calakmul, this raises a question about PROCAMPO. If people were "crazy for chile," what did they think about PROCAMPO?

PROCAMPO

"If it weren't for PROCAMPO, I would only plant chile," declared Roberto in Orozco. PROCAMPO continues to pay people a fixed sum for each hectare of land planted in pasture or subsistence crops. In 1994–95, the program paid $350 per hectare, an amount that increased to $440 in 1995–96. Payments were so large that they rivaled what families earned in cash crops. Furthermore, PROCAMPO had few of the drawbacks of cash cropping, since payments arrived even when harvests failed.

In addition to its connection to NAFTA, PROCAMPO came with a series of objectives, none of which received publicity in Calakmul. A government pamphlet noted PROCAMPO aims to:

1. Compensate for subsidies offered to farmers of other countries [that is, the United States and Canada].
2. Offer lower prices on staple foods to national consumers.
3. Encourage productive reconversion of farmland and environmental preservation.

Campesino poverty has long subsidized "national consumers" (Hewitt de Alcántara 1992; Reyes Osorio et al. 1974). New here is the way state agents added to this assignment the burden of environmental conservation. PRO-CAMPO's conservation tasks were not specified. State officials, nonetheless, made exaggerated claims to the program's role in environmental protection. In the same brochure, authors asserted PROCAMPO would "stop environmental degradation, give rise to the conservation and recuperation of forests, as well as reduce soil erosion and the contamination of water caused by excessive use of agrochemicals, in order to benefit the environment and sustainable development."

At Calakmul, PROCAMPO's environmental aspect centered on threats to deny payments to people who fell older growth forests. Following the original survey, ingenieros visited individual parcels to map the location of agricultural fields. The maps documented land cover types against which agents could check compliance with the law. As we saw, PRO-CAMPO's few staff meant supervision was unlikely. Still, people in Calakmul applied their own twist to forestall penalties. Before their parcels were mapped, some campesinos felled older forests to have secondary growth eligible for cultivation. Calakmul's Reserve director estimated a loss of 200 hectares to this tactic. Later assessments of PROCAMPO's impact added the program may have increased deforestation as people used the funds to open pastures (Klepeis and Vance 2003). PROCAMPO was a thorn in local environmental programming and later became a scapegoat. By 2001, Reserve officers found in PROCAMPO an easy defense against their inability to affect farm practices. They complained that the larger state apparatus gave the lion's share of funding to programs supporting deforestation.

Without the program's broader context, campesinos quickly deduced that PROCAMPO was like any other government payment, with all the complications this entailed. San Lorenzans and Orozcans were unfamiliar with the program's connection to NAFTA. But, they did not miss the fact that 1994 payments took place just before the country's presidential election. They knew government agents used PROCAMPO to buy support. Given the size of payments, they were willing to discuss the sale of their allegiance. Table 6.2 shows that PROCAMPO payments in Orozco could equal 75 days, or two and a half months, of wage labor. PROCAMPO payments in San Lorenzo were larger still because of the ejido's favorable ecology. In San Lorenzo, payments could equal 101 days or more than three months of wage labor.

PROCAMPO, more than any other program, played a complex role in farm management and ejido relations. In San Lorenzo, a father and his

Table 6.2 Household PROCAMPO Earnings

	Orozco (12 households)	San Lorenzo (33 households)
Average number of hectares inscribed in PROCAMPO per household	3.1	4.6
Average income from PROCAMPO per household based on $440/hectare	$1,496	$2,024
Equivalent of average income in wage labor days (based on $20/day)	74.8	101.2

three sons, who worked the same fields, felt forced to open separate plots, so authorities would recognize the individual merits of their PROCAMPO claims. In this case, PROCAMPO subtly changed the family's solidarity while simultaneously increasing forest fragmentation. Jerónimo, in Orozco, complained PROCAMPO limited his ability to take advantage of tractors lent by the Regional Council. The Council demanded removal of all tree stumps to protect their equipment. With six hectares promised to PRO-CAMPO, Jerónimo did not have time to clear his fields for the tractors. Here, the bonanza of the short-term payment countered Jerónimo's long-term goal of mechanized agriculture and, perhaps, sedentarized farming. In Orozco, ejidatarios limited poblador access to PROCAMPO by harassing those who signed up for more than a hectare or two. When a poblador PROCAMPO recipient left Orozco, ejidatarios assumed the prerogative of assigning the payment to another ejidal member. In this case, PROCAMPO served as a tool of coercion. Coercion became systematic when a secondary market in PROCAMPO payments opened up. Families in financial crisis found they could cede years of payments to loan sharks. By 2001, PRO-CAMPO disciplinary measures centered on identifying these loan sharks and returning payments to their original recipients.

Because PROCAMPO attempted to shape farm practices, it paralleled and was sometimes seen as interdependent with other subsidies.[3] Not all aid programs, however, centered on farming. Development proselytizing took many forms, as even religious preachers offered a few kilos of corn meal in exchange for attendance at services. Secondary to farming concerns, in government aid, were health care and children's education. By 2001, health and education would supersede conservation and farming as Calakmul's principal areas of government support. Turning to children's scholarships, I highlight the social engineering aspect to many subsidies. At the same time, scholarships coincide with PROCAMPO in demonstrating how ejidal members used their autonomy to rework those aims.

In Solidarity with State Aid

The scholarships supported first-, second-, and third-graders at risk of dropping out of school because of their parents' poverty. In addition to cash payments of 118 pesos monthly, children received a *despensa*, or bag of basic foodstuffs worth about $25.[4] Despensas were a popular form of aid in many development projects and were offered on the assumption that cash payments would be misspent (on alcohol or cigarettes). Overall, ingenieros viewed despensas as a softer subsidy. Effective even during vacation months, the scholarships (including the despensas) annually equaled eighty-six days of wage labor. People depended on monthly scholarships for a steady stream of income, although during my research, payments arrived irregularly.

The scholarships were part of a nationwide program known as PRO-NASOL, the National Solidarity Program or, more simply, Solidarity. Throughout Calakmul, the moniker "Made with Solidarity" was emblazoned across water catchment tanks, school buildings, rural stores, and the headquarters of the Regional Council. Solidarity's role in myriad projects could be confusing, partly because the program was a self-conscious attempt to tie development to the program's figurehead, Salinas de Gortari. (For an overview of Solidarity, see Cornelius et al. 1994. For the program's origination in the World Bank's reevaluation of its treatment of the poor, see Díaz-Polanco 1997.) Recall that Calakmul's conservation-development agenda was originally forged with the help of Solidarity organizers. Initially, the Regional Council was named the "Solidarity Regional Council." Council leaders dropped the "Solidarity" when they found campesinos antagonistic toward such an overt appropriation of their struggles.

This aversion evidences that campesinos saw through Solidarity's rhetoric of personal empowerment. State agents used notions of empowerment to declare that Solidarity offered the kind of poverty relief most desired by Mexico's people. Ideally, Solidarity paid for proposals that arose from campesino self-reflection, where campesinos requested help with their most urgent needs. Solidarity officials asserted funding would not constitute a handout. Instead, projects would come to fruition only if campesinos contributed labor or funds. In this way, Solidarity structures resonated with the participatory planning processes prevalent in international development circles (Chambers 1994). Throughout Mexico, Solidarity committees, like the Regional Council, were set up to coordinate these activities. Programs such as the scholarships required additional subcommittees at the ejidal level (for an assessment of the scholarship program nationally, see Gershberg 1994). The false quality of a government-arbitrated empowerment was not lost on people accustomed to similar condescension within ejidal regimes. At the same time, Solidarity's resonance with persuasive social movements meant that such empowerment was not entirely negated.

The false empowerment stemmed from the way Solidarity required recipients to identify as poor. In this way, the programs reinforced social hierarchies just at the moment when those hierarchies were supposed to be undermined. This process was evident in a scholarship pamphlet shared with me by parents in San Lorenzo. Pamphlet authors proposed the grade schoolers themselves choose recipients. The authors suggested designating "a special day" when children would "freely and spontaneously" elect scholarship winners. Through games and other activities, the children would consider who among them had the most financial need and the most academic interest (not academic achievement). Adults guiding the children should ensure only that elected children indeed presented financial need and that no single family received more than one scholarship.

Orozcans and San Lorenzans disregarded these guidelines to the extent that I never heard mention of them. The San Lorenzan who shared the pamphlet did so as a gesture of goodwill and gave no indication he had read the material. Instead, the ejidos' parent-teacher associations chose scholarship recipients. Most ejidatario families with a school-age child received a scholarship. Rather than focus on first- and second-graders, scholarships followed a single child throughout his or her grade-school years. Upon the child's graduation, parents and teachers passed the scholarship on to a younger sibling. The notion that scholarships support school attendance was watered down as the money became a critical component of a family's overall subsidy profile. However, people generally agreed that scholarship funds should be spent on household necessities. San Lorenzans reprimanded a father who used scholarship monies for his personal dental work.

Numerous programs mimicked Solidarity's reflective decision making. Thus, the potential radicalism such processes held was somewhat weakened. Solidarity drew on critiques of government practices in Latin America dating back to the 1960s. At the time, liberation theologians and other activists sponsored campaigns of self-reflection as a tool of consciousness raising among impoverished people. Peasants explored how their poverty was the result of government disregard and certain economic structures (Boff 1988). Peasants then discussed solutions to these obstacles and, in subsequent decades, pressed for altered economies and politics (Alvarez et al. 1998). In their application of this formula, Zapatista organizers emphasized that outsiders must follow the lead of community-based decisions and place themselves at the service of campesinos (Leyva Solano and Franco 1996). In appropriating liberation theology, Solidarity authorities rarely included this notion of service. Instead, Solidarity structures aimed at preventing the militancy that resulted when peasants throughout Latin America, having their proposals meet violent government opposition, turned to armed struggle (Harvey 1998).

I say this radicalism was weakened but not negated in Calakmul, because local authorities were only partially successful in stanching rebellion. At the Regional Council, Solidarity opened a space where campesinos could request and rationalize development aid. As we will see in the next chapter, campesinos both within and outside the Reserve-Council alliance took this opportunity and ran with it, demanding ever increasing aid. In order to understand the economic motives for these demands, I assess the programs overall for the amounts they contributed to household incomes.

Patchwork Household Economies

Hardly a week passed in Orozco or San Lorenzo without a visit by a government or NGO agent to address ejidal members' health, economic development, or land management. A government agent visiting Orozco admonished ejidal members to participate in his aid project because: "This area is screwed. This area is incredibly screwed. (Está fregada esta zona. Está fregadísima esta zona.)" Orozcans and San Lorenzans agreed with this assessment, but they disagreed about how to better their situation. As they struggled to control the projects, they argued about the role of subsistence farming in the household enterprise. These disagreements touched on identity differences and the fact that aid benefits were not evenly distributed. Table 6.3 shows how these arguments arose from and reflected the way families were positioned very differently in regard to various income sources.

The table examines the percent contribution of income from cash crops, wage labor, and subsidy programs for six Orozcan and four San Lorenzan households. The households are listed according to the male

Table 6.3 Sources of Household Income as Percent Contribution to Overall Income

House-hold	Chile/Chihua Sales	Misc. Sales	Wage Labor	Conservation or Development Wages	Children's Scholarships	PROCAMPO	Conservation-Development Despensas	Percent of Income Subsidies	Total Income
Orozco									
Jerónimo	61%	23%	0%	0%	10%	0%	6%	16%	$5,941
Gerardo	60%	6%	9%	0%	20%	0%	5%	25%	$2,903
Venancio	30%	0%	16%	15%	22%	10%	7%	39%	$5,827
Paco	47%	12%	22%	15%	0%	0%	4%	53%	$1,350
Eusebio	0%	0%	50%	0%	38%	0%	12%	50%	$1,562
Romero	5%	2%	93%	0%	0%	0%	0%	1%	$4,084
San Lorenzo									
Ramón	69%	0%	4%	0%	18%	0%	9%	27%	$3,312
Alejandro	5%	0%	0%	33%	19%	32%	11%	95%	$5,584
Carlos	10%	8%	22%	1%	6%	44%	7%	58%	$4,039
Melitón	0%	0%	28%	18%	0%	45%	9%	72%	$1,935

household head so readers might connect this data to information elsewhere in the book. The chart's final column tallies the household's peso amount of earnings. The column "Miscellaneous Sales" includes products other than chile or chihua, such as corn, eggs, and sales from a family-run store. Under the title "Conservation-Development," I have separated out household income stemming from state programs. For San Lorenzo, none of these wages and despensas were derived from Reserve-Council sources. For Orozco, all such wages stemmed from the Reserve-Council, while roughly half the despensas arrived from the same source.

The information for Orozco covers the six months from January to June 1995; the information for San Lorenzo covers three months, August–October 1995. Because of the different time periods, data collection in Orozco missed PROCAMPO distribution as well as the chihua harvest. Data collection in San Lorenzo missed the chile harvest.

In risking a comparison between wage labor and state-directed economic realms, I standardized the daily wage to 20 pesos. This way, I demonstrate a best-case scenario for household income. The standardization, further, smoothes out the abrupt change in the peso's value during Mexico's financial crisis of 1994. The crisis precipitated a decline in the peso's worth from 3 to 7 pesos to a dollar. Returning to table 6.3, at $20/day for wage labor, each $1,000 in earnings was the equivalent of 50 days of work. During their respective time periods, Orozcans earned between 67 and 300 days in wage labor equivalency (again, for a six-month period) and San Lorenzans earned between 50 and 275 days in wage labor equivalency (for a three-month period). Note, however, that during this same period, the peso's decline was causing real wages in Mexico to fall 25 percent (between 1994 and 1996; see Pastor in Soederberg 2001).

Table 6.3 is provocative both for what it relates and what it fails to relate. Families like those of Jerónimo and Venancio, who controlled development aid as it entered the community, received a relatively small proportion of income from state sources. These families tended to be better off, and development programs were one of several strategies they used to make ends meet. Extremes in access to aid reflected Orozco's and San Lorenzo's different social and ecological settings. Romero (in table 6.3) was a poblador, denied access to aid. Ejidatario families like Eusebio's participated very little in development programs, but their income was so low that sporadic inputs provided significant earnings. In San Lorenzo, Alejandro stood out as he combined farming with work as the village health promoter. During the study period he and a son participated in a state-sponsored workshop that caused the percentage of household income from development aid to balloon to 95 percent. At the same time, this figure likely underestimates Alejandro's earnings. Neighbors complained Alejandro illicitly charged a fee for his services and sold medicine provided free to him.

This kind of corruption was so common in Calakmul that most people believed it was impossible to eradicate. In chapter 7, I address corruption in conservation-development programming. Calakmul's Reserve director thought state agents could only work toward a lesser corruption, and he implicitly tolerated a certain level of corruption among his associates. Ejidal corruption was a controversial topic in which the men profiting from development projects deflected charges by arguing that aid programs were not distinct from subsistence work. Rather, projects rewarded people's hard labor in the fields and compensated campesinos for the vagaries of subsistence work. This argument held particular weight when applied to conservation, and I return to it in the following chapter. To my discomfort, I learned how effective this assertion was in cross-class settings when I reported my research findings to Orozcans in 1995.

Before an assembly of men and women, ejidatarios and pobladores, I profiled the incomes of three anonymous households. I expressed concern about people's reliance on aid and its unequal distribution. Don Venancio, with whom I had a close relationship, grew impatient as I portrayed the extent to which he and others benefited from development projects. Pacing back and forth, he retorted I could not possibly understand these matters since I had never worked in the fields as a campesina.

Venancio might be less defensive if he knew that campesinos are not unique in their dependence on government support. In the United States, an estimated 25 percent of farm revenue derives from government subsidies, a figure that predates the aid approved in 2002, which increased state farm subsidies by 70 percent (Fitzgerald 2003; *The Economist*, August 17, 2002).[5] But, in Calakmul, subsidies created conflicts for reasons unlikely to be found in the United States. Because there were few legitimate ways campesinos could become wealthy, wealth accumulation often carried an air of corruption. Furthermore, the power that accompanied wealth ran contrary to the stock of moral rectitude people ascribed to subsistence work and the ejido. When I asked Orozcans about wealth differences in their community, people resisted my questions: "We are all equal here." At first, I thought these evasions arose from a miscommunication, and I reworded my questions. As I encountered continued discomfort, I saw that wealth could not be divorced from the power structures

Table 6.4 Program Tendencies in their Contribution to Household Income, Factionalism, Conservation, State Power, and Campesino Identities

Programs	Household Income			Factionalism			Conservation			State Power			Campesino Identities		
	↑	Neutral	↓	↑	Neutral	↓	↑	Neutral	↓	↑	Neutral	↓	↑	Neutral	↓
Chile/Chihua	✓				✓				✓			✓	✓		
Wage labor	✓				✓				✓	✓				✓	
Conservation-development	x*	✓					x*	✓		✓				✓	
PROCAMPO	✓				✓				✓	✓			✓		
Scholarships	✓				✓				✓	✓					x*

Note: For each category, the chart offers three possibilities. In the first column, the programs may improve, promote, or strengthen the issue under consideration. In the second column, the programs have no tendency in either direction. The third column shows which programs may have the effect of harming, decreasing, or weakening an issue.

*Indicates a program that could have either a positive or a negative effect depending on circumstances.

around which Orozcans had built a wall of silence. People whose wealth expanded beyond their physical labor (for example, to trucks and the ability to hire workers) attracted continued income in a way that maintained power differences (Collier 1992). In Orozco, people were unsettled at the idea of commenting on such distinctions. (San Lorenzans, as usual, were spirited in discussing wealth differences.)

Table 6.4 explores this issue further by suggesting how aid affected the key issues of ejidal factionalism, environmental protection, state power, and campesino identities. Because these are tendencies, I note their variations in specific circumstances. For example, wage labor could increase state power, when the state itself is a large-scale employer. (As of 2001, the municipio of Calakmul was the second largest employer in the county, after the army.) Wage labor taken up with neighbors may have no effect on the state, while wage laborers who travel to the United States might subtly undermine the power of the state altogether.

What is clear from the chart is conservation's uncertain place in Calakmul society. Within household economies, conservation had an ambivalent role. Within area ejidos and Reserve-Council programs, however, conservation became part of factional politics, while simultaneously increasing state power. Because conservation programs focused on subsistence work and reinforced campesino identities, we see both the material for conflict and arenas in which this conflict played out. To my way of thinking, the question of subsistence work is crucial and worth revisiting because it gets to the root of people's ability to live at all, let alone live with conservation.

Gambling with Subsistence

In 2001, increasingly impatient with campesino demands for land, a few environmentalists in Calakmul complained that campesinos received only 20 percent of their income from subsistence farming. These figures resonate nationally, where officials estimate between 70 and 80 percent of campesino income derives from nonagricultural activities (Correa 2001). We already saw how campesino supporters feel such arguments reduce corn production to a financial figure and dangerously commodify people's ability to feed themselves. The debate highlights the various ways people with a secure financial situation flirted with policies that gambled campesino subsistence. Reliant on aid for survival, campesinos played along with this game, giving it an aggressive edge and, ultimately, failing to be as independent as they might desire.

As we saw in the previous chapter, campesinos in this game transformed their poverty into a performance. Campesinos had to maintain the semblance of a precarious subsistence to justify the state programs that formed a central, if insufficient, component of their livelihood strategies. In this way, campesinos mimicked the state's own development discourses in order to capture the state's attention (Escobar 1995; Gupta 1998). An appearance of poverty was easy to conjure. Campesinos never knew when payments would arrive and, without a local bank where they might invest their money, found long-term financial planning difficult. Also, the price of basic goods meant that a daily wage of $15 to $20 did not go far. Table 6.5 lists the costs of items that regularly appeared on families' shopping lists. Families like that of Eusebio's in Orozco could afford the minimum necessities of salt, laundry detergent, and cooking oil. They lived on little more than US$1/day, while the wealthiest families in Orozco and San Lorenzo earned US$8/day.

Part of the Reserve-Council's novelty lay in providing a stage where campesinos could vocalize and perform this poverty to national and international audiences. Prior to the Reserve-Council, campesinos tended to be limited to local and state audiences, especially ingenieros on their visits to

Table 6.5 Costs of Basic Groceries, Xpujil, 1995

Item	Cost (in pesos)
Nescafe coffee, 100 gr	8.60
Sugar, 1 kl	2.40
Salt, 1 kl	1.00
Corn meal for tortillas, 1 kl	1.00
Tomatoes, 1 kl	3.00
Onions, 1 kl	3.00
Vegetable oil, 1 lt	5.00
Chicken, 1 kl	7.00
Beef, 1 kl	14.00
Laundry detergent, 1 kl	4.60

area ejidos. Uncomfortably, research such as my own, ushered in by conservation's presence, aids in expanding an audience for this performance. We researchers therefore risk reinforcing campesino-state relations that are not only ethically fraught, but increasingly demand that campesinos depend on unreliable aid.

Calakmul in the 1990s was flush with state aid, but this local crest belied a declining system of federal aid and worsening corn prices. In 2002, federal recognition of a rural crisis led to the announcement of new financial supports for the agricultural sector. Prior to this, Otero notes that "by 1994, only 8.6 percent of [Mexico's] ejidatarios had some technical assistance, down from 59.6 percent in 1990" (1999:48; data drawn from de Janvry et al. 1997). Documenting the effects of NAFTA, Mexico's weekly magazine, *Proceso*, painted a somber picture (one corroborated in an Oxfam study; see EFE News Service 2000). In 1995, Mexico's federal government dedicated 6.4 percent of its budget to agrarian concerns. By 2000, this figure was just 2.9 percent. PROCAMPO payments during this time were reduced in real terms from US$100/hectare to US$70/hectare. Between 1996 and 1999 the price of corn fell 45 percent in real terms (see Correa 2001). Mexican economists, the article cites, view this situation as underpinning increasing labor migration out of Mexico's countryside. Frank Cancian writes, government programs in Mexico have long "pulled and pushed [peasants] out of corn farming" (1992:27). Calakmul would follow national trends, when migration to the United States exploded at the end of the 1990s.

In the meanwhile, two programs, available in the late 1990s, indicated how moving people from a subsistence-oriented poverty to a market-oriented poverty required campesinos' continued disciplining and self-reproach. The children's scholarships were replaced by a program called "Progress." Of Calakmul's 4,600 families, 3,200 received Progress, which allowed families to enroll more than one child in a similar scholarship program.

Progress was introduced to ejidal members at the same time as a program called "Fight against Extreme Poverty," referred to locally as simply "Poverty." "Poverty" offered recipients free corn meal and a vitamin enriched powder that, mixed with water, tasted something like chocolate milk. Although ejidal members knew the difference between the two, they often mixed up the programs' names. "Progress" became confused with "Poverty," and one Orozcan stumbled in describing a program as "Progress *toward* Poverty" (emphasis added).

Perhaps the most telling evidence that state aid was a gamble was the way campesinos ascribed it a limited role in their overall well-being. When I asked residents in Orozco and San Lorenzo to rank their neighbors according to localized wealth categories, not a single person mentioned government aid as a marker of wealth. Instead, they remarked that wealthier people owned cattle, trucks, a store, and often hired people on their farms. Individuals noted as the wealthiest invariably brokered projects as they entered the ejidos. Still, it is instructive that campesinos distinguished between a government-directed economy and a more privately oriented domain. Campesinos suggested enduring wealth rested on both sustained government inputs and transformation of those inputs into autonomous enterprises. One had to be savvy and manage aid toward a larger end.

When the Reserve and Regional Council launched their conservation-development programs, the groups knowingly walked into this development setting. Conservation-development projects attempted to affect people's subsistence work in ways that went beyond PROCAMPO or Calakmul's market for cash crops. The projects aimed to reorganize and expand the mix of subsistence and market strategies while changing basic farming practices. The odds against achieving these goals were sizable. Authors of Calakmul's conservation-development agenda worked toward a diversified economy. Yet, state efforts, revealed in their calculations, mimicked market trends away from diversity. In 1998–99, the 722,650 hectares of municipal land surrounding the Reserve included 9,315 hectares planted in corn and 1,966 in chile, for a total of 11,281 hectares (INEGI 2001b). Land in pasture, orchards, and other cultivars do not appear in state reckonings. If this were not challenge enough, the Reserve-Council took on Calakmul's political, as well as economic, management. As we will see, Reserve-Council managers had little choice in this regard. And, these political endeavors, rather than the agenda's environmental and economic aspects, would prove the agenda's undoing.

7

Conservation's Political Space

Here, my task is to consider the precise way conservation was linked to development and how this process reinforced political and financial inequalities, as well as poverty as a basis for campesino identities. I begin with a description of the parent program to Calakmul's conservation-development agenda, a community-forestry initiative in neighboring Quintana Roo state. Reserve Director Acopa, chief architect of Calakmul's agenda, had worked previously in Quintana Roo and drew heavily on this initiative. Calakmul's NGOs additionally studied and worked with the Quintana Roo model, while ingenieros and researchers moved between the two sites. Following this description, I relate how Acopa transformed the Quintana Roo model into something unique to Calakmul. Acopa was the principal negotiator among Calakmul's ejidal communities and Mexican and international conservation communities. San Lorenzans and Orozcans dealt with him at Regional Council assemblies. Additionally, campesinos, seeing his overall power, might petition Acopa for any number of personal needs. Acopa had his detractors, some of whom would alter the course of regional conservation-development. Nonetheless, most agreed that he was a consummate cultural and political broker. Part campesino, part ingeniero, part political boss, Acopa both translated across all these audiences and maintained the tensions among them.

Following this bird's-eye perspective, I consider what conservation-development programs looked like within Orozco and San Lorenzo. The two ejidos had different relations to the Regional Council, and this translated into different configurations of acceptance and resistance. Their internal hierarchies also affected project implementation. I found only a handful of campesinos participated in the Regional Council's programs out of a desire to protect area forests. Most engaged the projects, as they did other aid programs, out of economic necessity and out of concern that, if they rejected these programs, none more would be offered. Campesinos most active in the Regional Council were generally men anxious to position themselves as brokers between their ejidos and development agents.

Women's motivations for working with the Council were different still (cf. Agrawal and Gibson 2001). Unlike Calakmul's ejidos, Council assemblies were not sex-segregated, and women had an equal voice and vote in Council affairs. One board position was reserved for a women's representative. At the Regional Council, women found the only place in Calakmul where they could hold formal power. The Council also offered some job opportunities that, although they did not address the overall scarcity of jobs for women, offered a few alternatives to positions as waitress and sex worker that otherwise counted among women's few opportunities.

These different appropriations of the Reserve and Council's work complicated the Council's claims to be representative of Calakmul's campesino community. Campesinos sidelined in the new sustainable economy began to demand an alternative aid structure for Calakmul. In particular, Ch'ol Maya, whose subordination in Mexican society was duplicated at the Council, drew on Zapatista and PRD discourses to infuse a heretofore ignored ethnic dimension to Calakmul's development scene. During Easter of 1995, they staged a strike that eventually led to the demise of the Council's conservation-development agenda and a shift in emphasis toward traditional conservation measures—large-scale ecotourism and a reserve isolated from surrounding communities. I close this chapter with a description of the strike and its aftermath.

This ferment advocates a reading of conservation narratives in light of people's diverse plans for their own and Calakmul's future. Conservation work at Calakmul took place in the context of numerous contests. Notably absent from these pages are the arguments taking place within the ruling PRI, as I was less able to ascertain their role in Calakmul. Extending to Campeche's capital and Mexico City, maneuvers within different wings of the PRI were decisive in Acopa's appointment as director, in the federal support he received, and the agenda's later decline. Such maneuvers also located Acopa's main rival in the local offices of the National Indigenous Institute (INI). The director of INI declared economic development his main concern, and since he believed indigenous people lived in all of Calakmul's ejidos, he saw the entire region as falling under his jurisdiction. This inattention to indigenous concerns would prove crucial in the Easter strike. The importance of these supralocal machinations should not be forgotten for an additional reason. A longtime observer of events in Quintana Roo, Renee Foster, notes that, in the 1980s, conservation-development required the political support of just a few key individuals, namely the state governor and people close to him (personal communication 2001). As we saw in chapter 1, Calakmul's conservation-development began in a similar atmosphere. By the mid-1990s, growing government bureaucracies in southern Mexico meant increasing competition among Campeche state and federal offices. Rival state agents could then take advantage of local discontent to commandeer conservation programs and funds.

None of this would have been possible without a decade of work in community forestry upon which Acopa and others based their ideas. The Quintana Roo programs continue to this day. As a model, community forestry in Quintana Roo offers lessons in political survival as well as the practicalities of conservation-development.

The Plan Piloto Forestal: A Model for Calakmul

The state of Quintana Roo shares Calakmul's history of forest exploitation, including the rapacious practices of large logging concerns, who cheated campesinos out of the value of their timber. (For this overview, I draw from Flachsenberg and Galletti 1998; Galletti 1998; and Hostettler 1996). In the early 1980s, when concessions owned by Quintana Roo's principal logging concern expired, local foresters and social scientists took advantage of a political opening—support from Quintana Roo's state governor—to institute a new, ejido-based system of exploitation. The Plan Piloto Forestal, or the Pilot Forest Plan (PPF), as it was called, was designed by forest specialists from the German Association of Technical Cooperation (GTZ). German staff members were instrumental in its implementation, and German funds, channeled through a binational agreement known as the Mexican-German Accord, made the Plan a reality.

The PPF had four objectives, and its authors were unabashed in asserting the political quality of these aims. First, the Plan would facilitate campesino participation in forestry in ways that went beyond the customary sale of standing timber. Second, the PPF would diversify exploitation beyond the most valued species of mahogany and cedar. Third, the Plan would work with campesinos to develop sustainable logging and land-use management plans that would transform forests into long-term sources of income. Finally, the Plan would improve access to markets and the quality of timber sold in order to elevate the prices campesinos received for their timber.

To achieve these goals, PPF staff pushed for "the rapid emergence of a new social institution capable of standing up for its rights" (Galletti 1998:34). The PPF sponsored the creation of the Society of Ejidal Forest Producers of Quintana Roo. In 1996, the Society counted among its membership ten ejidos with a total of 2,030 ejidatarios and 289,280 hectares of ejidal land. Ejidatarios within member ejidos elected representatives to the Society. These delegates, in turn, oversaw the work of the Society's ingenieros. Rather than rely on university-trained foresters, the Society offered campesinos training in logging skills. Numerous researchers also worked closely with the PPF to provide information on forest dynamics and to create a scientific basis for sustainable harvests (Primack et al. 1998). The "Collaboration Triangle" of forest communities, researchers, and advisors would become thematic throughout lowland forested areas of Mexico, Guatemala, and Belize.[1] The word *advisor* includes technical staff but more specifically relates to another group of people. Advisors usually have advanced academic degrees and form the principal interface between campesinos and donors. In Quintana Roo and Calakmul, this structure was viewed as subverting traditional hierarchies. Campesinos would lead the work of researchers, ingenieros, and advisors, rather than vice versa.

PPF advisors insisted on democratic decision making as intrinsic to campesino empowerment and natural resource management. In this way, PPF advisors saw themselves as transforming the Society into a "political force" (Galletti 1998:39) and "an important new element in civil society" (ibid.:43). The idea was not easily implemented. PPF advisors struggled with the way democratic norms could become hostage to ejidal factionalism. Local PPF advisors sometimes clashed with national Mexican-German Accord staff who preferred a top-down approach that entailed working through the Quintana Roo state government.

Acopa and the Regional Council would imitate the PPF's democratic structure and duplicate the Plan's central component as their flagship conservation measure, the creation of forested reserves within ejidos. During the time of its broadest reach, PPF's members held an estimated 500,000 hectares in ejido reserves. Reserve-Council documents show 47,500 hectares in ejidal reserves at Calakmul, although more land was pledged informally. Interestingly, these initiatives received weak recognition from international conservationists, who pioneered the idea of protected areas. In 1995, Conservation International collaborated with NGO and peasant organizations to develop maps of protected areas in the lowlands of Mexico, Guatemala, and Belize. At a presentation of draft versions of the maps, environmentalists working in Mexico pointed out the missing ejido reserves. With their inclusion, the peninsula would have appeared swathed in environmental protection. However, the published map, perhaps for reasons of logistic ease, presented only state-designated protected areas.

Maps could overlook but not negate the way, in both Campeche and Quintana Roo, campesinos were effectively working out a buffer to protected areas. Within their reserves, campesinos working with PPF ingenieros divided up forests into plots that could be logged on a twenty-five-year rotation cycle. In addition to carrying out the logging themselves, ejidal members began to process raw logs and market final products. The idea was that campesinos could earn more from their timber if they were also active in the more lucrative aspects of creating wood products. The innovative PPF was putting into practice an environmentalist mantra: "If conservation pays, conservation stays."

The Society of Ejidal Forest Producers remains active today, whereas the Regional Council is a shell of its former self. What explains the difference? People close to the PPF note the organization experienced variable levels of state support. Significant government backing of the Plan ended in 1986. Subsequent survival depended on adherence to ejidal forest management as the group's central mission and flexibility in reacting to changing policy scenarios (Galletti 1998:43). I wonder whether the extent of the Plan's international connections also might have provided a cushion against policy fluctuations. Certainly, the Plan's ecological viability came under question. The presumed rates of growth underpinning the twenty-five-year rotation cycle turned out to be problematic for some species, as did ideas regarding how to encourage certain valuable trees (Snook 1998; Whigham, Lynch, and Dickenson 1998). Disconcerting as these findings were, they were manageable. From the start, PPF authors knew that little ecological research had taken place in Quintana Roo and future learning was likely to alter land use models. Also, the PPF's well-defined mission provided a mechanism for incorporating and responding to changing ecological knowledge.

At Calakmul, the PPF model would be transformed and expanded significantly. The Regional Council counted more than forty-five member ejidos at its peak.[2] The Council included 1,296 ejidatarios and 303 women members. More people benefited from its programs, as participation was not strictly limited to Council members (Ericson 1996). Forestry concerns played a central role at the Council, but the group also undertook or collaborated on road construction, water infrastructure, and a whole series of small-scale, conservation-development projects that included agroforestry; management of tree nurseries; organic agriculture; ecotourism; wildlife management; chicle, palm, and allspice collection; herbal medicines; handicrafts; and environmental education. The Reserve and Council's missions, aimed at improving well-being through natural resource management, were more diffuse than that of the PPF. The Council's expansive membership base also made the group more vulnerable to intra-campesino disputes. These factors might have been countered with some significant social anchor. Although international actors would play an important role at Calakmul, they were not as active in program design and implementation as the German contribution to PPF. From the beginning, the Reserve-Council alliance depended heavily on state support, in particular funding from the National Reforestation Program (PRONARE), Solidarity Forestry (Solidaridad Forestal); and a federal program aimed at indigenous peoples, the Regional Solidarity Funds (Fondos Regionales). As we saw earlier, this financing came with significant strings attached.

The Reserve-Council alliance did not last long enough to receive scrutiny regarding its ecological impacts. Nonetheless, in a meeting with Reserve and Council staff, representatives of Mexico's federal environmental agency (then SEMARNAP) heralded their work as a national example. Calakmul's conservation community was creating "new and rational ways to take advantage of the environment . . . based on the people, with the people, and for the people." The populist aspects of Calakmul's conservation-development contrasted with a certain authoritarianism discernible in the Reserve Director's influence. Rather than contradict one another, these qualities were combined and embodied in Director Acopa, who saw himself mandating campesino empowerment through conservation.

The Reserve Director's Political Ecology

In 1995, Deocundo Acopa was in his midsixties and had spent a lifetime in southern Mexico's forests. His parents met on a plantation where his father worked as a shepherd and his mother as a cook. At some point in his mother's life, her skin had been branded to mark her as someone else's property. Stories of the plantation may have contributed to Acopa's keen sense of politics, but he also recognized that the hard scrabble of plantation life followed the family's move into the difficult life of logging. By the age of twenty-five, Acopa's father was captain of a logging unit and responsible to a sawmill for his unit's profits and expenditures. Logging brought about a real improvement in the family's standard of living. Acopa received an education in Mexico City, studying at a private high school before following his father into logging. When I asked Acopa whether he considered himself a campesino or an ingeniero, he responded that he was an *obrero*, a worker, although one with much education.

In his office and at Doña Belén's restaurant, Don Deocundo, as everyone called him, agreed to a series of interviews in which he outlined his notion of conservation-development. Enveloped in a cloud of cigarette smoke, periodically punctuated by his smoker's hack, Don Deocundo projected a personality much larger than his stature.[3] He loved to lecture. Visiting environmentalists might find themselves captive to his speeches well into the night. To foreigners, he expounded on the minute differences between logging and chicle collection or the thousand and one contingencies impinging on a given conservation program. A staunch nationalist, Acopa seemed to use these talks to emphasize how little foreigners knew about local ecology, culture, and environmental management. International donors found in Acopa a wily negotiator. To campesinos, Don Deocundo reminisced about Chiapas, Veracruz, and Tabasco. Unusual for a government agent, Acopa eagerly waved campesinos into his office, where he would conjure obscure regional foods, phrases, or customs. These talks aimed to show that Don Deocundo was a man of the people, someone worth listening to. Campesinos found in Acopa a person who assumed the mantle of former power holders while maintaining a campesino's modest standard of living.

Although Acopa forsook the violence of past caciques, people feared violence would be perpetrated against him. On one occasion, a drunken police officer shooting his gun in the air was immediately presumed by Reserve staff to be an attempt on Acopa's life. Threats of violence would follow subsequent Reserve directors, a point attesting to the import Acopa vested in the position. Later Reserve officers would produce one municipal president and one highly competitive candidate for the president's seat.

The fact that this more personalized power took place via programs ostensibly aimed at campesino empowerment was not lost on Acopa's detractors. At a conference organized by an international conservation group, activists from Chiapas complained Acopa was an old-style PRI political boss. They viewed his close ties to the ruling party as more telling than his populist statements. These activists also criticized the hype surrounding Calakmul's conservation-development agenda. For all the campesino participation, up close the programs largely depended on Acopa himself for their funding, their implementation, and their bravado. "What happens when Acopa is gone?" critics asked.

This intertwining of political and conservation objectives permeated Calakmul and was indicative of how activists throughout Mexico were using the popularity of environmentalism to foster (variously defined) social change. Acopa's most important decision in this regard was to focus his attention and resources *outside* reserve limits. The electoral reasons for doing so were outlined in chapter 1. To environmentalists, he argued that ecological systems were self-contained and relatively predictable. Kept to themselves, ecological systems needed no human intervention. Social systems, in contrast, were dynamic and could impinge on the Reserve's ecological integrity. Protecting the Reserve required managing the social and political processes surrounding its borders. In this sense, Acopa invoked a realpolitik, saying: "Conservation has to accept the social, and it has to begin from the social."

Acopa's challenges in beginning from the social were twofold: a) the penalization of subsistence activities that generated campesino animosity toward conservation, and b) the demands of international donors that conflicted with the context at Calakmul. His counter to both points entailed working from within the campesino community to develop locally generated understandings of conservation. Acopa asserted: "One shouldn't try to control people's creativity, but encourage it. If you study all of humanity, you'll see that we evolved as a function of creativity. . . . So, from there, you have to control that this creativity goes toward people's own understanding and find that equilibrium, where they [campesinos] are completely in agreement with what is a reserve and, even more so what is conservation. So these things can serve campesinos."

Note Acopa's shift from *encouraging* campesino creativity to *channeling* that creativity in a certain direction, then on to supporting a campesino empowerment. This blending of populism and authoritarianism was emblematic of Acopa's ideas and programs. In the context presented above, one of campesino ideas, the blending took on a relatively mild form. In the context of land and campesino autonomy, Acopa's ideas held a potent appeal as he argued that conservation required campesinos to control natural resources.

Acopa's approach in this regard echoed activists from throughout Latin America: "How can people protect land they do not control?" (Bunch 1986). This premise, however, reversed national policy. Salinas's charge that campesinos "care for the Reserve" (chap. 1) resonated with ejidal tenures. Campesinos would be responsible for the Reserve without owning it or being able to assume the authority that such responsibility implied. Acopa argued to the contrary. Campesinos, he said, effectively owned the Reserve, as Mexican citizens and to the extent their actions determined its future. If Reserve policies paralleled ejidal land tenures, Acopa viewed the latter as problematic: "On private lands, the land tenure defends nature a little bit. There's a reason to defend and improve the land. It's clear who the owner is, whose decisions count, and who benefits from the land. Of course, private property doesn't guarantee conservation, but it's an incredibly important step." In the absence of private property, Acopa sought to create among campesinos secure feelings of ownership and responsibility, all the while taking advantage of the way ejidal tenures provided him access to area communities.

Acopa built these feelings by invoking past legal structures that connected land use and ownership. He then subverted those concepts in a
particular way. In earlier centuries, Mexico's forested lands were considered legally as *tierras ociosas, tierras baldías*, lazy or wasted lands. In
the twentieth century, state agents translated this concept to mean that
land was not worked if trees were not felled. Unlogged, unfarmed land was
open to claim, and authorities might reappropriate such sites from ejidal jurisdiction. Although this concept has changed in a legal sense, the
connection between farming land and owning it endures. Ejidatarios in
Orozco and San Lorenzo, for example, regularly claimed as their own
hectareage they farmed (often decades ago) in their ejidos' common lands.

Acopa saw that by working forests, campesinos could make stronger
land claims to both their ejidos and the Biosphere Reserve. It seemed in
Acopa's thinking, the two entities stood as proxies for one another. The
Reserve-Council encouraged the creation of extractive reserves in small
ejidos, even though Acopa knew places like San Lorenzo and Orozco could
not sustain extractive activities. Experience of ejidal reserves, he hoped,
would help campesinos form a connection to the more distant, abstract
Calakmul Biosphere Reserve. Acopa was ambivalent toward the Biosphere
Reserve itself, viewing it as politically necessary but contrary to his ideas of
conservation. Conservation, he stated, "is the practice of rational [natural
resource] use." Pointing to Zoh Laguna's aged sawmill, he defined rationality as: "What do I want? Do I want a mill that finishes off the forest,
or do I want a forest that will sustain my mill?" The answer was clearly the
latter, but Acopa could not work with campesinos vis-à-vis the Reserve in
creating a sustaining forest. Campesinos could undertake such practice
only in their ejidos. Not coincidentally, these ideas of working forests
resonated among Veracruzanos, Tabasqueños, and Chiapans alike, who
agreed that forests occupied a separate social world, and people's proper
role in forests was to work (see Haenn 1999).

Acopa's notion of working forests both reconfigured ongoing activities and went well beyond those to which campesinos were accustomed. Where the PPF focused on logging and, later, chicle extraction,
Acopa believed a greater number of forestry activities were required. Noting that campesinos would protect only what they found valuable, he
declared, "Biodiversity is diversity in use." Projects that focused on just
one aspect of the forest tended to insert communities into the boom-and-
bust cycles typical of Calakmul's history. The resulting economic instability led campesinos to rely on farming and cattle ranching. To counter this
trend, Acopa considered the projects as working in concert to address

deforestation from different angles. When I suggested that the diversity of projects could just as easily lead to total forest destruction, Acopa responded that may well be. The projects were still in an experimental phase. In the meantime, each project was supposed to communicate ideas of rationality. The example of wildlife management demonstrates this ideal.

The wildlife management program aimed to show the economic value of hunted species and then follow up with a management plan. Ejidatarios participating in the faunal project assessed the species and number of animals present in their communities. Accompanied by Reserve-Council ingenieros—and supplied by the project with boots, flashlights, and other items—ejidatarios ran nightly transects and documented evidence of wildlife in their communities. Ejidatarios also volunteered to document animals killed for household consumption. Hunters were supposed to bring their kills to a designated person who noted the species and its sex, weight, and approximate age. At the end of a year, ingenieros presented an estimate of the total kilos of wild meat consumed in a village along with its cash equivalent. With information on animal populations reinforced by data on the cash importance of game meat, campesinos had a basis to begin managing their wildlife for long-term hunting.

This same format followed for the Reserve-Council's other projects. Technical staff provided the scientific knowledge to assess existing resources and suggest sustainable extraction patterns. Staffers conducted the paperwork and negotiated government bureaucracies for harvesting permits. Campesinos formed supervisory committees for each Council project active in the ejido. Members of these committees carried out the actual harvesting as well as other logistical tasks. Repeated throughout the breadth of the Reserve-Council's sustainable-development projects, this structure, Acopa asserted, should allow campesinos "to see for themselves that the forest is being destroyed."

In addition to the core group of programs noted earlier, Acopa and the Council actively experimented with other possibilities. With no viable model for sustainable development at this scale, they continuously sought ways to meet environmental and economic goals. For example, Acopa and the Council worked to revive Zoh Laguna's sawmill and train women in handicrafts that they might sell to tourists. The question of how campesinos might profit from wild cats was the most prickly. Jaguar pelts fetched a high price on the black market. In 1995, a Calakmul man killed two jaguar and sold their skins to pay for his wife's medical operation. Acopa schemed that high-end ecotourism might answer the problem. He entered into negotiations with a tour operator who had led hunting trips to Calakmul when jaguar were legal to kill. The idea was to create an exciting adventure where tourists would track jaguar and photograph, rather than shoot, them. The project held huge risks. Deep in the woods, a campesino guide might be bribed to turn his eyes as a tourist's camera was set aside for a rifle. Acopa surmised the idea was still worth exploration. Large cats, however, are elusive. People rarely ran across one, so how could the Council assess where and how many animals were out there? They decided to experiment in one of the larger ejidos. Throughout the ejido's extensive forests, ejidatarios and technical staff hung sheep carcasses to attract the animals. The experiment initially worked. Technical staff and campesinos were able to count jaguar and puma when they approached the carcasses. Unfortunately, in the following weeks, large cats preyed on sheep herds and came uncomfortably close to people's homes. People viewed the Council as guilty of giving the animals a taste for sheep. Ejidatarios then shot three cats to stop the predation.

Knowledge of Acopa's philosophy might soften the impact of such embarrassing failures. This philosophy was widely available to researchers, environmentalists, and Reserve-Council ingenieros, but relatively few of Calakmul's campesinos knew of its details. Acopa disseminated his ideas to researchers and environmentalists through a consortium that further included the ingenieros and managers of the Reserve, Council, and various NGOs. At their quarterly meetings, these groups coordinated efforts and defended their distinct interpretations of conservation-development. The small size of the group allowed for pointed communication on controversial questions. In contrast to his participation in consortium meetings, Acopa depended on the Council's monthly assemblies to broadcast his ideas to campesinos. Acopa stood on the sidelines of these meetings in which the Council's campesino managers addressed an audience of as many as 300 people. Acopa would step forth to adjudicate disagreements or interject his philosophy in explaining a given project. Assembly delegates listened to him closely, but this listening did not always translate into a reproduction of his ideas in other circles.

Orozco's Council delegate, Don Venancio, repeated the kernel of Acopa's philosophy that most caught on with campesinos: "cuidar no significa no tocar pero controlar (caring [for the environment] doesn't mean not touching it, but controlling it)." Venancio relayed this to me in defending himself against neighbors who had accused him of hunting in the ejido's reserve, where, at the urging of Council ingenieros, ejidatarios had banned hunting. Neighbors complained that Venancio participated in this program in order to convert the reserve into his private hunting grounds. Venancio said people were accusing him in reference to a deer he had actually killed in his milpa. In any case, he complained, his neighbors were really jealous of the bicycle he had received from the faunal project to help run transects. This embedding of Reserve-Council projects in ejidal disputes was common. In these contexts, as well as in their opposition to environmental regulations, Council delegates often grabbed onto Acopa's notion of use to defend existing practices. Venancio and a Council manager from another ejido unknowingly repeated one another when, on separate occasions, they advertised that they were maintaining forest on their farm parcels both to protect the environment *and* so their children would have somewhere to plant in the future.

Most campesinos were unable to clarify this apparent contradiction, although Acopa's ideas of a working forest could form a bridge between past and present forest use. In our conversations, Acopa asserted that his role as advisor meant he could not impose his ideas. He could only convey them to campesinos' democratically elected representatives, who, in turn, were charged with reporting Council affairs to their ejido assemblies. Acopa was well aware that most Council representatives arose from the sort of factionalism described in chapter 5. He knew that Council representatives often kept news to themselves, preferring to monopolize their connections than open them to their neighbors. When I pointed out the extent to which these fractures damaged his overall project, Acopa threw up his hands in frustration. He could not be responsible for internal ejidal affairs. Council managers were known to deliver water to their ejidal neighbors and then charge for what should have been a free service. Acopa complained, "What can I do if the people put up with this?!" Acopa's support of campesino empowerment coincided with the broadly shared belief in ejido autonomy. Although Acopa was bent on influencing ejidal affairs, he considered determining ejidal structures as practically and morally beyond his abilities.

Acopa's position shows how the notion of ejidal autonomy could be employed in multiple ways. Campesinos used the notion to defend themselves against unwanted government intrusion. State agents put the notion to work differently. Given the extent of the state's interference in ejidal affairs, ejido autonomy was an imaginary, moving target. State agents could locate that target in various places to rationalize flaws in development aid and their own powerlessness. Acopa's defense of campesino and ejidal autonomy supports the archipelago metaphor of ejidal-state relations. More than the ingenieros or other officials thus far mentioned, Acopa was explicit in elaborating how poverty acted as a bridge between campesinos and governing authorities. His descriptions in this regard show how a conservation mapped onto development could add to wealth hierarchies new power differences structured around environmental problems.

Mediating Power and Wealth Differences

The following conversation took place after the strike described at the end of this chapter. The strike dealt a serious blow to Acopa's authority, and during its aftermath, he argued defensively for both his programs and his tactics. Acopa complained his new rivals for state aid had failed to appeal to authorities in a way that would maximize their return. Their blunt demands for $500,000 contrasted with Acopa's more calculating style. He begins by discussing his efforts to train Council managers to negotiate directly with the state, a process he called "interlocution":

> Interlocution is people's capacity to identify and treat their problems, the capacity to negotiate with institutions in general. It's the capacity to negotiate, but with convincing words (Es la capacidad de negociar, pero palabreada). What happens is you negotiate on the basis of your problems. You have a problem, for example, they [the strikers] want $500,000 to work 500 hectares. You can't just say to the government "give me $500,000 for 500 hectares." The government will want to know, "How are you going to pay me?" You have to have the whole scenario identified: first, who is going to receive the money; second, what do they want it for; third, how many people in each ejido will receive the support; fourth, does the money go to the individual or the ejido; fifth, what [is the] time frame. As a principle of negotiation, if you want the money no strings attached (regalado), say that up front. It's a given that you have to work with a group, like Solidarity. You have to pull together a justification for your request.
>
> I don't want to fight with the governor. I want to negotiate with him. So, I say, "Mr. Governor, in 1991 there was a drought that left us completely destroyed. In 1992, it rained hard enough to break the highways in two and ruin our milpas. We lost our milpas. In 1993, there was some drought and more or less we got by. We weren't able to replace what we'd lost in previous years, but we also didn't lose. The year 1994 brought the mother of all droughts that lasted into 1995. As you can see, Mr. Governor, we have not been able to recuperate everything we have invested. We've been on the losing end four years straight, without Solidarity, without anything, because we

already owed from past projects. So, we want you to help us. But, let's keep something straight. If our corn harvests go really well, and we can produce at least two tons per hectare, we'll pay back those $500,000. But, if we don't get two tons per hectare, you can forget about seeing your money. Because, at that point, it's not our problem. We fulfilled our commitment. We planted and gave it all we had. But, if luck doesn't come our way, and it doesn't rain, it's no longer our problem." Then the governor has to think of a response: "I'll give you the money, and part of it will be a loan and part of it will be a grant." This is where a negotiation, an interlocution, begins. What you're doing is training people to be good interlocutors for their problems. One doesn't fight, but negotiates, and thus gets more things (bajo esta premisa consigue más cosas).

Here, we see themes resonant with past chapters: campesinos' duty to plant and the government's duty to compensate poor harvests; reliance on the state to compensate for Calakmul's agricultural conditions and obfuscation of the extent of that reliance; the central role of collectivism in accessing state aid; and Solidarity-type expressions of poverty through reflection and petition. Acopa effectively blended all of these in an effort "to get more things."

While on the one hand this approach appears a simple selling out, Acopa's position was more complicated than that. In many ways, he paralleled the local intellectuals in Florencia Mallon's assessment of post-colonial state-making in Latin America: "By choosing to mediate between their locales and the national political culture, local intellectuals also choose to enforce at least some of its tenets. . . . In this sense, the more effective they are as mediators, the more they must also take on the role of enforcers" (1995:285).

Note, in Acopa's remarks, the unrealistic expectation of corn harvests. We saw in chapter 6 that average harvests in Calakmul ranged between 800 and 1,200 kilos per hectare. Acopa would negotiate from the premise of 2,000 kilos per hectare. In Acopa's estimation, campesinos entering this hypothetical negotiation should operate from a losing strategy. Campesinos would employ what one Calakmul ingeniero describes disparagingly as campesino blackmail, "el chantaje campesino." They would transform their subsistence needs into an aggressive demand for aid and alleviation from environmental strictures. In Acopa's description, campesinos' performance of poverty was central to their negotiations with the state.

Overall, Acopa's reckoning responded to government demands, as well as the mathematical and verbal accountings international donors required of local grantees. His skill in this area made Acopa indispensable, especially as international donors refused to work directly with ejidal members. By demanding some mediating institution (or NGO), donor agencies invigorated the role of advisors in peasant organizations. Gabriela Vargas-Cetina considers people like Acopa the new middlemen, agents who do the work of global organizing and administration by translating across linguistic and cultural boundaries. Such advisors also create the (democratic) organizations that are acceptable to donors (Vargas-Cetina 2002). This structure was especially obvious in the aforementioned conference sponsored by international conservationists. In his behavior at the conference, Acopa showed he was not only aware of his unique position, but he was keen to share it with campesinos.

The meeting included a day in which U.S. representatives taught attendees how to formulate work plans and evaluate and report on project success. Some campesinos at the meeting asked if they might absent themselves, saying the discussion was incomprehensible to them. Conference organizers responded by splitting the group in two, so campesinos might share their experiences among themselves. I watched closely as the Regional Council's representatives did not join their fellow campesinos. Instead, the managers accompanied Acopa in sitting with ingenieros, advisors, and international representatives. Acopa and the Council's managers refused to be denied an audience. However, without the entree provided by the Reserve director, it was less likely that the Regional Council would have been able to negotiate directly with international agents.

Acopa's other contribution to campesino-state relations entailed refining and elaborating verbal performances and inculcating these in his protégés. He spoke with daring, clearly enjoying the drama of it all. Following his lead, Council managers spun their own colorful tales. They responded to donors' bureaucratic tendencies in kind, by arming themselves with facts and figures. They anticipated questions, having at ready the number of hectares in their reforestation program, the number of tree saplings distributed, the number of ejidos and ejidatarios participating in their projects, and the cost effectiveness of their projects over alternative possibilities. If these numbers were somewhat exaggerated, Reserve-Council supporters might overlook such mistakes. International donors, in any case, had few means to see past the smoke and mirrors. For a while, Mexican authorities chose to turn a blind eye to these inventions. Officials from the National Reforestation Program met with Reserve, Council, and

NGO staff in February of 1995 to review four years of work. In the meeting, one administrator expressed disbelief at an ingeniero's claim that 92 percent of the Council's reforested trees had survived. The ingeniero backtracked immediately to a figure of 60 percent, claiming 40 percent of reforested saplings were lost to drought. The administrator then offered his own surprising admonition, "I would put it another way. Despite the drought, there was a 60 percent survival rate. This level of achievement has had considerable impact."

This kind of tolerance could not last forever, but the impetus to change came from within the campesino community rather than from state or environmentalist circles. The campesino strike of 1995 undermined the Reserve-Council's authority as Calakmul's political and ecological leader. Following those events, Campeche agents took advantage of campesino demands that the state governor resolve their frustrations with the Regional Council. Campeche authorities moved to usurp the federally funded Reserve-Council alliance. Just six months after PRONARE staff reviewed the conservation-development agenda with kid gloves, Campeche authorities held a similar meeting whose tone was not nearly as congenial. Campeche authorities interrupted, contradicted, criticized, and generally threw their weight around to emphasize that power relations had changed. It is hard to say whether campesino critics of the Reserve-Council were in the majority. However, as we will see, critics voiced their concerns in a way that demanded attention, regardless of their numbers. Before turning to the events that ended the Reserve-Council alliance, I examine the Council's monthly assemblies and quotidian experiences of the programs.

Conservation-Development at the Regional Council

The Council's premier role in Acopa's plans was on display every month at Council assembly meetings. Before dawn on a Saturday morning, Council trucks fanned out across Calakmul to collect Council delegates. Ejidatarios voted two men to represent their interests at Council assemblies. An ejido's UAIM could also vote two representatives. Council assemblies lasted all day, with anywhere from 100 to 300 people milling about the open-air meeting hall. Board members—voted from within the ranks of assembly delegates—and technical staff reported on expenditures and project activities. They also described negotiations with donors for future projects. At Acopa's insistence, donors and researchers (like myself) requested permission from the assembly to work in the area. Individual ejidos petitioned to participate in certain projects. Families in crisis might ask the assembly for cash to pay for a child's operation or to replace a house lost to fire. In these cases, delegates passed around a hat and needled ingenieros with jokes about their high salaries. In short, Council assemblies knit together Calakmul's diverse actors in a setting designed to foster campesino authority.

Council assemblies were the only public forum at a regional level and helped constitute Calakmul as a coherent region. As a barometer of political events, the assemblies paralleled ejidal assemblies and Solidarity-type organizing. Ideally, campesinos would meet in their ejidos to assess local development needs. These requests would then pass through the hands of Council delegates to the group's board of directors. Area development would respond to these requests. In practice, Council delegates could resist but not alter the projects thrust upon them. Delegates might harass government agents with whose work they disagreed (see below), but in general they encouraged the continued flow of aid regardless of its content.

Commonly, Council assemblies, like their ejidal counterparts, were long and tedious affairs. At this scale, it was even harder to follow the intricacies and subtext of political jockeying. Ten or twenty people dominated discussions, and skeptical delegates always searched these people's words for hidden motives. Otherwise, most people seemed to pay little attention to the proceedings. They socialized and enjoyed a free lunch, paid for by the Regional Council. Delegates usually entered assemblies already having voiced certain differences in regional gossip. Council assemblies, then, tended to focus on questions for which informal communication failed to produce a compromise.

Council governance was closely tied to this constant flow of information traveling in gossip networks. It was fruitless to analyze assembly events without prior grounding in the parallel conversations taking place in Calakmul's gossip networks. But, it could also be difficult to get a handle on those parallel conversations. The variety of voices and opinions could be dizzying. In casual talk on Xpujil's streets, at Doña Belén's tables, or in a Council truck, someone would allude to how fed up people were with some Council manager or ingeniero. He or she was *grillero*, a blustery troublemaker, or *prepotente*, trying to make himself powerful. It mattered if the person making the assertion was influential, but mostly it mattered that people were talking. The force of public pressure was brewing. In the days before a Council assembly, gossip escalated as it centered inevitably on corruption accusations. I would attend the assembly expecting a fight, and more likely than not, nothing happened. The point of complaint might not even come up because critics, having tested the waters, found insufficient support for their position. A brief example of the disjuncture between gossip and Council assemblies will show how campesinos used the two spheres to work through different kinds of disputes.

Don Raimundo, a Council board member, was out of a job when his ejido recalled him and replaced him with another delegate. The Council's board, however, ignored the ejido's decision for weeks. Raimundo stayed on until the argument came up in an assembly. Through gossip channels, Raimundo's neighbors complained he charged for water delivered freely to the ejido by Council trucks. Ejidal members asserted Raimundo used control of the Council's heavy machinery to dig a private pond on his farm parcel. He appeared to use control of scarce water resources to set himself apart. These issues never arose in the assembly discussion of his case. There, his neighbors contended Raimundo's absence from the ejido hurt his work as ejidal president, and he never reported to them on Council affairs. Around this time, corruption accusations in Calakmul's gossip networks were mounting against other Council board members as well. People viewed Raimundo as the first to feel the full blow of public wrath. In a protracted debate, Raimundo sat emotionless and stone-faced as hundreds of delegates disputed his future and, by implication, his personal character.

The discussion began quietly enough. A delegate stood to ask the assembly what the group should do, since Raimundo's ejido had replaced him as representative, but he remained on the Council's board. This set off a debate over whether an ejido or the board had the right to decide who would act as an ejido's delegate. Some delegates defended Raimundo, citing a need for continuity in project management. Others worried ejidal members would attack the Council for not following the ejido's wishes. Delegates voted by a show of hands that Raimundo remain in office, but, by the mood in the room, the question was not settled. Delegates chose to vote a second time. Board members hung before the crowd a poster-sized sheet of paper that contained "yes" and "no" columns. In a dramatic show, each delegate walked to the front of the hall and marked publicly whether they thought Raimundo should stay or leave. The men voted first, and Raimundo appeared on his way out. But, Raimundo had been supportive of UAIM issues. The women's swing vote turned the election in his favor by just two ballots. Raimundo's allies tried to quiet the dissenters. They proposed the board visit Raimundo's ejido to discuss the matter. Many delegates concurred, but dissenters remained resentful. People rumored that, following the assembly, Raimundo received death threats. Raimundo left office shortly thereafter, as animosity surrounding him grew beyond the board's influence. Threats of violence confirmed the limits to their control. Raimundo's fellow board members feared they were next in line for censure.

If we took into account Council events alone, Raimundo's case emerges as an institutional problem. What were the relative jurisdictions of the ejido and the Regional Council? In light of the ejido's troubled autonomy, this question was pressing enough. Through gossip, however, people added multiple dimensions to the dispute. Did Raimundo steal Council and ejidal funds? Were delegates reining in Raimundo before he grew so powerful he was no longer answerable to his neighbors? To what extent was Raimundo a fall guy for increasing dissatisfaction with the Council as a whole? Parnell argues that gossip in rural Mexico can work as a public ranking of political players (Parnell 1988). In effect, gossip serves as a kind of election poll, although one that could be much more emotionally charged. People could mention things in private—such as corruption and death threats—that they would not say before the Council assembly. For outsiders, this disconnect between acceptable public and private speech could be especially confusing. Donors might hear rumors of malfeasance, but outsiders were challenged to gauge the severity of the public's feeling and develop adequate responses to personnel complaints.

With all its ambiguities, Raimundo's case was a moment of clarity in Calakmul's games built on wait-and-see. Politically active campesinos considered the *process* of mustering alliances and financial capital as important as any final outcome. They worked hard to forge connections, access cash, and throw doubt on their opponents. I once heard praise for a Washington, D.C., politician whose acumen extended to tracking multiple power networks, games within games, and the many possibilities posed by shifting alliances. By such standards, I thought, Calakmul was brimming with masterful political players. People closely watched current events with an eye to the future. Who would act next, where, and with whose backing?

Reading this, readers might wonder, what happened to reforestation, environmental education, and all the conservation programs? For many people active in the Regional Council, these political processes *were* conservation. Council debates centered on controversial personalities, financial expenditures, and the conduct of projects. Campesinos *never* debated whether the Council adequately lived up to conservation ideals. To the contrary, delegates argued when they felt conservation programs went too far in constricting their work (see below and Haenn 1999). Council delegates mapped conservation onto familiar critiques of power holders. Who controlled the programs and profited most from them? Why did projects tend to concentrate in some ejidos and not others? Which ingenieros were trustworthy and why did some technical staff waffle in fulfilling promises? For those at the center of the conservation-development agenda—delegates plus approximately twenty-five ingenieros, Council board members, and other NGO staff—the agenda's substance was power through conservation-development. This point could take people a long way from questions of ecological management, as the next section shows.

Drive-Thru Conservation

No description of Calakmul's conservation would be complete without a discussion of trucks. The programs relied on the Reserve and Council's fleet of vehicles, which transported goods and people to Calakmul's most remote ejidos. I learned about Calakmul's peculiar brand of truck culture from my first days in the area. With a nod from Director Acopa, I accompanied ingenieros and Council managers on some of their constant visits to area ejidos. We delivered saplings for reforestation and agroforestry projects. We investigated jaguar, deer, and tapir rumored to be captive or killed. We checked on the progress of various projects, including construction of cabins for ecotourists visiting archaeological ruins. Always, we stopped to greet friends, especially in Xpujil. As market town and crossroads, Xpujil functioned as Calakmul's communications network. A slow crawl through Xpujil announced the importance of a truck's occupants. It also gave people a chance to survey the latest information. Drivers looked out for people they knew and stopped to exchange words. With a few hand signals, people on opposite sides of the street could ask, "Any news?" and learn in response, "Nothing happening," or "Wait up, I have something to tell you." The Reserve and Council's trucks were traveling offices, where campesinos might make petitions, coax staff into fulfilling promises, or simply assert their influence by letting Xpujil's public see they were connected. The density of this communication was such that rushed ingenieros avoided Xpujil's crowded intersection if they wanted to get somewhere in a hurry.

Reserve-Council trucks pulled people into the conservation-development agenda by traveling filled with people who had hitched a ride. The demand for rides was such that one Canadian donor considered outfitting his program's truck with benches. The idea created a stir among Reserve-Council ingenieros, who suggested this level of comfort was taking ideas of campesino empowerment too far. Drivers would be under even greater pressure to give people rides. In later years, ingenieros talked about the finer points of who received rides and who sat where in the truck.

These details of hierarchy were readily legible to campesinos. Once, driving my Volkswagen bug from Xpujil to Orozco, I offered a ride to a few Orozcans waiting for public transport. They were not people I frequented with often, and they were surprised by my invitation. Wouldn't I rather wait on my close acquaintances who were also in Xpujil and would need a ride later on? I responded in the negative but learned that campesinos viewed the networks embodied in ridership as closed or, at a minimum, semipermeable.

Emblazoned with Reserve, Council, and NGO insignias, trucks inscribed these hierarchies in a more public manner. Although there were fewer trucks than ingenieros, certain ingenieros and Council managers were assigned or effectively monopolized particular vehicles. This fact fueled talk about who was operating which vehicle, when, where, and for what purpose. Any truck's arrival to an ejido merited notice. In Orozco, people passed word of a vehicle's visit, commenting on who received the visitor and speculating about the reason for the visit. Trucks made social networks visible, although the content of those relations could still be obscure. Two other ways the vehicles signaled power included monetary concerns and a truck's macho signification.

The cost of a truck was beyond the finances of most campesinos (and most ingenieros, who generally did not have their own vehicles). The few campesinos I knew who owned a vehicle used them sparingly. Association with any truck, thus, brought campesinos a measure of prestige because they were significant wealth markers. Newer, more expensive trucks indexed greater power. Dodge Rams sat at the top of this ranking and were operated by people like the Reserve director. At the bottom sat campesino vehicles, which tended to be decades old. I found automotive literacy, in this regard, important to communicating with conservation-development staff. Arriving in Calakmul, I was an automotive simpleton. When I left, I could distinguish a truck's manufacturer by its grate, having spent months talking in terms of "the Dodge," "the Ford," and "the three-ton truck."

Reserve-Council staff were overwhelmingly male, and, for some, trucks were important to projecting their gendered identities. Almost none of Calakmul's women (and relatively few campesinos) knew how to drive. Male drivers might bestow favors to certain women by allowing them to travel comfortably in the cabin. A truck parked in an odd location advertised a sexual tryst. A few ingenieros viewed sexual conquest as part and parcel of their jobs. Men also expressed themselves by traveling at preferred speeds up to 100 mph. The wear this placed on Reserve-Council vehicles was considerable, and the alliance maintained its own garage. Individual driving habits were controversial (if unchanged), especially in the event of an accident. The only trucks faster than the Council's were the municipal police, who broadcast themselves by appearing to fly over dirt roads in menacing black Rams. Unlike the police, Council board members and ingenieros were accountable to the Council's assembly of delegates.

Delegates did not see accidents as gendered events but as recognizable indices of waste and decadence. Accidents were the one transgression ingenieros and Council members could not hide (although they occasionally undertook surreptitious repairs). Car accidents always inspired heated quarrels at Council assemblies. Faulty drivers found themselves in extremely awkward positions. Delegates turned accidents into simple tales of right and wrong, what someone should or should not have been doing. Delegates used the vigorous disciplining of those involved in accidents as a way to demand a more general accountability. Car accidents often revealed excessive alcohol consumption and the use of trucks for personal errands. That is, accidents hinted at a larger hijacking of Reserve-Council resources for personal advancement. Acopa argued with delegates on the need to regulate the use of trucks: "The Council has grown too big. You all are handling big money, big politics, and a big organization." But, delegates always agreed to charge drivers only the cost of repairs. One accident incurred an astonishing $10,000 bill, and the driver, a board member, tried to squirm his way out of responsibility by pleading a common poverty: "Look, we're not chauffeurs, we're campesinos. We've had a machete in our hands since birth . . . and all we earn here is a day's wage." Delegates would not let him off, although they knew he had no means to come up with the funds. In opting for this system over a more formal regulation, delegates retained a measure of accountability while recognizing that unfettered mobility, both social and physical, was crucial to the Council's success.

Conservation-Development in Orozco and San Lorenzo

The hustle and bustle at Reserve-Council headquarters contrasted with the chimerical presence of conservation-development in Calakmul's ejidos. Periodically, a Reserve-Council truck would appear. People might gather around as an ingeniero held an assembly or distributed some goods. Ingenieros would leave and talk of conservation would subside until the next visit. A stranger visiting Orozco or San Lorenzo might find visible evidence of the programs hard to discern. In 1995, Council projects had not affected ejidal ecologies as much as they had altered ejidal politicking. Calakmul's ejidos were also the site where campesinos expressed their depth of opposition to conservation. Resistance in the context of Reserve-Council assemblies had to take into account the programs' financial and political import. At home, campesinos spoke more openly and worked actively to defend their subsistence work. In particular, they rallied to counter regulations against felling and burning forests. In this section, I address the contentious question of fire after an overview of Reserve-Council programs in Orozco and San Lorenzo.

Reserve-Council visits were a weekly occurrence in Orozco, where ejidal members received no fewer than five Council projects. San Lorenzans received four projects, but their greater distance from Zoh Laguna (a two-hour drive versus half an hour to Orozco) meant fewer ingeniero visits. In both communities, the Council's agroforestry program provided fruit trees as well as precious hardwoods of mahogany and cedar. The Council's environmental education program showed ejidal residents a video of Walt Disney's *The Lion King*. The movie was meant to humanize wildlife in a way that got people thinking about protection. Orozcans' nearness to Zoh Laguna meant their children received greater attention from the education program. Grade schoolers traveled to the Zoh Laguna zoo and participated in a drawing contest. In the contest, children depicted idealized plants, animals, and archaeological ruins. One child, absent when the assignment was explained by the school's teacher, stood out by drawing people felling forest in preparation for a burn. He received a special prize by Council ingenieros who acted as judges. Seeing how the teacher imposed his own notions of environmentalism on the students' drawings, the ingenieros wanted to emphasize the Council's message that protection could entail resource use.

Council projects brought together ejidal members in different configurations, although the main beneficiaries were those families who dominated the committees charged with project implementation. Environmental education was open to all children. Wildlife management (in Orozco) and sustainable timber harvests (in San Lorenzo), both of which involved common lands, required assembly oversight. Participation in agroforestry and organic agriculture was aimed at individual households, and these programs were generally brokered by male family heads. Handicraft projects were among the few opportunities available to women.

On the whole, these arrangements reinforced the power of men's ejidal assemblies over caciques of the past. This came about as the Regional-Council allowed for multiple contacts between the ejido and its organization. Many caciques responded to this change by transforming themselves from patrons (in which a leader doles out goods according to his/her prerogative) into brokers (acting as point of contact between two distinct groups; see Gupta 1998). These new leaders organized factions around family and ethnic ties (cf. Agrawal and Gibson 2001). In these positions, caciques still functioned as doorways through which aid entered area ejidos, but now this work was under constant challenge. Rival factions vied for control of Council programs, as was the case in Orozco, leaving disaffected ejidal members on the sidelines. San Lorenzo offered a distinct encounter between aid programs and ejidal factionalism. San Lorenzo's two factions assigned programs to one or the other group. A minority faction participated in the Regional Council, while roughly two-thirds of the community's households received aid from other sources. The two groups shared programs only when necessary.

Regardless of these disagreements, faced with certain threats, ejidal members could quickly set aside their animosities. Dealing with government agents, ejidal members refrained from positioning themselves as Veracruzanos, Tabasqueños, Chiapans, men, or women. Instead, they worked together as "campesinos." This identity had profound implications for conservation. A common identity based on subsistence farming coincided with common understandings of the environment as a place of work (Haenn 1999; Murphy 1998; Schwartz 1999). Conservation policies touched on people's economic vulnerability, but they were also situated within the strongest arena for organizing. As "campesinos," people in Calakmul could present a united front against conservation threats to their work.

Still, learning the extent people opposed conservation was not so easy. They were hesitant to condemn conservation for fear of losing its accompanying development aid. Orozcans, with their geographical nearness to Zoh Laguna, let down their guard only when pushed to exasperation. They claimed to follow the law closely because "we're more conscientious, and we're also a little afraid." San Lorenzans were more openly anticonservationist. Their feelings were so strong, my work would have been hampered had I presented myself as an environmentalist. During my first days in the ejido, San Lorenzans tested me when a hunting party distributed game meat. As a crowd gathered to admire the kill, the hunters grew awkward with my presence. They invited me to a taco and joked that, if I reported them, they would be sure to tell authorities I had eaten the contraband. In their own way, ejidal members in both communities required my allegiance to their environmental stance in exchange for their confidence.

This demand made sense as I learned that people fundamentally distrusted the motives that lie behind environmental programming. Orozcans and San Lorenzans viewed deforestation as either a positive trend ("when I fell forest, it's for good") or an impossibility ("the forest always grows back"). And, they commonly viewed protected areas as nonsensical. They were bewildered by ideas of setting aside land people would not work. Faced with this incomprehensibility, people looked for the true meaning of conservation in motivation (Brydon 1996). They believed conservation served as a screen for elite attempts to control financial and ecological resources. These sentiments were rarely expressed at the Reserve-Council, but, as the case of fire shows, they were familiar assertions in Calakmul's ejidos.

The 1995 burning season saw a rash of forest fires in Calakmul, and firefighters soon arrived to combat the flames. Campesinos have good reason to want to control fires. Mainly, they say, an out-of-control fire can affect a neighbor's parcel and be the start of an argument. I never heard this commonsense plea circulate among state or NGO agents, who instead urged people to protect forests. Because they took this approach, the firefighters' work was controversial. People rumored many of the fires were set intentionally. A fire that eliminated a parcel's older growth forest could be advantageous if it freed the owner from future state supervision. With fires continuing unabated, exhausted firemen held an assembly at the Regional Council to discuss fire control techniques. They suggested methods in timing burns and constructing firebreaks. The crowd of 300 people impatiently rebuffed the suggestions, saying, "They talk as if it's so easy," and, "If we do all this work, when will we do the work that feeds us?" Despite open opposition, authorities asked each ejido to submit a schedule of when people would burn. The schedules would allow authorities to have teams on hand for rapid response to rogue fires. Because the timing of a burn depends on weather as well as other factors, campesinos cannot say with precision when they will burn. In Calakmul's ejidos, these logistical concerns received less attention than other issues.

In Orzoco, the demands maddened Jerónimo. Jerónimo sat on every Reserve-Council committee operating in the ejido, but, on the topic of fires, he proffered strong words against government agents and environmentalism more generally: "They want to make idiots of us (quieren hacer pendejo). They want us to burn at four in the morning. Nobody burns at that hour. Then they want to send someone out to supervise the burn. We've been doing this for a long time! We know what we're doing! They said that if you're going to burn five hectares, you have to clear five hectares of firebreak. When am I going to do that?! Let them do it! How many years have they spent making milpa anyway? They can throw me in jail if they want to. I won't do what they say." We were sitting in his kitchen, when Jerónimo's wife eagerly jumped into the conversation: "They just want to get money out of us. Every time they say we need official permission to burn, they mean they want an excuse to get a bribe. If all this was really important, the governor would have attended the meeting personally." This mention of the governor presaged by just a few weeks demands that the governor intervene to restructure development aid in Calakmul. In the meantime, the couple's sentiments were widely shared by Orozco's ejidatarios, who convened to discuss the firefighters' requests.

At the meeting, ejidatarios built a collective front against the government's demands. Ejidatarios complained the firebreaks required additional labor on their part with no compensation. They agreed not to submit the schedule, citing the specter of collective punishment: "We don't want anyone coming to damage our work, because if they come and there aren't any firebreaks, it will hurt everybody." They worried the fire control program was an excuse to investigate whether they were felling older growth forest. And, they agreed with Jerónimo's earlier assessment of the injustice of the situation: "What we are going to care for is the [Calakmul Biosphere] Reserve, and we are not going to care for the forest, because the government gave it to us. If the government prohibits something on the land it gives, why give it in the first place?" Here, Jerónimo located the problem in government ambivalence about land tenure and campesino control of environmental outcomes. From this perspective, Council members who resisted government directives were exerting their own brand of ownership. Resistance contrasted with Acopa's emphasis on forest use. Campesinos might find ownership in leaving reforestation saplings to languish (as in the year 2001, when every ejido I visited hosted a pile of long-neglected saplings) or in transferring a researcher's radio collar from a hunted jaguar to a village dog.

As a weapon of the weak, this recasting of aid into a mechanism for autonomy contained an uncomfortable paradox. Aid programs were indispensable to campesino survival. Campesinos enacted a kind of land

ownership by selectively subverting a central pillar in their own livelihoods. At the same time, campesinos viewed the *misdirected* quality of aid
programs as demanding such subversion. In San Lorenzo, Juan echoed
Jerónimo's position, although the two men did not know each other:
"Well, the government should come and explain exactly why it doesn't
want [us to fell forest]. If the government gave us land, it gave us land to
work. Then after giving us the land to work, it doesn't want us to fell. Then
what it should do is give us other lands, give us the support to be able to
live from one or two hectares, with mechanized agriculture or something.
Because, we can't live from the forests if we don't work them. A lot of
people say, 'If we listen to the government, we'll die of hunger.' "

Unlike Jerónimo, Juan did not participate in Council projects, but
he still saw the need for agricultural programs. As federal authorities reneged on constitutional promises to the peasantry, Juan suggested certain
kinds of aid could substitute for land distribution. Aid and land distribution were interchangeable to the extent they both made campesino livelihoods possible. This substitution did not resolve campesino demands for
land. Indeed, under pressure from campesinos, Reserve officials held out
the possibility of opening new sites for colonization throughout the 1990s.
In Juan's estimation, however, aid did ameliorate tensions surrounding
land distribution and land tenure.

This relief came at the cost of long-term, sustained interactions
between campesinos and the state, as aid programs required constant
monitoring. Defending themselves against unwanted government intrusion in this regard, campesinos employed a three-pronged approach. As a
first line of defense, ejidal members rarely turned down a project offered
to them, even if they counteracted projects they found to be flawed. Interestingly, this tactic also has been employed by NGOS seeking international
funding. In both cases, people participated in an overly ambitious series of
projects to attract further funds (Christen et al. 1998). As a second line of
defense, ejidal members cultivated their ejido's image as an upstanding
member of the development world. Presenting a unified, tranquil front
required that ejidal members monitor one another. Orozcans constantly
fretted their divisiveness would have adverse effects. Even with programs
directed toward individual producers, like PROCAMPO, Orozcans worried
that if someone failed to fulfill his or her contract, "they damage all of us
because [the ingenieros] won't trust us." San Lorenzans were more secure
in this regard. In negotiating with ingenieros, the ejido's strongman, Esteban, demanded development aid as his due, and he cared little what
ingenieros thought of him.

Campesinos' third line of defense lay in fostering a reputation for rebelliousness. A mild form of this approach took place at soccer games, where NGO and Reserve-Council ingenieros played against ejidal teams. Campesinos taunted their opponents: "We're going to fell the forest to get rid of you all!" The Regional Council, with its PRI credentials, offered a place where ejidal members could sometimes vent anger at conservation policies. Ingenieros, however, believed this rebelliousness was relenting under the weight of aid programs. They compared Council assemblies in 1995 with more argumentative meetings of past years, when a state governor might have been shouted down. By 1995, Council delegates were applauding the governor with a standing ovation when he signed before them a binational aid package for the region.

Perhaps some forms of rebelliousness were softening at Calakmul, but other forms were taking on greater poignancy. Orozcans, San Lorenzans, and ejidatarios throughout Calakmul subjected Reserve-Council projects to ejidal factionalism. Ingenieros noticed, but refused to address, the dissent of ejidal members who felt sidelined in the new sustainable economy. Reserve-Council staff considered these problems as "internal to the ejido." Nonetheless, in the spring of 1995, these problems became all of Calakmul's problems as disgruntled campesinos forced a change in governance and, consequently, in conservation planning.

Reforming Conservation-Development

During Easter week of 1995, I followed Mexican tradition and took a holiday. On a second-class bus, with the radio blasting, I first heard reports of a strike in Xpujil. The announcer's voice was lost in the wind blowing through the bus, but I knew something important had happened. Xpujil did not usually make headlines.

I returned first to Zoh Laguna. Calakmul's gossip network was in full force, and people shared their diverse opinions about the previous days' events. The strike appeared spontaneous, but in retrospect people made out its clandestine organization. The strike began as a Holy Week pilgrimage. A group of Catholics planned to process north, past numerous ejidos, and then through Xpujil to attend services in Zoh Laguna. Pilgrimage organizers solicited cash and food items to support people's journeys. The pilgrims never arrived at Zoh Laguna. Instead, the group stopped in Xpujil, where, joined by hundreds of supporters and curiosity seekers, the group closed Xpujil's highway for three days. Strikers charged tolls to passing drivers, demanding higher fees from foreign nationals and chauffeurs of more expensive vehicles. Protestors stole equipment from Council trucks caught in the fracas. A woman who had contributed food to a pilgrimage organizer was frustrated to find the same man demanding she pay to pass through Xpujil. Tractor-trailer drivers refused to pay the tolls, and Xpujil became clogged with trucks. The situation grew critical. The road passing through Xpujil is one of only two highways connecting the Yucatán peninsula with the rest of Mexico.

The protestors requested Campeche's governor personally negotiate their list of demands. The governor in question came to power through Calakmul's votes-for-development deal, and he traveled to Xpujil to settle the strike. Chief on protestors' list of demands was a resolution to the water situation. Strikers requested the government supply water trucks and dig deep wells. Protestors pressed for paving the road running south from Xpujil, along which thousands of people traveled. They additionally demanded a $5,000 credit per chile producer for an estimated 1,500 campesinos. The program for children's scholarships was three months in arrears, and protestors demanded the government fulfill payments. Apart from these regional requests, individual ejidos made their own demands for electricity, the dismissal of incompetent schoolteachers, and resolution of land tenure questions. Many of their requests had been made before, but were stalled somewhere in the government bureaucracy.

The emphasis on water lends to an interpretation of the strike as a conflict arising from scarce resources. Ethnographic information, however, shows such explanations to be facile (cf. Peluso and Watts 2001). By focusing their demands on those aspects of household economies outlined in chapter 6, protestors implicitly criticized the conservation-development agenda. In the question of water, protestors made a revealing request. Citing corruption at the Regional Council, they insisted government funds be channeled through their own, new, campesino organization. The protesters did not argue over environmental resources. Instead, they clamored for state attention and equity in development aid.

To press their point, protestors engaged the governor in theatrical displays of poverty. They fed him a plate of unsalted beans and a glass of the murky brown water typical of area water supplies. The governor conceded few points but assigned a team to look into matters. Within days, new water trucks arrived in Calakmul painted to announce their role in an "emergency water plan." Children's scholarships were disbursed quickly. The following year, the state paved the southern road. Chile credits were not forthcoming. Nonetheless, the strikers were successful on a larger scale. Policy makers and NGOs alike immediately began to think beyond the

Regional Council to reckon with the new players. Campesinos throughout Calakmul sought to take advantage of this political opening. Following the strike, no fewer than four new campesino organizations formed to rival the Regional Council.

In Zoh Laguna, people noticed, but did not elaborate on, the fact that most strikers were Ch'ol. For some time, Acopa and other government agents overlooked Ch'ol as a political constituency, arguing the group was "closed" to outsiders and had no identifiable leaders. (No ingeniero spoke Ch'ol, although the Council's board included one member who did.) Authorities maintained this position even as Ch'ol voiced their concerns in public, organized ways. In the Reserve and Council headquarters of Zoh Laguna, Ch'ol pobladores staged a series of sit-ins during 1994 and 1995 to force that ejido's officials to recognize their candidates for office. Their carefully constructed ignorance continued as Reserve-Council staff overlooked the strike's indigenous character—the organization arising from the strike called itself the "New Indigenous Campesino Union"[4]—and focused on how the strike undermined their preeminence. In later years, Mestizos formerly active in the Reserve-Council would describe the new Union as better organized, more enduring, and more politically astute than the Regional Council. Where campesino organizing had become a modus vivendi for Council board members, the new organization displayed closer adherence to campesino empowerment. Mestizos in regional governance, however, would follow the Reserve-Council in disregarding or working to neutralize the Union's influence. In 1995, relations between the Reserve-Council and its opponents were extremely delicate. During the strike, Council board members had received death threats, and they traveled with caution. The strike, supposedly aided by Zapatista organizers, left many to wonder whether Calakmul was about to erupt in armed conflict. In responding to the situation, state authorities focused on generic campesino identities and rhetorically marginalized those peasants whose indigenous identities shaped a distinct campesino experience. In practice, Acopa and the Regional Council called on their extensive organization in Calakmul's ejidos to reestablish their authority and made no overtures toward the question of ethnic difference.

I watched these events take place in Orozco, where the tensions described in chapter 5 were now brought to bear on those seeking alternative political expression in the new Union. Adolfo Gilly (1998) describes the Mexican state as ruling via revolts like that of Easter 1995. How do campesinos partake in this process? Discussions in both Orozco and San

Lorenzo were revealing for what people thought constituted legitimate grievances against the state and how, among themselves, campesinos opened and closed different paths of resistance.

Disciplining Ejidal Members

In Orozco, the strike's opponents and participants squared off in the continuing struggle over control of the ejido and development aid. Gerardo, one of Orozco's Ch'ol officers, had stamped the ejido's seal on a list of protestors' demands. A quietly ambitious man, Gerardo seemed to strain against the ejido's hierarchy. Gerardo asserted the strike was not ethnic in character and cited the presence of Mestizo organizers. Nonetheless, the excitement of the largely indigenous movement caught his attention. Gerardo told neighbors he was ready to take up arms. Even neighbors who were pleased the strike gave the government its comeuppance hesitated to accompany Gerardo into armed conflict. "It seems those people do not want to eat," declared one man of the war advocates. Orozcans who were deeply involved in the Council's projects especially worried that Gerardo's actions implicated the ejido as a whole and threatened the flow of development aid. In the run up to the assembly that would deal with Gerardo's actions, I solicited opinions on the strike.

I spoke with Venancio while he was making a rare visit to the home of his rival Jerónimo. The two were discussing a unified response to the strike. Both men dominated the ejido's Reserve-Council projects. They described the protestors as political neophytes, whose tactics were inadequate to the goal of maintaining development aid. Jerónimo's wife inspired hearty laughter when she described the protestors, disparagingly, as "like the Indian (como el indio). The Indian won't go or stay. He's like the dog who eats everything and leaves no food for his master (patrón)." A Mestizo critique of the indigenous protest was palpable. At the same time, the group did not alter its antigovernment sentiments, noted above. At base, they concurred with a more balanced assessment of the strike offered by a Ch'ol poblador: "Some say the strike was good, because the government doesn't fulfill its promises. Others say it wasn't good because the government does help some. What if we do too much, and the government gets so angry it doesn't give us anything?" Egalitarian aspects of the protest discomfited those adept at working within a hierarchical state. This hierarchy, in turn, intimately affected intra-ejidal relations. At Jerónimo's home, the group opined Gerardo would have some gall appearing at an impending meeting to resolve the scholarship problem. One should not publicly protest the state one day and then stand in line the next to receive state benefits.

At his home, Gerardo defended himself by asserting a critique with which almost any campesino could agree. The strike was necessary, because "the government doesn't fulfill its promises." He went on to repeat the protestors' demands, adding: "I had to be there because there's strength in numbers. Many people don't have the money to pay for water, and that's why we struck. Not for any other reason." The protestors' treatment of the governor was necessary, he said, because the governor can solve problems through his relationship to Mexico's president: "The governor talks with his president because he's ordered by him, just like Xpujil is ordered by [then municipal seat of] Hopelchén. The governor orders all the institutions in the state."

In both Orozco and San Lorenzo, people described the stratified state using a kinship analogy of father and son. Mexico's president was a kind of father to Campeche's governor. People acknowledged a common subordination within this hierarchy, but they disagreed on appropriate campesino conduct within that position. These distinctions sat at the heart of San Lorenzo's factionalism, where each side argued for different kinds of relationships to the state. The leader of one faction explained his support for adherence to state laws: "Campeche is still our father, even if the state hasn't always cared for us. That's the name on our birth certificate [ejidal decree], and you can't change a birth certificate." In the ejido's early days, he continued, the father was not there to support his "child." Now, the state was interested in the ejido, and ejidatarios should follow suit by complying with laws devised, in his estimation, to benefit the community. Faithfulness to the law was very much a minority position throughout Calakmul. Esteban, the rival faction leader, rejected it out of hand: "We don't want the government to love us, we want it to give us something." In both Orozco and San Lorenzo, people differed on whether their connections to the state should be based on a morally imbued, paternalistic social contract or on more narrow self-interest. People combined these positions creatively so that, in Gerardo's case, opposition to the state could be construed as righteous in that it aided the governor to fulfill his prescribed role as patron.

In this ambivalent space, Gerardo rebuilt his relationship with Jerónimo. Both men agreed the governor needed reminding of Calakmul's development needs. "He has a lot on his mind," they concurred and was surrounded by people who were not sympathetic to campesinos. The strike allowed campesinos to bypass those gatekeepers and negotiate directly with the governor. Jerónimo and Gerardo, however, were able to reach this compromise only after Gerardo received a public reprimand in Orozco's assembly. The reprimand came about when Council supporters forced their fellow ejidatarios to state their allegiance to the Regional Council and, by extension, to the PRI.

At the assembly, Gerardo's father briefly defended his son by asserting that someone needed to be present at the strike, because ejidal officials were "sleeping in their houses" and neglecting the community's problems. Ejidal officials would not be waylaid. They were under considerable pressure themselves. Privately, Orozco's president Guillermo worried, "The governor is going to have my neck because our seal was on the list of demands." As ejidal president, he was responsible for the seal. Ejidatarios, displeased with his work, had taken the seal away from Guillermo but left him in office. Guillermo coordinated with fellow Council supporters to allege that the ejido could not belong to both the Regional Council and the Indigenous Union. Throughout Calakmul, the Council demanded its members choose between the Regional Council or the fragile, new organization. This count took place within ejidal assemblies under the guidance of each ejido's Council delegates. Where the protest offered the anonymity of a crowd, the count required people to personally identify with the opposition, often in the face of ejidal pressure to do just the opposite. Nobody in Orozco chose to challenge the status quo, and all voiced at least a grudging support for the Regional Council.

The Municipio of Calakmul

For very different reasons, Reserve Director Acopa agreed with Orozcans' depiction of strikers as neophytes. Acopa conceded the strikers' ingenuity in political performance. He knew he had been upstaged. But, he thought protestors had wasted an opportunity by making small, short-term demands. They should have pressed for the creation of a new municipio for Calakmul. As a principal political organization within Mexico, municipios command a great deal of money, four to five times the amount handled by the Reserve-Council. Furthermore, these monies are relatively certain. Conservation-development depended on state and NGO funding cycles lasting just one to three years. At the end of a cycle, donors could decide not to renew their support. By spearheading the campaign for a municipio, Acopa and Council board members hoped they would dominate the new institution. Indeed, many actors central to the Reserve-Council alliance later occupied municipal offices. Campeche officials, however, moved to assure that Acopa and his closest collaborators would have no part in Calakmul's new governing structure. Campeche officials worked to displace Acopa by arguing against his particular brand of conservation.

The governor's cultural advisor was the spokesperson for this new conservation, and, following the strike, he suddenly took on an important presence in Calakmul. His rambling and contradictory critiques attested to the weight of opposition bearing down on Acopa. The advisor dissected the failures of each Council project and extended his invective to the PPF. The people in Quintana Roo, he said, had been duped by their German sponsors. The Reserve's recent management plan was, he claimed, a useless document. The advisor both criticized Acopa for failing to build tourist cabins inside the Reserve and complained Acopa was involved in programs about which the Reserve Director knew little, specifically the ecotourism project.

This incoherence revealed the extent to which complaints against Acopa had little to do with conservation. Instead, the advisor exclaimed, "Acopa should have the political structure in the palm of his hand, and he doesn't have it." Incredulous that Acopa had no advance warning of the Easter strike, the advisor offered this alternative job description for Reserve director: "If Acopa had simply organized a few plant nurseries, that would have been enough. . . . The work of a Reserve director is political work, policy making. He shouldn't have been going about inventing things like ecotourism. His job was to influence the politics in the area without being obvious, that's what the projects were about. He had the 'façade' of being a Reserve director." (He uttered "façade" in English.)

It is impossible to say whether Acopa was pushed out of office or left voluntarily. A diplomatic evaluation might note the Easter strike effectively pushed up Acopa's plans to take on new duties. In late 1995, Acopa moved to Chiapas and attempted (with mixed success) to replicate the Calakmul formula there. The governor's advisor was influential in naming Acopa's replacement, and conservation at Calakmul found itself on a new path.

Conservation-development's final decline came about in the year after I finished my research in Calakmul. Thus, I give a sketch of events following Acopa's departure. Roughly, the municipio of Calakmul was established in late December of 1996. The Regional Council and Biosphere Reserve became separate institutions. State funding focused more narrowly inside Reserve limits, and the newly formed Indigenous Union supplanted the Council as the main beneficiary of state funding for agrarian concerns. Reserve-Council ingenieros recall that as Council board members saw the end of their tenure in sight, they became increasingly avaricious of Council funds. Donors, already hesitant toward the Council's environmental ambivalence, retreated when funding cycles came to a close. The conservation-development model continues to operate in Calakmul, under the auspices of a few NGO and state offices. By 2000, however, the political import of these programs had diminished. The municipio of Calakmul worked to coordinate the activities of no fewer than twenty-nine state agencies, of which environmental agencies were only four. The scope of intervention in people's lives had expanded (theoretically, at least) to reflect a broader social order whose many facets— from hygiene to diet, child rearing, recreation, and housing construction, as well as points mentioned previously—now came under the purview of state planning efforts (Scott 1998). The contribution of environmental agencies to household economies remained challenged by new state programs and remittances from international migration. Most disappointingly, campesinos' voice in this setting was crowded out by the many professionals who now oversee the state's expanded infrastructure. In a 2001 meeting of thirty-four state and NGO organizations working in Calakmul, only three of forty-eight people in attendance were campesinos. Overall, environmental programming at Calakmul now leans toward the "fortress conservation" typical of protected areas elsewhere in the world (Brockington 2002).

Students of peasant movements will see a familiar story in the rise and fall of conservation-development at Calakmul (cf. Peet and Watts 1996). Questions of charismatic leadership, the role of money in buying out militancy, the mediated quality of social movements, and accusations of corruption are common themes in that field (Edelman, 1999). These topics took on greater potency at Calakmul, as environmentalists, new players in the development scene, became enthralled by both the mystique of collective action and the hybrid ideas arising from this iteration of Calakmul's social movement. Individuals like Acopa saw that it would be impossible to create a notion of environmental management distinct from agrarian concerns, and they drew on Mexico's long history of peasant organizing and cacique performances to combine the new with the old in a dynamic way. Peasant movements, however, are also known for considerable fluctuation in membership and influence. This point made it difficult to ally peasant-based conservation with the long-term goals of environmental protection.

As we saw, this fluctuation is connected to changing state practices. The social contract contained in Article 27 offers diverse positions from which the state may alternate attention among campesino sectors, first to indigenous people (the Union of Maya People), then to Mestizos (the Regional Council), then to indigenous people again (the Indigenous Union). Within these shifts, we saw how, at all levels of governance, control of natural resources and control of people became bound up with one another. Some agents used control of people to affect control of resources, while others sought the reverse. In this setting, the environment became a kind of social actor, albeit one whose presence in Calakmul's political scene was always controversial. This controversy rested on more than the fact that campesinos doubted the motivations behind ecological prescriptions. Where agrarianism had long formed part of state political structures in Mexico, *sustainable* development was an innovation. The Reserve-Council, in some ways, represented an attempt to inculcate sustainability within dominant discourses. Their failure to do so shows the challenges to working at the intersection of environment, development, and governance. Resistance came, not just from campesinos, but also from state agents who were accustomed to other ways of doing business. Sustainability's marginal role in state practices overall meant that, once the political winds shifted, the Reserve-Council agenda could be quickly forgotten.

Nonetheless, in the conclusions I describe why it would be wrong to abandon community-based formulas altogether, as some advocates of protected areas assert. Also, I suggest practical means to ameliorate questions of public relations and ideological shifts. I carry into that discussion a principal lesson from this chapter. In pursuit of their interests, Calakmul's diverse sectors sought less to obtain wealth from the environment than to use each other to gain access to the state, which was viewed as the primary source of wealth and power (cf. Coronil 1997). The state's own wealth derived not from conservation but from tourism, oil revenues, and other endeavors. From this perspective, even in a setting that appeared designed for conservation, the environment was always a minor concern, except in the context of campesino subsistence.

8

A Sustaining Conservation

The closer I looked at Calakmul's conservation setting, the more I saw within Pandora's box. In the previous chapters, I assembled a story that appears clear in retrospect, but, in the field, the contradictions associated with conservation could be puzzling. To name just a few of these tensions, we saw oppositions between state power and ejido autonomy, campesino empowerment and campesino dependency, local conditions and global transformations, idiosyncratic environmental threats and systemic ones, and personal change and institutional change. These contradictions are inherent to conservation because, although people are central to conservation activities, protected areas are designed to exclude a majority of people from making decisions about a specific territory. This central contradiction quickly becomes a contest between conserving land and sustaining people, which then engenders a series of confusions about where responsibility for conservation lies and what tactics best serve natural resource management. Conservation practitioners are not alone in contributing to these contradictions. Practitioners, however, do build, sometimes unwittingly, on local history, identity, power differences, and state practices to promote their cause.

Conservation programming thus has created a trap for itself. Protected areas, conservation's most asocial and people exclusive tactic, seem to best preserve natural resources (Bruner et al. 2001), yet people remain crucial to conservation's long-term effectiveness (Kottak and Costa 1993). At Calakmul, these people include (among others) ejidal members, diverse peasant groups, agents in the tourism industry, the military, state authorities who authorize road construction, and scientists who explore the area's uniqueness (cf. Bebbington 2000). It seems to me that conservation needs a new definition that better matches conservation goals with the means to achieve those goals. This definition would also have to acknowledge and work with the contradictions typical of any political setting (see chap. 2), but especially those that surround natural resource management. In this closing chapter, I set out to define this new *sustaining conservation*.

Working within the biosphere reserve's spirit of experimentation, I develop a theory of a sustaining conservation by drawing on a multidisciplinary mix of thinkers. From feminist theory, I seek a concept of justice. From political theory, I utilize a definition of sustainability. Drawing on state formation theory, I reconsider the diffuse quality of power as well as identities and movements that now affect environmental thinking in Calakmul. State formation theory also helps me consider the challenges posed by unintended uses of conservation. Altogether, these points lead me to identify a consensus among practicing and academic conservationists regarding frameworks for negotiating natural resource use. Finally, I return to phenomenology and theories of figured worlds to bridge cultural barriers and reckon with the power differences that have complicated conservation at Calakmul and elsewhere.

I crafted the idea of a "sustaining conservation" in response to specific critiques of conservation-development and community-based approaches to natural resource management. In their influential books, writers John Oates (1999) and John Terborgh (1999) argue that a focus on local people has distracted conservationists from their main task at hand. Rather than venture the hazards of social work, conservationists should stick to what they know and do best, that is, protected area management (for various positions on this debate, see Wilshusen et al. 2002; *Conservation Biology* 14, no. 5). Given my experience at Calakmul, readers will not be surprised to learn that I disagree with this position. I revisit the issue below to show that fencing parks off from local people often translates into a larger project of maintaining power and resources in the hands of elites (cf. Dunn 1988; Johnson 1999; Lewis 1989; West and Brechin 1991).

My main concern in defining a sustaining conservation entails the most pernicious aspect of conservation at Calakmul. In chapters 6 and 7, I described how campesino subsistence was a pawn in state-peasant relations and, by extension, conservation practices. Both campesinos and state agents toyed with campesino subsistence as they sought diverse goals. The state's subsidy offerings mean few people in Calakmul starve, but many, living on beans and tortillas or simply tortillas, do go hungry. People in Calakmul manage to survive bodily, but at the cost of their future security. The insecurity of their lives stems partly from the nature of subsistence work but, more important, from the rhetoric and actions of state authorities.

A sustaining conservation would avoid this particular contradiction between subsidies and insecurities by acknowledging the importance of people. A sustaining conservation would use the mechanism of natural resource negotiations to foster an atmosphere of social justice and transparency in policy prescriptions. The idea here is to move conservation into the arena of the public good, where now it is essentially privatized—in the hands of private organizations, donors, and states that are, effectively, private institutions. At the core of these negotiations would be a new definition of sustainability, one resistant, although not immune, to manipulation. I begin my case for a sustaining conservation with an examination of justice and sustainability.

Justice and Sustainability

Throughout the book, I have avoided defining sustainable development in order to emphasize the concept in practice. Readers may now bring a healthy skepticism to the abstract debates that have surrounded the topic. In the international arena, the definition that guides the United Nations (UN) and other groups was outlined, in the Brundtland Report, as one based on needs. The Brundtland Commission claimed that sustainable development was that which "meets the needs of the present without compromising the ability of future generations to meet their own needs" (WCED 1987:43). Since then, the definition of sustainable development has not changed significantly. The 1992 Rio Declaration on Environment and Development asserts: "The right to development must be fulfilled so as to equitably meet developmental and environmental needs of present and future generations." The declaration also gives broad authority to define these needs via "the sovereign right to exploit their own resources pursuant to their own environmental and developmental policies."[1] UN agencies view economic development, social development, and environmental protection as "interdependent and mutually reinforcing pillars."[2] As we have seen, in practice, these pillars rest on the willingness of national and local actors to implement the ideas behind them (cf. Keys 1998). At Calakmul, such economic, social, and environmental pillars were so closely tied to political ends as to mute their individual merits.

Critics of the UN's approach to sustainable development have assailed the issue as an imposition. It distracts from existing economic concerns by asking people to think about the future (Wilbanks 1994). Resisting this aspect of sustainable development, people in places like Calakmul have reworked the concept, viewing it as "a strategy for sustaining development, not . . . an infinitely diverse natural and social life" (Esteva 1993:16). Remember Don Venancio, who was saving his forest so that he and his children could have somewhere to plant.

Political theorist Andrew Dobson scrutinizes the language of sustainability to show how the idea contains a central contradiction (2000). This contradiction allows people to take the notion in different directions. The development part of sustainable development includes the notion of progress inherent to development theory (see chap. 2). Progress, in development terms, assumes industrialization and the increasing consumption of raw materials, both of which contradict ecological dynamics. The physical environment cannot provide an ever-increasing amount of raw materials, nor is the environment infinitely flexible in absorbing wastes. In other words, notwithstanding human ingenuity (Denevan 1983), economic activities influence a physical environment that we are ultimately powerless to understand, much less control. I see in this dichotomy between progress and an uncontrollable ecological world a likeness to the contradictory position of rural communities in development discourses. In development narratives, villages and ejidos are subject to progressive forces because they are, by definition, unprogressive places (Escobar 1995; Pigg 1992). In the rhetoric of both sustainable and traditional development, notions of controlled change converge on places where neither control nor change is practically possible. Thus, when Dobson argues for a definition of development that meets the goals of sustainability, he is also arguing for a development that views rural people as inherently necessary to the process. In both cases, the new definition would have to define environment and local people as agents of change who have their own particular logics and their own (sometimes competing) goals. When a sustaining conservation takes people and environment as equal in concern, it recognizes that sustainability is not the work of individuals, that is, the lone ejidatario felling forest, but the work of social networks that are mutually dependent on one another and the places that concern them (Latour 1987; Whatmore and Thorne 1997). Sustaining a particular environment thus requires sustaining the social relations that made that environment possible (Mendes 1989).

This clarification on the social quality of conservation still leaves a central question. Sustaining what for whom? If a needs-based definition is too vague, what idea of natural resource management could structure negotiations among diverse players and resist the kinds of manipulations we saw in earlier chapters? Seeking a meeting ground between sustainability and social justice, one that carries a "defence against obfuscation," Dobson alters the framework of needs while retaining an emphasis on future generations (1998:243). His definition amounts to a need for each parent generation to provide the next generation *all* the environmental resources enjoyed by their seniors. That is, all of us must ensure that our children inherit all the environmental resources made available to us. This is a preservationist view that allows for as few substitutions as possible. One tree species should not replace another that may become extinct. Just the same, this is not conservation for conservation's sake. Instead, the focus is on children, a consideration appealing to people, like those in Calakmul, for whom family is their primary concern. The centerpiece of this sustaining conservation would consist of negotiations that make the ideal of preservation feasible. As we saw, some people at Calakmul do have to make stark choices. They hunt large cats to protect their sheep or to raise money for an operation. A sustaining conservation would not view such activity as criminal but as *preventable* given the right governing framework. A sustaining conservation would offer a forum where campesinos could go if they felt in the position to have to hunt. Preservation does demand that today's parent generation tolerate points they dislike or find threatening in the environment. By preserving jaguar, today's campesinos leave to their children the threat of cattle depredation. But, people also leave their children the thrill of the hunt, and negotiations would have to find a way to make this trade-off worthwhile.

This definition of sustainability allows accountability to flow in all directions because all people would need to play a role in resource preservation. The focus would be not just on campesinos. A clearer definition of sustainability that expands the field of accountability makes a step toward sorting out the rights and responsibilities in resource management of both individuals and nations. People in places like Calakmul can preserve forest so their children have somewhere to fell, but they may also demand that elites, for example, change air and car travel to secure fossil fuels for the next generation. The demand for these kinds of trade-offs have already been voiced in the international arenas (UN 2002).

Importantly for my analysis of justice, the revised definition situates sustainability within cultural production and reproduction, historically issues of keen concern to subsistence farmers. In places like Calakmul, the success of a sustaining conservation would rest on valuing people's work in raising their families and shifting authority in natural resource management away from the private sector and toward a public sector accountable to future generations.

Many critiques leveled against protected areas doubt the justice of strict enforcement precisely because of threats to livelihoods. They ask whether it is right to deny people access to land, when people need those resources to survive (Colchester 1994; Peluso 1992; Pimbert and Pretty 1995). Fortwangler has cataloged a list of conservation abuses from across the globe that include forced relocations, denial of social services, false promises of development, intimidation, extortion, and even torture (Fortwangler 2003:32–33). In some areas, conservation programs clearly need to make up for lost faith. But, what norms of justice are relevant to these efforts?

Ideas of justice, fairness, and goodness change over time, appear different from the perspective of distinct actors, and undergo multiple cultural constructions. Residents of the United States and Europe once saw no problem in the indiscriminate killing of wildlife. Former U.S. president Theodore Roosevelt prided himself on his hunting accomplishments. Today, few people would ascribe to this position, and certainly, few people would defend an *unjust* conservation. Consider the idea of punishing a man who sells jaguar pelts to pay for his wife's medical treatment. Developing locally specific justice norms can be a complex task. Elsewhere, I explore campesinos' simultaneous use of democratic and patron-client norms and their implications for a just conservation at Calakmul (Haenn 2003). I conclude that transparency, inclusion of public opinion at the policy formation stage (as opposed to the implementation stage; see chap. 7), and a commitment to campesino participation in negotiations are necessary to clarify a contradictory justice setting. The consensus I report on below takes these logistical concerns farther in asking that actors in conservation settings specify their understanding of justice. I want to add to this discussion a more abstract notion of justice, one applicable to diverse multicultural and policy settings.

I suggest a justice *perspective* is more useful to addressing conservation settings than any set of specific rules (Mohanty 2002). A justice perspective demands we look at the meaning of fairness from the position of specific actors and, from there, delineate a hierarchy of injustices, both perceived and actual. The plurality of meanings and perspectives will be overwhelming at first. As a guide through this multitude, Mohanty asks, whose perspective reveals the broadest occurrences of injustices? That is, who constitute a society's most vulnerable members? Who has least recourse and the least resources when faced with powerful decision makers? By answering this question, local people, policy makers, and conservationists alike can use this perspective from the margin to inventory the ramifications of a particular policy for society as a whole. The inventory can then serve as a basis for rectifying injustices in culturally satisfying ways.

Mohanty proffers that the most comprehensive justice perspective is that of Third World indigenous women (ibid.; cf. Rocheleau et al. 1996; Shiva 1988). Because Third World indigenous women tend to be the most socially marginalized, their position reveals the greatest examples of injustices at different levels. Putting this approach into practice, we can appraise the fairness of Calakmul's conservation-development agenda from the perspective of Orozco's Ch'ol women. The agenda bolstered Mestizo men in already male-dominated decision-making institutions. Its experimental projects focused on men's earning potential, especially in areas that had little to do with household subsistence. Because of this, the projects took men away from activities that secured a family's food. The agenda incorporated men into expanding circles of influence, from the ejido, to the Regional Council, to national and international arenas. As we saw in chapter 7, when conservation agents undertook sexual conquest, the agenda took on an overt sexism. With its overriding focus on forests in a place where water was women's chief environmental concern, the agenda failed to appeal to women as agents in human-environment relations. This brief list of local manifestations largely excludes injustices at the national and international levels. Conservation at these broader scales was entirely inaccessible to indigenous women.

My point here is that conservation-development did not always distinguish between men and women (although sometimes it did), since Mestizo women and many men of all ethnicities were similarly excluded from conservation-development's decision making and benefits. These exclusions came about because conservation-development at Calakmul employed local ethnic and gender norms in unreflective ways. Even though these hierarchies were the order of the day, their presence and incorporation into conservation measures nonetheless merit consideration (Brosious 1999). Indigenous women's perspectives aid in this process by providing insight into all the ways conservation-development stemmed from some people's prerogatives and not others. Overall, women's perspectives help build a conservation that benefits the greatest number of people and is just from the broadest perspective.

Local Knowledge, Local Conservation

Successful and fair environmental management requires dealing with sociocultural issues in specific ways and relies on an in-depth knowledge of the local scene. In previous chapters, I argued that when conservation becomes part of the fabric of local power structures, campesinos participate in environmental programming for political as well as economic reasons. Recapping the cultural specificity of politics at Calakmul, I use this section to revisit everyday forms of state formation. I examine trends in campesino organizing that have a growing effect on conservation possibilities. In earlier chapters, I noted that a crucial aspect of state formation in Calakmul is the idea that the state holds the majority share of a limited supply of power. Here, I remind readers that academic theories of power describe it as diffuse and contradictory. Power is "contradictory because, even when a person or an institution succeeds in concentrating power, other people may generate other sources of power" (Schoenbrun 1998:12). This definition of power illustrates why governance is a process open to unexpected change and contradictions. In these paragraphs, I show how Zapatista ideologies and their calls for "autonomy" comprise a new source of power that is altering governance models. Zapatista ideas resonate in particular ways with a sustaining conservation. Just the same, both these positions must reckon with local histories and existing governance norms. I summarize key aspects of Calakmul's cultural setting before turning to questions of autonomy.

Calakmul offers a set of qualities that arise out of its history as an agrarian frontier and a tradition of land use negotiations in which state agents work through the ejido and campesino organizations. Among these qualities, we saw that, for state agents and campesinos alike, public compliance and private resistance are common. People commonly accede to projects or ideas only to subvert them later. Theatrical performance is a valued political activity, but performance alone is insufficient. Protagonists must ground performance in occasional deeds that leave little doubt of their willingness to act aggressively. This leaves the area susceptible to strikes and protests, which state agents may accommodate to facilitate their rule (Gilly 1998). Strikes can serve as an impetus for state authorities to shift their attentions. Within the ideals set forth in Article 27, authorities can invoke new ideologies to justify changed political arrangements. These shifts contribute to negotiated settlements that hold a momentary quality. Impermanency in accords also stems from the sense that a satisfying democracy requires appeasing dissenters. This process is distinct from the winner-take-all norms prevalent in the United States (see Guinier 1994). It requires attention to minority positions, even if their proponents cannot muster sufficient support to occupy public offices. Minorities can quickly gain a kind of majority status or, at least, an influential place at the negotiating table. Minorities do so by developing relevant patron-client ties or creating performances that demand state attention. These factors pose challenges to transparency in governance. Transparency is hindered further by the use of corruption accusations to address issues ranging from embezzlement and extortion to personal animosities and doubts regarding a leader's representativeness. Crucially, Calakmul's uniqueness arises from ejidal autonomy in natural resource management and the fact that past state projects have been foisted on ejidal members with an attitude of "participate or we won't help you at all."

Revisiting these qualities from a justice perspective, I see a government that defines itself less via quality of life issues and more on bare-bones competition. "The state seeks control, control, control," an assistant Reserve director explained ominously. On the one hand, this commonsense understanding appears daunting. These hierarchies are the state's reason for existence and become naturalized in everyday forms of state formation. On the other hand, ideas of a fractured state demonstrate how a place's particular position in regional, state, federal, and global structures can open fissures in the façade of government power (Bebbington and Batterbury 2001; Ferguson and Gupta 2002; Rubin 1997). At Calakmul we saw this in the rivalry between Campeche state and federal authorities and the opportunities posed by international conservation initiatives and NAFTA (an impetus to the Zapatista uprising; see chap. 4). Historically, caciques and men like Reserve Director Acopa gained their power by bridging these positions. Given the enduring importance of advisors (Zapatista-inspired groups also rely on these individuals), campesino leaders likely will continue to play a crucial role in campesino-state relations and conservation. A sustaining conservation would take into account how external groups can be influential in fostering a specific political atmosphere.

Campesino frustration with the quality of government leadership has generated numerous protest movements. To date, the Zapatistas have been arguably the most savvy in using their identities as campesinos and, more potently, as indigenous people to exploit the fissures in government rule. Their experience of the Mexican government has been so alienating as to lead them to demand autonomy or self-rule. Using their identities to change both the structure and content of governance, Zapatista demands for autonomy have become an important trend in campesino organizing, and the idea has consequences for a sustaining conservation. As we saw, Chiapas functions as a shadow political realm to Calakmul. People in Calakmul readily draw on events in Chiapas to gauge their own situation and press for change. Although a formal agreement regarding autonomy does not exist between the Zapatistas and state authorities, areas under Zapatista control have declared themselves autonomous and are undertaking experiments in self-rule (Rus et al. 2003).

At this point, it is necessary to point out that the definition of autonomy is by no means fixed. Although the idea has been a central negotiating point between the Zapatistas and Mexican authorities, in practice the word *autonomy* carries two distinct notions (both in Mexico and throughout Latin America). The first entails a legal and political project intended to reshape the nation-state. Díaz-Polanco argues the Zapatistas fall under this description by calling for a series of changes that recognize indigenous peoples, towns, and communities as new political subjects (1997:17; see also Stephen 1999). If this aspect of the movement is successful, the autonomy movement would allow indigenous groups to appoint community officials, establish court systems, and promote indigenous language and cultures. The second notion better describes the situation at Calakmul, especially the negotiations that followed Easter 1995. In this autonomy, people see the possibility for independence, but the specifics are left undeveloped. Instead, "this tendency advances through the elaboration of a kind of catalogue (more or less exhaustive) of demands" (Díaz-Polanco 1997:17), among which autonomy may be only a vague addition to the list. This kind of autonomy is open to manipulation by those who quickly transform political ideologies into demands for increased aid. At the same time, these vague expressions of autonomy give voice to the depth of rural discontent and require that local development needs be addressed regardless of larger policy goals.

The novelty of autonomy may be unclear to people accustomed to government neglect and ejidal independence. In an insightful analysis, Mattiace conveys the problems indigenous leaders have had in translating autonomy concepts into governing institutions (2003). The movement has posed a number of unanswered questions, including the exact nature of state relations to an autonomous area. Much of what she cites as "autonomy in practice"—local election of leaders, community jurisdiction in judging and punishing crimes—are points that Calakmul's people would recognize from their ejidos (although the autonomy movement would extend these prerogatives in significant ways).

Just the same, autonomy movements require attention by those interested in conservation. Above, I listed the local, cultural qualities to Calakmul's political setting. I hinted these qualities challenge a truly public, participatory natural resource management. Zapatista ideologies draw on local cultural qualities to offer the inverse of these ideas. The autonomy movement gives campesinos and indigenous people alike a forum for distancing themselves from existing political norms. The movement delimits state authority and acts against the notion that states should hold a majority share of power and wealth. The movement also gives rural residents a language, including a feminist position, with which they can assert that governing structures should not come one-size-fits-all. One of the Zapatistas' most vital innovations in campesino organizing has been its attention to marginalized people and its equal treatment of men and women. Women occupy leadership roles, and the movement's platform calls for women's freedom to chart their lives (Harvey 1998). Autonomy goals, thus, open the possibility for creating a local governance responsive to Calakmul's uniqueness while linking justice perspectives to both local and national justice norms. The movement's self-conscious reworking of existing power hierarchies resonates with national struggles to alter the legacy of PRI rule through decentralized authority, an eradication of corruption, and clean elections.

Among their demands for self-rule, Zapatistas include collective rights over natural resources and greater authority in dealing with outside agents (Gomez-Rivera 1999). Autonomy ideals would assign campesinos greater authority in natural resource management. Autonomous movements, thus, would limit the role of state and environmental groups in land use decisions. Autonomy proponents cannot guarantee environmental protection. I believe, however, that because the movement demands campesinos be recognized as political equals, autonomy ideals hold the possibility for more straightforward and genuine land use negotiations. We have seen, at Calakmul, how the intense political jockeying around conservation inspired a split in local society between those adept in manipulating environmentalism and those who were not. Negotiations based on autonomy ideals can bring forward the kinds of hidden resistances we saw within ejidos and at the Regional Council. This move would counter the false compliance that a hierarchical conservation encourages, because, rather than institute a fractured social field that requires a broker to bridge diverse positions, autonomy ideals view broad-based popular participation as a premise for governance. And, since the Zapatista movement emphasizes cultural survival, its ideologies are amenable to the revised notion of a sustaining conservation. A sustaining conservation that focuses on cultural survival would give special consideration to those natural resources that are closely tied to indigenous and campesino lifeways. Still, autonomy is not a panacea. People like Don Jerónimo and Don Venancio, adept at working with a state built on inequality, may not thrive in such a setting. A justice perspective, however, should be attentive to how changing dynamics create new marginalized groups, and some of the prescriptions mentioned below could be geared toward easing the anxiety of such individuals (see tables 8.1 and 8.2, this chapter).

A sustaining conservation should draw on existing lessons in campesino organizing, which have already laid the groundwork for future conservation responses. Years following the decline of the Regional Council, I asked David Bray, a central actor in Mexico's community-forestry setting, what happens next? Given the cycling of projects, what can campesinos and supporters of sustainable development hope for in the future? He placed his faith in campesinos, that the projects would leave behind people with new skills and new awareness. These people become a project's living memory and may be called on in the future, when political winds shift again. He had in mind people like Don Ignacio in San Lorenzo. In 2002, Ignacio's impressive stand of mahogany, cedar, and allspice trees sat alongside a small pasture where more than a dozen sheep grazed. Don Ignacio continued to plant corn and chile, and he was experimenting that year with tomatoes. He boasted a two-meter firebreak surrounding his fields. Bray's assessment of people like Ignacio parallels research into campesino movements. Although the organizations themselves may be fleeting, individual actors provide enduring links across disparate struggles (Edelman 1999). Conservation's social justice question at the moment of sustainable development's revival becomes how to facilitate the dissemination of this knowledge without re-creating the hierarchies of the past.

At some point, state attention will focus, again, intently on campesinos (Collier 1987). I have indicated this attention may meet a campesino community invigorated by ideas of autonomy or invigorated by ideas of patron-client relations. But, will it focus on environmental protection and, if so, what kind? In their calls for self-rule over natural resources, the Zapatistas take a strongly nationalistic stance. They describe themselves as "men and women who are not content to see their country handed over to foreign power and money" (communiqué of January 1, 1996; EZLN 1997). The international quality of environmental programming, however, is unlikely to go away. A sustaining conservation is necessary, not least because campesino organizations view natural resource management as a priority and find a hierarchical conservation unacceptable (cf. Peet and Watts 1996).

Today, international conservationists lament how difficult it is to operate in Calakmul, with its large number of unique ejidos and lack of a few identifiable power holders. I view this moment differently. As I argued earlier, a sustaining conservation must pay attention to multiple social groups. Calakmul offers an opportunity, indeed demands, that conservation programming do so and move away from traditional hierarchies. Individual ejidos, ejidatarios, and families require case-by-case solutions to land management. Orozco and San Lorenzo are so different ecologically and socially that I doubt the same land use planning arrangements would work in both places. The negotiating framework surrounding conservation would have to address questions of fairness in a situation in which distinct ejidos receive different environmental treatments. In the following sections, I describe an emerging consensus that would make this kind of negotiation mechanism possible. Before that, I want to outline additional challenges to a sustaining conservation, in particular the unintended use of conservation frameworks.

A Resilient Conservation?

Earlier, I mentioned critiques that call for a renewed focus on border enforcement and an abandonment of the conservation-development agenda (see Margolius and Salafsky 1998 for a description of this agenda at a global level). At Calakmul, a fortress conservation is unlikely to endure and not only because it fails as a social strategy more generally (see chap. 2). Both campesinos and government agents are accustomed to negotiating with one another through the ballot and campesino organizations (however problematic those negotiations may be). A conservation that denies the possibility of negotiation frustrates these political norms. Such a move truncates the possibility of dealing with conflicts and discredits the small-scale experimentation of innovative actors.[3]

It follows that a rigid or "exclusive" (Fortwangler 2003:35) conservation framework will be less resilient to changing times and linguistic slipperiness. Inflexibility reinforces the sense that local people are somehow incompetent at managing their own resources. Unfortunately, this notion is already a salient theme in conservation. Once, waiting at the Cancún airport, I picked up *Time* magazine's Latin American edition to find proposals distinct in tone, but not intent, from Terborgh's assertions. Terborgh writes that "the well-organized societies of the industrialized world are the ones most concerned about biological diversity," and the "freewheeling societies of many tropical countries" display an "overall lack of social, economic and political maturity" (Terborgh 1999:13). *Time* listed eight "promising strategies" for conservation (McCarthy 2002:47). All strategies entailed transforming donor countries, environmental groups, and their private backers into arbiters of Third World ecology: debt-for-nature swaps, ecotourism, marine reserves, wildlife corridors, philanthropy, indigenous control, carbon credit offsets, and the purchase of timber concessions. The only people other than financiers and conservation professionals deemed competent managers were indigenous people (see Fortwangler 2003 for international agreements that explain this preference). The idea that environmental solutions are located extra-locally coincides with the notion that wealth and development are imports to marginalized areas (see also West 2000; Pigg 1992). These overlaps in development and environmental hierarchies produce confusing results. Slash-and-burn farmers can be demonized for their supposed backward-ness, pitied for their poverty, and praised for their low level of consump-tion (Li 1999).

These confusions are reflected in protected area models and the way people play fast with environmental rules. In a global survey of park policies, O'Neill writes that, in the 1980s, numerous countries responded to international pressure by creating minimal park systems (O'Neill 1996). This trend continued in the 1990s, when the number of national parks throughout the globe more than quadrupled (Brechin et al. 2003:ix). Parks and environmental policies were often symbolic gestures meant to boost a government's image to international audiences. Little real conservation took place on the ground. O'Neill (1996) concludes that the success of any protected area rested on whether state officials believed conservation would enhance their authority.

As a biosphere reserve, Calakmul, as I illustrated in chapter 1, was similarly imbued with political meanings. Biosphere reserves are a cate-gory of protected areas recognized by UNESCO for both their biological diversity and their potential for reconciling conservation with sustainable resource use. In UNESCO's words, biosphere reserves "serve in some ways as 'living laboratories' for testing out and demonstrating integrated manage-ment of land, water and biodiversity."[4] To fulfill this mission, a biosphere reserve has three parts. The core area "consists of minimally disturbed ecosystems" (USMAB 1990:52). Legally, core areas should be regulated un-der the strictest of protection laws. Surrounding the core, the buffer zone includes lands where "resources and activities . . . are managed in a way that helps to protect the core area" (ibid.). Enveloping the buffer zone is a transition area, which "may contain settlements, croplands, managed for-ests, areas for intensive recreation or other economic uses" (ibid.). The biosphere reserve model incorporates land use negotiation as a central conservation practice, but, in places like Calakmul, the model served as a way to exert force in situations of unequal power. The core of Calakmul's Reserve sat flush with the Reserve's eastern border, technically leaving no buffer zone to manage. The notion of a transition area never entered these discussions, nor did I ever hear mention of the concept. People in the local conservation community argued this structure had a political rationale, namely, to check the expansion of ejidal lands. Additionally, conservation-ists privately murmured that the Calakmul Biosphere Reserve was declared in 1989 only because, in 1988, Salinas de Gortari entered office under accusations that he stole the election (*The Economist*, June 28, 1997). He looked to environmentalism as one way to gain legitimacy with the international community. These political maneuvers challenge the scientific underpinnings of biosphere reserves. The scientific dubiousness of the Reserve's limits was such that, a decade after the Reserve's founding, a group of biologists and other physical scientists proposed its reconfiguration (Galindo-Leal 1999).

The manipulation of conservation at Calakmul may have gone beyond the "living laboratory" imagined by UNESCO, and the reformulations did not end with Acopa. The Biosphere Reserve continues to serve as a field upon which innovative political performances take place. From my office in the United States, I scan the internet for tidings from Calakmul, and during the year 2000, three reports caught my eye. The first entailed the January arrest of eighteen men inside Calakmul's Reserve. Military troops came across the group, who were rumored to be guerillas. Further investigation showed the men did come from Chiapas, but authorities described them as members of an elite hunting club, people of "great economic power." The group had traveled to poach inside the Reserve because, they said, a Zapatista presence in Chiapas forests prohibited them from practicing their hobby in that state. The men paid a fine and returned home (Chim 2000).

The second report offered stranger camouflaged identities. Newspapers disclosed a helicopter hijacking inside the Reserve. In May, a group of tourists hired a helicopter to take them to Calakmul's main archaeological site. There, a group of men, wearing Zapatista-type masks, emerged from the forests. They reportedly shouted their sympathies with the Zapatistas and took control of the helicopter (subsequently found in Nicaragua). Later accounts showed the tourists, guerilla identities, and hijacking were a ruse (*Diario de Yucatán*, May 12, 2000), while guards on duty at the time report the masks and Zapatista connection were fictions invented by the press. Instead, the helicopter was hired purposefully to transport something or someone out of the country. A national commentator questioned how a hijacking could take place in a militarized area, where army officers had at their disposal equipment to prevent such a crime (Hernández López 2000). In response, municipal authorities explained Calakmul's "natural conditions" lent themselves to harboring illicit activities (*Diario de Yucatán*, May 13, 2000).

Both accounts show the Reserve plays a role in national fantasies, which project a guerilla presence onto southern forests.[5] Some people take advantage of those fantasies to create a sense that Calakmul remains a lawless frontier. An air of lawlessness allows people to use the Reserve for

unintended purposes while providing cover for both environmental degradation and the lack of political will to carry out conservation measures.
Note that Campeche state has fewer than ten officers assigned to investigate environmental infractions throughout its territory. This work is further challenged by the poor quality of scientific messages emanating from
state officials and media outlets.

Conservation's legitimacy is further undermined by the inaccurate
representations of the Reserve found in the third report. In the fall of
2000, authorities staged an exhibit about Calakmul in the state capital and
documented the Reserve's endangered species (*Diario de Yucatán*, October 19, 2000). Remembering that Calakmul is landlocked, I was surprised
to find the Reserve supposedly houses endangered manatee, flamingo, and
marine turtles! Later, a government-issued poster touting the Reserve
included depictions of scarlet macaws, a species not found in Calakmul.
As rationales for conservation, in the public realm, continue to lack scientific coherence, what sense might campesinos see in proceeding with
conservation practices? At present, the ideologies, representations, and
hierarchies that undermine conservation at Calakmul have no significant
counterweight. In the following section, I imagine what such a counterweight might look like.

A Socially Just Conservation: The Emerging Consensus

Among academic and practicing conservationists, a group of people
have begun to theorize a socially just conservation, one I view as consonant with a sustaining conservation. Although these people emphasize
relations between parks and people, they also respond to the way a focus
on local people can overlook larger threats to the environment (road
construction and logging concessions to name a few; see Bowles and
Prickett 2001; Schwartzman et al. 2000; Wells et al 1999:4). Alongside
systemic and corporate threats, small-scale sustainable development can
only appear to fail. Contributors to the consensus locate the answer to this
problem in more expansive natural resource negotiations. I add to this
consensus the need to carefully handle cultural information, an explicit
rendering of political positions, and a discussion of personal and institutional change.

In summarizing this consensus, five themes stand out: defining conservation as a process rather than an outcome; accountability for all parties; a deeper understanding of social and political structures; a willingness
to admit conservation's experimental quality and learn from mistakes; and
the need for checks and balances. Table 8.1 summarizes Brechin et al.'s

Table 8.1 Key Elements to Conservation Negotiations

Element	Questions	Issues in Biodiversity Conservation
Human dignity	Who benefits? Should biodiversity be granted moral superiority relative to human welfare? On what grounds?	—Establishment of explicit moral parameters for social processes associated with conservation interventions. —Accounting for principles of social justice: 1) full participation; 2) self-representation/autonomy; 3) self-determination
Legitimacy	Is the process considered appropriate and just by those most affected?	—Social control built on strong agreements, fair enforcement, strong organizational and institutional arrangments, and constructive dialogue.
Governance	Who decides? Based on what authority? Who participates and how? How will decision making take place? Parameters for accountability and enforcement?	—Establishment of "rules" or "norms" and responsibilities for decision making, accountability, enforcement, and participation
Accountability	To what extent is each party holding up its end of the bargain? How effectively are participants pursuing their goals?	Responsibility: —Rights imply responsibilities —Appraisal focused on social and political process *in addition to* other indicators —Distingish between problems of implementation and conceptual inadequacy

Table 8.1 *continued*

Element	Questions	Issues in Biodiversity Conservation
Adaptation and learning	How can we systematically adapt and learn from experience	—Constant reflection and experimentation —Organization and social learning
Nonlocal forces	To what extent does environmental change result from large-scale commercial enterprises? How are local practices driven by wider political economic process?	—Scale of intervention —Focus of conservation objectives —Strategic political alliances

Source: Adapted from Brechin et al. 2002

position within the consensus, while table 8.2 compares the group with other authors.

In brief, the consensus heralds a conservation that views human dignity as equal to nature protection. To achieve this goal, policies surrounding conservation must be perceived as legitimate. Protection must take place in a setting where government and private sector actors as well as subsistence workers work within systems of accountability. Accountability requires that policies retain some relevance to local cultural constructions of ecology, land use, power, and governance. Policies need not rigidly adhere to cultural norms. Few societies agree on a shared set of unchanging ideals, and dominant norms may be designed to exclude certain groups. Instead, if policies take place within an explicit and ongoing processual atmosphere of learning and adjustment, people can work through ideological and practical differences. At Calakmul, experimentation was the order of the day, but practitioners were forced to be defensive about this in response to donor requirements for assured outcomes. Finally, the consensus notes that a focus on subsistence workers must take into account broader political and economic settings. For example, as state authorities promote large-scale tourism in Calakmul, is an emphasis on slash-and-burn farming as a threat to forests appropriate? At what point does tourism become a larger threat than household activities? (See chap. 6.)

I find the emerging consensus valuable in addressing some main

Table 8.2 Emerging Consensus Regarding Effective Community-Based Conservation

Wyckoff-Baird et al. (2000)	Wells et al. (1999)	Brechin et al. (2002)	Hemmati (2002)
Know the meaning, value, and rights to natural resources; know who benefits least and most from conservation actions.		Governance	Good governance is a "fundamental value" for sustainable development.
Research and address underlying social factors behind environmental threats.	Local people are often not as threatening to protected areas as other factors.	Nonlocal forces	Stakeholders vs. shareholders
Identify partners with authority and legitimacy		Legitimacy	Participants need to check back with constituents.
Consider groups normally marginalized from the public arena.		Human dignity: Who benefits?	Be attentive to gender, culture, and power differences.
Encourage local-national linkages to ensure mutual accountability.	Requires high level political support, close communication with local governments.		Strengthen (inter)governmental institutions while focusing on voices, not votes.
	Requires flexibility to adapt to changing field needs.	Adaptation and learning	Learning is a "derived" goal.

issues at Calakmul. By arguing for conservation organizations to specify their activities, the authors respond to campesino anxieties that authorities might use conservation to expand their reach into campesino lives. In the private sector, Brechin et al. call for local and international NGOs to define their commitments to a particular place, stabilize the expectations of all affected parties, and set the boundaries of accountability (2002:53). This move would respond to campesino experiences that those in power do not fulfill their promises. Long-term commitments would counter notions that conservation, like past development initiatives, is inconsistent over time. Sustained contact among state and private conservation groups and local people would require a negotiating forum wherein changes in conservation could be addressed. State formation theory (see chap. 2) tells us to expect contradictions and conflict as part of the normal course of these relations. Brechin et al. emphasize that efforts to work through such contradictions must be voluntary (2003:170). In this regard, negotiating forums at Calakmul failed. Rather than resolve contradictions, they tried to make contradictions palatable. Negotiating forums have rarely been voluntary. Future forums would need to take into account the subtle ways people might be forced into "participation."

This last point coincides with the notion that conservation strategies and global prescriptions should operate only at the most general levels (Brechin et al. 2002). Conservation narratives, like their counterpart in development, tend to favor checklists and bulleted points that guide practitioners through a series of steps. Harkening back to ideas of progress (chap. 2), readers get the sense that fulfilling the steps will be sufficient to a successful outcome. Brechin et al. (2002) repeat this structure, but they also say they hope to undermine it. I suggest we do away with it altogether. Consensus ideals are general enough to operate at a global level, but beyond that Calakmul's conservation setting offers issues, such as ejidal tenure, that require unique responses. In this sense, the elements noted in tables 8.1 and 8.2 serve as guides for thinking about solutions, rather than specific recommendations.

My discussion, thus far, supports a gesture within the consensus toward a more intensive use of social science (Brechin et al. 2003; Brosius et al 2003). Recalling the topic of regional cultures (chap. 2), remember that conservation programs rest on how well environmental managers know the people involved. At Calakmul, state and private sector environmental actors, assigned the job of working with people, usually were nonlocals, trained to deal with plants and animals (zoologists, biologists, or the veterinarian who implemented PROCEDE). In addition to these concerns, anthropologists fear that, for conservation practitioners, social science may become reduced to just one aspect of complex realities (Brosius et al. 2002). Economics, land tenure, or some other matter takes the fore, when, as we have seen, the intertwined quality of social topics makes it nearly impossible to respond to conservation challenges via a single issue. The attraction to a single response is understandable, but this tactic carries, perhaps, the greatest risk in creating an unjust conservation. At Calakmul, for example, a focus on land tenure would likely translate into a focus on ejidatarios, to the exclusion of women and pobladores. Rather than narrow the field out of which conservation options might arise, work in phenomenology and figured worlds (chap. 2) alerts us to the need to expand options. If conservation demands new ways of relating among people and environment, conservation practitioners should then create new experiences out of which these relations might arise. I return to this point below.

Anthropologists, of course, are keenly aware of the cultural differences among both national and international actors as well as conservation managers and local people. The depth of these differences, evidenced in the frustrations of Ch'ol protestors, can open or close particular paths of resource management. Because of this, I believe cultural information demands careful handling. For example, constructed identities can be confounded with land use practices, such that destruction becomes the central way many outsiders think about campesinos. For some nonlocals, campesinos have become, by definition, people who destroy the environment. Environmental destruction as an *identity* is degrading and makes sustainability all the more difficult to achieve. It requires people change who they are, not just what they do, a dubious prospect to say the least.

Thus, while I laud the emerging consensus and find it compatible with a sustaining conservation, I also believe these recommendations remain insufficient. For me, the consensus continues to struggle with three central issues. My first concern is that environmental problems may take on new characteristics, while underlying issues remain intractable. In earlier chapters, we saw how the sheer variety of mechanisms used to counter poverty reinforced (sometimes stemmed from) a sense that poverty itself was insurmountable. By multiplying conservation methods, the consensus risks creating a similar climate. My second concern is the failure to take a stance on how this model fits with existing governing ideals and hierarchies. Will this amalgamation sit within a liberal, conservative, or socialist tradition? Given experiences in Calakmul, I imagine that either authoritarian or socially just measures could easily serve to subjugate campesinos. Because process can shape outcomes, the question, who decides natural resource management? is hard to separate from, how should decisions get made? Both points take on greater weight in these multicultural settings, where some figures are clearly unwelcome. In Calakmul, this was the case for foreign national environmentalists. International actors, however, are unlikely to go away, and therefore the sentiment behind policy implementation—the justification for any stakeholder's presence—matters strongly. My third concern is that, in many places, conservation programs not only need to justify themselves; they also need to make up for a loss of good faith. History cannot be forgotten. Both researchers and conservation practitioners can contribute to rectifying past abuses by setting a new tone within environmentalism. I look at the question of political tradition before considering the issue of bridging historical and cultural differences.

Specifying Political Positions

Earlier, I proposed the justice perspective of marginalized groups as a useful first step toward building a sustaining conservation. At the local level, specifying political positions is a necessary second step. Some conservation professionals describe democracy, a green democracy, as the answer to this question (Diamond 2000). I find this response to be too specific for the general, international level of conservation. In particular, U.S.-style democracy can be construed as a particular cultural construction and alien to local governing norms. Because of this, at the general level, an emphasis on accountability, regardless of specific, local political positions, is crucial. If democracy is relevant to the local level, at that point we can ask, what kind of democracy? Parliamentarian? What kind of voting mechanisms would be involved? From this specificity, a sustaining conservation becomes transparent, offers a point from which negotiations are possible, and helps establish the parameters for accountability. When all parties to environmental negotiations specify political positions at the general and local levels, negotiating processes are better able to respond to hierarchies, declare their justice intentions, and establish a position that makes poverty alleviation and conservation possible.

The pragmatist might argue, in contrast, that few have the luxury of thinking in political abstracts. What counts are local governing structures and how conservation agents interact with these institutions. However, the participatory mechanisms espoused by the emerging consensus—with their implicit collectivism—have little history as a governing institution. Inexperience in representative governing has left participatory methods open to charges of implicit favoritism (West 2000). In places where government structures are nonexistent or weak enough to submit to encroachment from local and international NGOs, governing bodies arising from the consensus would chart new territories. Following Dobson, these new governing mechanisms will immediately encounter tensions.

Both democratic and authoritarian tendencies have been long standing and palpable within conservation (Dobson 2000). Conservation seeks
to be democratic because some of its proponents believe democracy to be
the most just form of governance, but conservation can also be authoritarian, when advocates insist that people will not willingly sacrifice for
the sake of ecology. Thus, to the extent new participatory bodies carry
with them old forms of relating, they will re-create many of the obstacles
and hierarchies described throughout earlier chapters. Specifying political
positions is one means of avoiding this repetition. Another means entails
examining the contradictions between institutional and personal reforms.

Thinking beyond Environmental and Development Hierarchies

Conservation has tacked back and forth between pushing for institutional reform and pushing for personal change. The emerging consensus and moves toward local autonomy are examples of institutional
reforms relevant to natural resource management. Demands that campesinos change the way they think about and interact with the environment
are examples of personal reform. A sustaining conservation asks that we
change the ways individuals work in groups as well as our orientation as
beings in the world (Jackson 1998). A social justice perspective further
requires we imagine events from other people's viewpoints. Here, I draw
on a participatory management exercise to show how a combination of
personal and institutional change might be affected to negotiate these
cultural differences.

Writers in development ethics, in their critiques of international
agents, have recently suggested the kinds of changes I describe as necessary
to fair and successful poverty alleviation. Development ethicists challenge
international conservationists and development agents alike, to cultivate
empathy, to work at identifying with others, and to recognize how "power
hinders learning" (Chambers in Giri 2002:217). Recall how the consensus described above requires continuous learning. Brechin et al. contrast
"single-loop" and "double-loop" learning (2003:169–179). In the former,
individuals use learning to assess their project's effectiveness. In the latter,
individuals go beyond project assessment to question the validity of their
original goals. Development ethicists promote this learning as a way to
force people to question their own presumptions. The work can be a
humbling task. However, not only is this modesty appropriate, but it is
necessary to multicultural settings.

In an example of such a multicultural setting, a group of Australian
researchers conducted the kind of collective land use planning envisaged

in the emerging consensus. Under the auspices of the Commonwealth Scientific and Research Organisation and the Department of Land and Water Conservation, Aboriginal peoples, agro-pastoral lease holders, state authorities, and representatives of conservation, mineral, and tourism sectors undertook a series of tasks that aimed at developing "portfolios." In the portfolios, the groups made sets of land use recommendations.[6] The process differed from traditional participatory planning associated with conservation sites. The time frame spanned four years. This long-term framework allows nascent ideas and social relations time to solidify and gain a broader currency. Researchers guiding the planning committed to three propositions. They sought environmental resilience in the face of constant change. They viewed people and the environment as integral to, rather than separate from, one another. And they assumed no one was in charge. Clearly, some individuals and groups had more influence than others. By refusing to mimic such differences in the participatory process, researchers embraced social complexity and evened the playing field a bit.

Subtly, this process included a theory of cross-cultural learning and personal change appropriate to a group of people whose ideas and interests differ markedly. The theory is compatible with anthropological notions of culture and phenomenology (Jackson 1998; Shore 1996) and poses thoughtful challenges to researchers and conservation-development agents alike. Drawing on psychology, moderators of the Australian case defined how, in our minds, people comprehend the world around them:

> People use experiences to build constructs which enable them to understand and predict events. People tend to accept information that confirms their constructs, and shed the rest. They may change the information to fit the constructs. The constructs are organised into mental models. The primary function of a mental model is simplifying complex reality. Simplification means that human perceptions are inaccurate because elements of reality are omitted. Because individuals select information and organise it differently, their mental models differ, and so do their interpretations of the world.[7]

The notion of a mental construct conveys the depth of cultural differences we can expect in conservation settings and the limits people encounter in grasping new situations. Our minds are built to learn, but in narrower ways than we may find useful. At the same time, our knowledge of mental constructs includes their undoing: "Direct experiences are often needed to challenge a person to change their constructs—'telling' is not usually enough. [Thus] our project . . . provided opportunities for

participants to learn about each others' mental models, without necessarily agreeing with each other. Such understanding is the first step in
communication, and perhaps to negotiation of win-win solutions."[8]

Although these findings apply to all parties in natural resource negotiations, for researchers, policy makers, and students especially, they in-
spire humility. They ask that we turn a critical eye toward ourselves.
The fields of academia and policy value assertive statements of certainty.
In contrast, the shape of human cognition demands consistent, radical
doubt. Without such doubt, we risk reinforcing our own, sometimes er-
roneous, ideas at the expense of taking in a multifaceted, contradictory
reality. By reinforcing our own ideas, we fail to comprehend other people's
worldviews.

Participatory planning and negotiated natural resource management do not resolve the problem of conservation and development hierarchies. Clearly, someone could enter and exit a participatory process with
her or his sense of hierarchy intact. Also, the cultural diversity of Calakmul
should remind us that participatory planning is, itself, a construct that
requires modification and adaptation. But, participatory planning centered on mutual learning and awake to our cognitive shortcomings can
soften existing hierarchies. The process provides a method for exploring
justice perspectives, by asking us all to consider what it might be like, as
campesinos do, to gamble today's subsistence on future survival. In negotiations where the particulars of a sustaining conservation are worked out,
cross-cultural learning helps participants imagine the contingencies of
raising families in diverse political, economic, and ecological settings.
Beyond participatory planning, I see the need for more and different kinds
of spaces for cross-cultural, experiential learning.

These spaces can be found everywhere people strive to learn how
another sees the world. The distinction here is that rather than ask, what
would I do if I were that person? we should ask, how would I see the world
if I had lived this person's life? Nuala O'Faolain writes elegantly about the
power of art in this regard: "to learn to hold on to the self while going out
of the self to enter into the [art] that someone else had made—to find a
poise between subjectivity and objectivity. . . . The change in the person comes in that; it isn't a matter of learning a technical vocabulary"
(1998:99). This is the kind of opportunity I have attempted to impart in
this book. According to the above formulation, books have a limited effect
in altering social relations, because they "tell" rather than create an experience. But, for those with active imaginations, who use reading to explore
what it is like to stand in another's place, I believe books are adequate tools

for learning. Also, writing responds to some ethical questions I have about participatory processes (and anthropological fieldwork). If conservation and development hierarchies are not reckoned with first, people who are the object of planning processes may easily become a site where others seek "experience." Art, books, and other venues can serve as effective substitutes for one-on-one experiences, a kind of training ground where readers may practice cultural relativism.

Final Thoughts

Observers of environmental affairs in Mexico have located the solution to ecological issues alternately in land reform (O'Brien 1998), in political alliances between campesinos and outside agents (the Plan Piloto position; see also Umlas 1998), in grassroots movements (Escobar 1995), and in strict enforcement of existing regulations. My examination of events at Calakmul leads me to believe none of these tactics alone will be effective. They additionally require a more broadly shared sense of a feminist-inspired egalitarianism, as well as an awareness of cultural diversity that counters power structures. This thinking beyond traditional conservation and development does not mean denying campesinos' economic and political demands. An unwavering and radical sense of human equality can be savvy to the hierarchies at hand. At Calakmul, I believe this sense of equality should include forums wherein conservation initiatives are negotiated and scientific rationales for conservation are elaborated in ways relevant to campesinos' lives.

Perhaps most important, this sense of equality must be applied in a way that the survival of campesinos and other subsistence producers is no longer a bargaining chip in conservation and development work. The sustaining conservation aims in this direction by establishing a forum in which contradiction in natural resource management can be worked out and sustainable development can ensure resources for today's children, as well as their parents. A sustaining conservation built on equality demands that all environmental practices come under scrutiny, and I see here a further contradiction in maintaining an environmental focus on subsistence workers and not on members of industrial and service economies. During the 1980s, when Calakmul's Reserve came into existence, one U.S. resident consumed as much energy as seven Mexicans (Escobar 1995:212; see Wilk 2002 for additional consideration of consumption and environment). These kinds of studies not only reveal unfairness in natural resource negotiations, but they betray the ways traditional development is environmentally unsound. My favorite U.S. park, the Great Smoky

Mountains National Park, has been beset by industrial air pollutants and other anthropogenic problems, although it sits a two-hour drive from the nearest metropolitan area (Peine et al. 1995; White 1995). Declared a half century before the Calakmul Biosphere Reserve and without the threats purportedly posed by subsistence producers, the Great Smoky Mountains National Park is successful in a way managers of Calakmul's Reserve can only imagine. Significant problems remain, nonetheless, leading me to wonder, if traditional notions of development are successful in southern Mexico, will Calakmul not meet a similar future? In the meantime, without a sustaining conservation, the boisterous characters in Calakmul will be sure to notice that local and international environmentalists rarely voice fears about their own environmental practices, only those of campesinos.

Until a sustaining conservation comes into force, conservation practices will continue to appear as political tools, caught up in a series of contradictions. Campesinos are well rehearsed in exploiting and resisting these fractures. On an evening in 1995, sitting on Orozco's public square, I talked with Venancio, Gerardo, and Paco about earlier Reserve management plans that suggested campesinos use only organic fertilizers. This assertion moved the conversation quickly onto the topic of how unreliable ingenieros were. Years earlier, the men had been promised a program in organic fertilizer, but the staffer never delivered. Gerardo noted, "Foresters and ingenieros only do what they have to in order to keep their jobs." Venancio agreed: "They always come here and do their thing and later nothing happens." The men recalled how, just the previous year, an NGO conducted research on tree use and people's farming habits. The organization promised trees for animal forage and plants that would fence in sheep. To date, the ejido had received nothing, and ejidatarios had not been advised if the program was in delay. The men recalled a similar failure in the Council's reforestation program. The staffers suggested that, before felling, campesinos have a forester examine their land for valuable trees. Later, technical staff were never available to carry through on the suggestion. Staffers gave a talk on the subject in the ejido's public square, leading Paco to complain, "They didn't even go to any of our parcels to show us what these trees might look like." While the men resisted the disciplining aspects of their connections to technical staff, they saw themselves in genuine need of advice. They preferred that ingenieros give concrete recommendations to particular situations, but technical staff rarely had the time or interest in such individualized attention. I asked the men why they did not press for a changed relationship with technical staff (and by extension state authorities more broadly). Why not complain to the staffers directly? The men's bravado deflated as Gerardo responded, "It's better if you let them do what they want." Paco concurred, "If they want to fool us, well, . . ." his voice trailed off. In Orozco, where circumstances left people highly dependent on state aid, campesinos suggested their most powerful defense against intrusive policies lay in a passive opposition made possible by ejidal autonomy.

Notes

Chapter 1. Conservation-Development at Calakmul

1. See http://www.unesco.org/mab/nutshell.htm, available February 4, 2004.

2. This surprise was a potent component in their negotiations. Public relations surrounding the decree were likely less than adequate at a time when Calakmul had almost no radio, television, or print media. Campesinos, however, did know of the Reserve, as resettlement of people living inside its limits took place in 1988. These sites were subsequently reoccupied and became the object of future relocation schemes.

3. In 1995, a federal agent charged with monitoring forest clearing was murdered by farmers under investigation for cutting older growth forest. The agent was rumored to be an extortionist. True or not, the rumor shows campesinos connected environmental laws to government corruption. I return to this point in subsequent chapters.

4. See the work of Friends of Calakmul, http://www.calakmul.org, available February 1, 2004.

Chapter 2. Theorizing Conservation and Development

1. Mexico's border with Guatemala is relevant here. Although incentives to colonize Chiapas had much to do with protecting Mexico from its southern neighbor (Pohlenz 1989) and likely influenced the Reserve's declaration (Folan and García Ortega 2003), authorities rarely expressed such anxieties in Calakmul. At present, no paved roads connect Calakmul to Guatemala, and relatively few people move across this portion of the border.

2. Based on reports from local government officials, I estimate the murder rate at Calakmul for 1994–96 at roughly 45 per 100,000 compared to a national rate of 17 to 19 per 100,000 (Rockett 1998; *La Jornada*, March 3, 1997). My estimate is not conclusive. Calakmul's police often learned of murders post facto through gossip, and they admitted their count may not be accurate.

3. Following Jeffrey Gould, one can see how "physical violence creates the conditions for the long-term exercise of symbolic" violence (1998:22). That is, state tolerance of violence is linked to larger movements to enhance elite claims to rule by discrediting certain identities and practices.

Chapter 3. Conservation's Hidden History

1. See Alonso (1995) for a comparable end to Apache autonomy via changing U.S.–Mexico relations.

2. All translations are my own.

3. I thank Reyna Sayira Maas Rodríguez, who came to this conclusion.

4. This figure is based on census data from the year 2000, which describes 25 percent of the Mexican population, or 24.6 million people, living in communities of fewer than 2,500 people (INEGI 2001a).

5. In some ejidos, people might piece together unconnected plots to form their allotment. People referred to this strategy as "trabajando en común (working in common)." The phrase led some policy makers and environmentalists to misinterpret the practice as a common property regime. In fact, ejidatarios always claimed private ownership over the lands they worked, although ejidal tenures might prevent campesinos from acting on these claims. Also, campesinos viewed working in common as a secondary strategy to be utilized only when expedient, for example, when hilly countryside made desirable flat land scarce. Campesinos agreed that defending land claims while working in common was more difficult, as people could rarely give disperse plots their full attention. Newcomers to Calakmul, sent by ejidatarios to work in common on surplus lands, often found these directives insulting, believing ejidatarios were consigning them to insecure situations.

6. The importance of different offices changed with Calakmul's municipio. Comisariado municipales became salaried representatives of the state, and this office displaced the Consejo de Vigilancia in importance. The Comisariado Ejidales continued to assert their primacy, and many ejidos effectively had two presidents. Whereas in 1995 an outsider asking for an ejido's "comisariado" would be directed immediately to the Comisariado Ejidal, in 2001 such a question received the response, "Which one?"

Chapter 4. The Migrant's Journey

1. The Fray Bartolome de Las Casas Human Rights Center lists 10,000 people as displaced by the war (EFE News Service, August 29, 2001). The Red Cross and others list the figure between 12,000 and 30,000 (Franco 2002).

2. Indicative of the rapid pace of change in Calakmul, by 2001 many of Calakmul's anti-Zapatistas supported the union that grew out of events described in chapter 7. The union has loose ties with the Zapatistas. Chiapan refugees rationalized their membership by insisting the group was not Zapatista per se, although the group "knows" the Zapatistas. This accommodation was, partly, a reaction to municipal authorities who proffered prejudicial remarks about indigenous people and generally ignored their demands. The union provided a unique and necessary forum for Ch'ol political expression.

3. Ejidal endogamy was practiced throughout Calakmul. In San Lorenzo, only two of the village's thirty-three households have no blood or marriage ties to other village households. Since the ejido's recolonization in the mid-1980s, eighteen villagers who entered San Lorenzo unmarried ended up in union with another villager. Only three people sought spouses outside the ejido. This fact is even more remarkable considering San Lorenzo's neighboring ejido lies just one kilometer to the south.

Chapter 5. The Fractured Ejido, the Fractured State

1. Julia Murphy (personal communication 1996) notes that staffers described factionalism in terms of whether or not an ejido was "organized." Organized ejidos were supposedly better able to implement projects. Working in one such ejido, Murphy found people worked hard to maintain a congenial image. Murphy suggests "organized" ejidos might appear so because they have positive relations with government agents who aid in fabricating the ejido's image.

2. Migrants might avoid the fee by establishing solitary homesteads on national lands, but few chose to work outside an ejido. Ejidos offered valuable services, most notably water. As we saw in chapter 4, people, thinking of their physical safety, saw ejidos as providing safety in numbers. Also, clearing land is an onerous job that few are willing to risk without some base in an existing ejido.

3. The ejidatario/poblador distinction is outlined in Mexico's agrarian law (Procuraduría Agraria 1993). Originally, the difference applied to communities that housed both farmers and full-time artisans or merchants. The law establishes that ejidatarios and the ejidal assembly decide issues relevant to agricultural lands. Ejidatarios and pobladores collectively should decide questions relevant to the *zona urbana*, or village center. At Calakmul, however, no settlement other than Xpujil supported a non-farming class.

4. Common lands may be undesirable because they lie far from an ejido's urban zone, where people cluster their homes. Also, common lands often contain taller forests that require more effort to fell than the secondary growth located in farm parcels. In Orozco, pobladores complained common lands were prone to flooding.

5. Again, ethnic constructions in Calakmul were undergoing rapid changes in response to the Zapatista movement. See chapter 7.

6. To help readers follow the overall argument, I have condensed the number of ejidatarios contributing to the meeting. I retained the flow by maintaining a literal transcription.

7. This statement is based on the 2001 survey of 153 households. Families with herds of approximately twenty cattle all cited an urban investor who provided the initial three or five cattle and financing.

8. The impact of this policy distinction could be considerable as roughly four-fifths of Mexico's closed forests are located on ejidal lands (Wexler and Bray 1996).

9. Ejidatarios could choose to set aside a piece of land that would be occupied by future ejidatarios as designated by the ejidal assembly.

Chapter 6. "Toying with Survival"

1. Mexico's forestry law takes as its starting point the need to conserve biodiversity. Article 13 notes that domestic use of forest resources, such as the creation of pastures, is subject to the norms established by the federal regulating body SEMARNAP (now SEMARNAT), the Secretary for the Environment, Natural Resources, and Fisheries. Otherwise, exploitation of forests for timber sales requires state authoriza-

tion, environmental impact assessments, and the development of environmental management plans (Articles 11 and 12).

2. Compare with Sandstrom's 1991 estimate of 2,400 kl or 5,280 lbs of corn for households in Veracruz.

3. For example, women in Orozco's UAIM hoped to transfer the hectareage they agreed to under PROCAMPO to a loan program known locally as "PRONASOL." The women believed PRONASOL officers were more lax in checking on whether they actually completed the promised work. The two projects were independent of each other, but women interpreted them as similar in the way they paid people to plant.

4. High school scholarships were also available. These operated under a different program, were fewer in number, entailed less money, and did not apply to summer months.

5. Nearly three-quarters of monies associated with the U.S. farm bill, however, benefited large-scale producers and people who earn more than US$250,000 a year (Fitzgerald 2003).

Chapter 7. Conservation's Political Space

1. See http://www.nrem.iastate.edu/projects/smaya/smayaf.htm, available February 9, 2004.

2. The organization continued to grow throughout 1995. New members need only request acceptance at the Council's monthly assembly. Participation in particular projects would then need to wait as new members became incorporated into project proposals.

3. Don Deocundo Acopa died of lung cancer in the spring of 2000. His passing and life's work were officially recognized by the Quintana Roo state legislature.

4. This was among the first names for the group that circulated. Later, the organization would become the Consejo Regional Indígena y Popular de Xpujil. Note the symmetry with the Regional Council's name, Consejo Regional Agropecuario de Xpujil. I believe the shift signaled the new group's political rather than military bent, as it adopted a language resonant with existing negotiating frameworks.

Chapter 8. A Sustaining Conservation

1. From the Rio Declaration on Environment and Development, available February 12, 2004, at http://www.un.org/documents/ga/conf151/aconf15126-1annex1.htm.

2. From the WSSD Plan of Implementation, available February 12, 2003, at http://www.un.org/esa/sustdev/documents/WSSD_POL PD/English/POIChap ter1.htm.

3. An example of this would be the ideas of Mario Mancilla Barillas who works in Petén, Guatemala. Mancilla argues against state- and NGO-sponsored social engineering. Instead, he defines the role of government in promoting the wishes of the general public and in refereeing social relations to guarantee people's physical security and the fairness of economic structures. When we discussed his position in 2001, I noted that what seemed like a progressive viewpoint in postwar Guatemala appeared

quite conservative in U.S. terms. He responded that his argument was iconoclastic. In my understanding, caught between a marketplace and governing authorities, neither of which premised the public or environment's well-being, Mancilla sought a liberating position, one dominated by a sympathetic rationality.

4. See the Man and Biosphere web page, available February 12, 2003, http://www. unesco.org/mab//nutshell.htmv.

5. For the press's ongoing preoccupation with guerilla activity in Calakmul despite the lack of supporting evidence, see the following articles (translations are my own): "There are no armed groups in Xpujil, only unhappy people, says the army," *Diario de Yucatán*, December 7, 1996; "Guerillas and drug trafficking are two grave problems in Xpujil, says [senatorial candidate] Layda Sansores," *Diario de Yucatán*, April 9, 1997; "It would be difficult for an armed group to emerge from Xpujil, opines a priest," *Diario de Yucatán*, January 8, 1998; and, with the contradictory headline, "Campesinos discard the idea of guerilla activity: Residents of Calakmul opine that military surveillance should be more extensive in the area, because [guerilla] 'are only in the forest,' " *Diario de Yucatán*, May 13, 2000.

6. The process also included a historical assessment of both the region and institutions working inside it. Considering the changes in Calakmul, I find the suggestion to formalize institutional memory provocative. International actors, new to Calakmul, encounter campesinos' demands for the first time and conclude these demands are incipient. The cycling of state attention to campesino organizations, which disposes of past groups as irrelevant to today's concerns, also serves to obscure the depth of campesino grievances.

7. For a full description of the project see, http://www.cse.csiro.au/research/Program2/nsw_rangelands, available February 17, 2004.

8. See note 7.

Works Cited

Acopa, D., and E. Boege. 1998. "The Maya Forest in Campeche, Mexico: Experiences in Forest Management at Calakmul." In *Timber, Tourists, and Temples: Conservation and Development in the Maya Forest of Belize, Guatemala, and Mexico*, ed. R. Primack, D. Bray, H. Galletti, and I. Ponciano, 81–97. Washington, DC: Island Press.

Adams, J., and T. McShane. 1992. *The Myth of Wild Africa: Conservation without Illusion*. New York: Norton.

Adams, R. 1985. "Settlement Patterns of the Central Yucatan and Southern Campeche Regions." In *Lowland Maya Settlement Patterns*, ed. W. Ashmore, 211–258. Albuquerque: University of New Mexico Press.

Agrawal, A., and C. Gibson. 2001. *Communities and the Environment: Ethnicity, Gender, and the State in Community-Based Conservation*. New Brunswick, NJ: Rutgers University Press.

Aguilera Herrera, N. 1958. "Suelos." In *Los recursos naturales del sureste y su aprovechamiento*, ed. E. Beltrán, 175–212. México, D.F.: Instituto Mexicano de Recursos Naturales Renovables, A.C.

Alcorn, J. 1981. "Huastec Noncrop Resource Management: Implications for Prehistoric Rain Forest Management." *Human Ecology* 9:395–417.

Alonso, A. 1995. *Thread of Blood: Colonialism, Revolution, and Gender on Mexico's Northern Frontier*. Tucson: University of Arizona Press.

Alvarez, S., E. Dagnino, and A. Escobar, eds. 1998. *Cultures of Politics, Politics of Cultures: Revisioning Latin American Social Movements*. Boulder, CO: Westview Press.

Antochiw, M. 1994. *Historia cartográfica de la península de Yucatán*. Campeche: Gobierno del Estado de Campeche.

———. 1997. "La Cartografía y los Cehaches." In *Calakmul: Volver al Sur*, ed. R. Ferré D'Amaré, E. Pino Castilla, and C. Vadillo Buenfil, 23–32. Campeche: Estado de Campeche.

Appadurai, Arjun. 1996. *Modernity at Large: Cultural Dimensions of Globalization*. Minneapolis: University of Minnesota Press.

Arizpe, L., F. Paz, and M. Velázquez. 1996. *Culture and Global Change: Social Perceptions of Deforestation in the Lacandona Rain Forest in Mexico*. Ann Arbor: University of Michigan Press.

Atran, S. 1999. "Managing the Maya Commons: The Value of Local Knowledge." In *A*

View from a Point: Ethnoecology as Situated Knowledge, ed. V. Nazarea, 190–214. Tucson: University of Arizona Press.

Azuela E. 1989. "Cultura política y frontera." In *El Redescubrimiento de la frontera sur*, ed. J. Hernández Palacios and J. Manuel Sandoval, 27–35. México, D.F.: Universidad Autónoma de Zacatecas, Universidad Autónoma Metropolitana.

Azuela, M. 1927. *Los de abajo*. Madrid: Ediciones Biblos.

Baranda, J. 1873. *La cuestión de Belice*. Campeche: Imprenta de la Sociedad Tipográfica.

Bebbington, A. 1999. "Capitals and Capabilities: A Framework for Analyzing Peasant Viability, Rural Livelihoods, and Poverty." *World Development* 27 (12): 2021–2044.

——. 2000. "Reencountering Development: Livelihood Transitions and Place Transformations in the Andes." *Annals of the Association of American Geographers* 90 (3): 495–520.

——. 2001. "Globalized Andes? Livelihoods, Landscapes, and Development." *Ecumene* 8 (4): 414–436.

Bebbington, A., and S. Batterbury. 2001. "Transnational Livelihoods and Landscapes: Political Ecologies of Globalization." *Ecumene* 8 (4): 369–380.

Beltrán, E., ed. 1958. *Los recursos naturales del sureste y su aprovechamiento*. México, D.F.: Instituto Mexicano de Recursos Naturales Renovables, A.C.

Benjamin, R. 1951. "Lo llamaban El Loco." *Reader's Digest* 21:121–125.

Boege, E. 1995. *The Calakmul Biosphere Reserve Mexico*. Paris: South-South Cooperation Program, UNESCO.

Boege, E., and R. Murguía. 1989. *Diagnóstico de las actividades humanas que se realizan en la Reserva de la Biosfera de Calakmul, estado de Campeche*. Mérida: PRONATURA-Península de Yucatán.

Boff, L. 1988. *When Theology Listens to the Poor*. San Francisco: Harper & Row.

Bowles, I., and G. Prickett, eds. 2001. *Footprints in the Jungle: Natural Resource Industries, Infrastructure, and Biodiversity Conservation*. Oxford: Oxford University Press.

Brandon, K., K. Redford, and S. Sanderson, eds. 1998. *Parks in Peril: People, Politics, and Protected Areas*. Washington, DC: Island Press.

Bray, D., M. Carreón, L. Merino, and V. Santos. 1993. "On the Road to Sustainable Forestry." *Cultural Survival Quarterly* Spring:38–41.

Brechin, S., P. Wilshusen, and C. Benjamin. 2003. "Crafting Conservation Globally and Locally: Complex Organizations and Governance Regimes." In *Contested Nature: Promoting International Biodiversity with Social Justice in the Twenty-first Century*, ed. S. Brechin, P. Wilshusen, C. Fortwanger, and P. West, 159–182. Albany: State University of New York Press.

Brechin, S., P. Wilshusen, C. Fortwanger, and P. West. 2002. "Beyond the Square Wheel: Toward a More Comprehensive Understanding of Biodiversity Conservation as Social and Political Process." *Society and Natural Resources* 15 (1): 41–64.

——. 2003. *Contested Nature: Promoting International Biodiversity with Social Justice in the Twenty-first Century*. Albany: State University of New York Press.

Brockington, D. 2002. *Fortress Conservation: The Preservation of Mkomazi Game Reserve in Tanzania*. Bloomington: Indiana University Press.

Brosius, J. P. 1999. "Analyses and Interventions: Anthropological Engagements with Environmentalism." *Current Anthropology* 40 (3): 277–309.

Brosius, P., and D. Russell. 2003. "Conservation from Above: An Anthropological Perspective on Transboundary Protected Areas and Ecoregional Planning." *Journal of Sustainable Forestry* 17(1/2): 39–65.

Bruner, A. G., R. E. Gullison, R. E. Rice, and G. A. B. da Fonesca. 2001. "Effectiveness of Parks in Protecting Tropical Biodiversity." *Science* 291 (5501): 125–128.

Brydon, A. 1996. "Whale-Siting: Spatiality in Icelandic Nationalism." In *Images of Contemporary Iceland*, ed. G. Palsson and E. Durrenburger, 25–45. Iowa City: University of Iowa Press.

Bunch, R. 1986. *Dos mazorcas de maíz: Una guía para el mejoramiento agrícola orientado hacia la gente*. Oklahoma: World Neighbors.

Cahn von Seelen, K. 2004. " 'This Place Was Paradise': Consumption as Metaphor and Material Concern on Mexico's Southern Frontier." Ph.D. dissertation, University of Pennsylvania.

Cancian, F. 1992. *The Decline of Community in Zinacantán: Economics, Public Life, and Social Stratification 1960–1987*. Stanford, CA: Stanford University Press.

Chambers, R. 1994. "The Origins and Practice of Participatory Rural Appraisal." *World Development* 22 (7): 953–969.

Champagne, M. 2002. "La sustentabilidad y las prácticas discursivas: Un estudio sobre la institucionalidad del desarrollo conservacionista en Calakmul, Campeche, México." Master's thesis, Centro de Investigaciones y Estudios Superiores en Antropología Social, San Cristobal de las Casas.

Chim, L. 2000. "Depredaban especies de la reserva de Calakmul." *La Jornada*, January 22, Internet edition, México, D.F.

Christen, C., S. Herculano, K. Hochstetler, R. Prell, M. Price, and J. T. Roberts. 1998. "Latin American Environmentalism: Comparative Views." *Studies in Comparative International Development* 33:58–87.

Clay, J. 1988. *Indigenous Peoples and Tropical Forests: Models of Land Use and Management from Latin America*. Cambridge, MA: Cultural Survival.

Cliggett, L. 2000. "Social Components of Migration: Experiences from Southern Province, Zambia." *Human Organization* 59:125–135.

Colchester, M. 1994. *Salvaging Nature: Indigenous Peoples, Protected Areas, and Biodiversity Conservation*. Geneva: United Nations Research Institute for Social Development.

Collier, G. 1987. "Peasant Politics and the Mexican State: Indigenous Compliance in Highland Chiapas." *Mexican Studies/Estudios Mexicanos* 3:71–98.

——. 1992. "Seeking Food and Seeking Money: Changing Relations of Production in Zinacantán, Chiapas." In *Economic Restructuring and Rural Subsistence in Mexico: Maize and the Crisis of the 1980s*, ed. C. Hewitt de Alcántara, 81–97. Geneva: United Nations Research Institute for Social Development.

———. 1994. *Basta! Land and the Zapatista Rebellion in Chiapas.* Oakland, CA: Food First.

Collier, J. F. 1973. *Law and Social Change in Zinacantán.* Stanford, CA: Stanford University Press.

CONAP (Consejo Nacional de Áreas Protegidas). 2001. *Plan maestro de la Reserva de la Biosfera Maya, 2001–06.* Guatemala: Editorial Serviprensa, S.A.

Cornelius, W., A. Craig, and J. Fox, eds. 1994. *Transforming State-Society Relations in Mexico: The National Solidarity Strategy.* La Jolla, CA: Center for U.S.–Mexican Studies.

Cornelius, W., and D. Myhre. 1998. Introduction to *The Transformation of Rural Mexico: Reforming the Ejido Sector,* ed. W. Cornelius and D. Myhre, 1–20. La Jolla, CA: Center for U.S.–Mexican Studies.

Coronil, F. 1997. *The Magical State.* Chicago: University of Chicago Press.

Correa, G. 2001. "La miseria en el campo, peor que en el porfiriato." *Proceso* 1289:10–13.

Corrigan, P. 1994. "State Formation." In *Everyday Forms of State Formation: Revolution and the Negotiation of Rule in Modern Mexico,* ed. G. Joseph and D. Nugent, xvii–xix. Durham, NC: Duke University Press.

Denevan, W. M. 1983. "Adaptation, Variation, and Cultural Geography." *Professional Geography* 35:399–406.

Descola, P., and G. Pálsson. 1996. *Nature and Society: Anthropological Perspectives.* New York: Routledge.

DeWalt, B. 1979. *Modernization in a Mexican Ejido: A Study in Economic Adaptation.* New York: Cambridge University Press.

DeWalt, B., and M. Rees. 1994. *Past Lessons, Future Prospects: The End of Agrarian Reform in Mexico.* La Jolla, CA: Center for U.S.–Mexican Studies.

Diamond, N. 2000. *Workshop Summary: Greening Democracy and Governing the Environment: Managing for Cross-Sectoral Results.* Washington, DC: Biodiversity Support Program.

Diario de Yucatán. December 7, 1996. "En Xpujil no hay grupos armados, sólo gente descontenta-dice el Ejército en Campeche." Internet edition. Mérida, Yucatán.

———. December 31, 1996. "Hoy decretaría su creación el Congreso de Campeche el municipio de Calakmul." Internet edition. Mérida, Yucatán.

———. April 9, 1997. "Guerilla y narcotráfico, dos problemas graves en la zona de Xpujil-Layda Sansores." Internet edition. Mérida, Yucatán.

———. April 9, 1997. "Hacienda, no Pemex debe dar el dinero por el petróleo." Internet edition. Mérida, Yucatán.

———. January 8, 1998. "Es difícil que surja un grupo armado, opina un sacerdote: La situación en la zona de Xpujil." Internet edition. Mérida, Yucatán.

———. May 12, 2000. "El secuestro de un helicóptero, amplia operación militar para localizar un grupo." Internet edition. Mérida, Yucatán.

———. May 13, 2000a. "En la selva el secuestro del helicópter lo pasó casi inadvertido." Internet edition. Mérida, Yucatán.

———. May 13, 2000b. "Campesinos descartan una guerrilla: Vecinos de Calakmul opinan que la vigilancia militar debe ampliarse en la zona, pues 'sólo está en la selva.'" Internet edition. Mérida, Yucatán.

———. October 19, 2000. "Llamado a participar en programas de conservación del medio ambiente y cuidado de especies animales." Internet edition. Mérida, Yucatán.

Díaz-Polanco, H. 1997. *La rebelión Zapatista y la autonomía*. México, D.F.: Siglo Veintiuno Editores.

Dobson, A. 1998. *Justice and the Environment: Conceptions of Environmental Sustainability and Theories of Distributive Justice*. Oxford: Oxford University Press.

———. 2000. *Green Political Thought*. 3rd ed. London: Routledge.

Dove, M. 1993. "Uncertainty, Humility, and Adaptation in the Tropical Forest: The Agricultural Augury of the Kantu." *Ethnology* 32:145–167.

Dumond, D. 1997a. "Breve historia de los pacíficos del sur." In *Calakmul: Volver al Sur*, ed. R. Ferré D'Amaré, E. Pino Castilla, and C. Vadillo Buenfil, 33–50. Campeche: Estado de Campeche.

———. 1997b. *The Machete and the Cross: Campesino Rebellion in Yucatan*. Lincoln: University of Nebraska Press.

Dunn, D. 1988. *Cades Cove: The Life and Death of a Southern Appalachian Community, 1818–1937*. Knoxville: University of Tennessee Press.

Durham, W. 1996. "Political Ecology and Environmental Destruction in Latin America." In *The Social Causes of Environmental Destruction in Latin America*, ed. M. Painter and W. Durham, 249–264. Ann Arbor: University of Michigan Press.

The Economist. 1997. "Democracy, Mexican-Style." 343 (8023): 33–34.

———. 2002. "Heartbroken: Is Rural America Really Such a Great Role Model for the Nation?" 364 (8286): 27.

Edelman, M. 1999. *Peasants Against Globalization: Rural Social Movements in Costa Rica*. Stanford, CA: Stanford University Press.

EFE News Service. 2000. "Mexico-NAFTA Deregulations of Corn Market Has Hurt Mexican Farmers," October 25, news wire report.

———. 2001. "Chiapas: Fox Greets Displaced Residents as They Return to Chiapas," August 29, news wire report.

Ericson, J. 1996. *Conservation and Development on the Border of the Calakmul Biosphere Reserve*. Master's thesis, Humboldt State University.

Ericson, J., M. Freudenberger, E. Boege. 1999. *Population Dynamics, Migration, and the Future of the Calakmul Biosphere Reserve*. Washington, DC: American Association for the Advancement of Science.

Escobar, A. 1995. *Encountering Development: The Making and Unmaking of the Third World*. Princeton, NJ: Princeton University Press.

———. 1996. "Construction Nature: Elements for a Post-Structuralist Political Ecology." *Futures* 28 (4): 325–344.

———. 1999. "After Nature: Steps to an Antiessentialist Political Ecology." *Current Anthropology*, 40 (1): 1–30.

Esteva, G. 1993. "Development." In *The Development Dictionary*, ed. W. Sachs, 7–25. Atlantic Highlands: Zed Books.

EZLN (Ejército Zapatista de Liberación Nacional). 1997. EZLN *documentos y comunicados*. Vol. 3. México, D.F.: Ediciones Era, S.A. de C.V.

Fairhead, J., and M. Leach. 1996. *Misreading the African Landscape: Society and Ecology in a Forest-Savanna Mosaic*. Cambridge: Cambridge University Press.

Farris, N. 1984. *Maya Society under Colonial Rule: The Collective Enterprise of Survival*. Princeton: Princeton University Press.

Ferguson, J. 1990. *The Anti-Politics Machine: "Development," Depoliticization, and Bureaucratic Power in Lesotho*. Cambridge: Cambridge University Press.

———. 1999. *Expectations of Modernity: Myths and Meanings of Urban Life on the Zambian Copperbelt*. Berkeley: University of California Press.

Ferguson, J., and A. Gupta. 2002. "Spatializing States: Toward an Ethnography of Neoliberal Governmentality." *American Ethnologist* 29 (4): 981–1002.

Finn, J. 1998. *Tracing the Veins: Of Copper, Culture, and Community from Butte to Chuquicamata*. Berkeley: University of California Press.

Fitzgerald, S. 2003. *Liberalizing Agriculture: Why the U.S. Should Look to New Zealand and Australia*. Washington, DC: Heritage Foundation.

Flachsenberg, H., and H. Galletti. 1998. "Forest Management in Quintana Roo, Mexico." In *Timber, Tourists, and Temples: Conservation and Development in the Maya Forest of Belize, Guatemala, and Mexico*, ed. R. Primack, D. Bray, H. Galletti, and I. Ponciano, 47–60. Washington, DC: Island Press.

Folan, W., and J. García Ortega. 2003. "Reserva de la biosfera de Calakmul: Los primeros esfuerzos." Paper presented at Simposio Calakmul: Sustentabilidad Impostergable, Campeche, Mexico.

Folan, W., et al. 1992. *Programa de Manejo de la Biosfera Calakmul Campeche*. Campeche: Centro de Investigaciones Históricas y Sociales, Universidad Autónoma de Campeche, Secretaria de Desarollo Social.

Fortwangler, C. 2003. "The Winding Road: Incorporating Power and Social Justice in Biodiversity Conservation." In *Contested Nature*, ed. S. Brechin, P. Wilshusen, C. Fortwangler, and P. West, 25–40. Albany: State University of New York Press.

Franco, P. 2002. "Rights—Mexico: 12,000 Displaced by Violence in Chiapas." Inter Press Service.

Galindo-Leal, C. 1999. *La gran región de Calakmul: Prioridades biológicas de conservacióon y propuesta de modificación de la Reserva de la Biosfera*. México, D.F.: World Wildlife Fund.

Galletti, H. 1998. "The Maya Forest of Quintana Roo: Thirteen years of Conservation and Community Development." In *Timber, Tourists, and Temples: Conservation and Development in the Maya Forest of Belize, Guatemala, and Mexico*, ed. R. Primack, D. Bray, H. Galletti, and I. Ponciano, 33–46. Washington, DC: Island Press.

García, R., et al. 1989. *La modernización forzada del trópico: el caso de Tabasco*. México, D.F.: El Colegio de México.

García-Gil, G., and I. March. 1990. *Cartografía temática básica y base geográfica de datos para la zona de Calakmul, Campeche*. Merida: PRONATURA, Península de Yucatán, A.C.

Garrett, W. 1989. "La Ruta Maya." *National Geographic* 176 (4): 424–479.

Gates, M. 1993. *In Default: Peasants, the Debt Crisis, and the Agricultural Challenge in Mexico*. Boulder, CO: Westview Press.

Gershberg, A. I. 1994. "Distributing Resources in the Education Sector: Solidarity's Escuela Digna Program." In *Transforming State-Society Relations in Mexico: The National Solidarity Strategy*, ed. W. Cornelius, A. Craig, and J. Fox, 233–253. La Jolla, CA: Center for U.S.–Mexican Studies.

Ghimire, K., and M. Pimbert, eds. 1997. *Social Change and Conservation: Environmental Politics and Impacts of National Parks and Protected Areas*. London: Earthscan Publications Ltd.

Gibson, C., M. McKean, and E. Ostrom, eds. 2000. *People and Forests: Communities, Institutions, and Governance*. Cambridge, MA: MIT Press.

Gilly, A. 1998. "Chiapas and the Rebellion of the Enchanted World." In *Rural Revolt in Mexico: U.S. Intervention and the Domain of Subaltern Politics*, ed. D. Nugent, 261–334. Durham, NC: Duke University Press.

Giri, A. 2002. *Conversations and Transformations: Toward a New Ethics of Self and Society*. Lanham, MD: Lexington Books.

Glick Schiller, N., L. Basch, and C. Blanc-Szanton. 1992. "Transnationalism: A New Analytic Framework for Understanding Migration." In *Towards a Transnational Perspective on Migration: Race, Class, Ethnicity, and Nationalism Reconsidered*, ed. N. Glick Schiller, L. Basch, and C. Blanc-Szanton, 1–24. New York: New York Academy of Sciences.

Goldring, L. 1998. "Having Your Cake and Eating It Too: Selective Appropriation of Ejido Reform." In *The Transformation of Rural Mexico: Reforming the Ejido Sector*, ed. W. Cornelius and D. Myhre, 145–172. La Jolla, CA: Center for U.S.–Mexican Studies.

Gomez-Rivera, M. 1999. "Indigenous Autonomy and the Strengthening of National Sovereignty and Identity." *Cultural Survival Quarterly* 23 (1): 41–44.

Gould, J. 1998. *To Die in This Way: Nicaraguan Indians and the Myth of Mestizaje, 1880–1965*. Durham, NC: Duke University Press.

Graham, E. 1998. "Metaphor and Metaphorism: Some Thoughts on Environmental Metahistory." In *Advances in Historical Ecology*, ed. W. Balée, 119–137. New York: Columbia University Press.

Greenberg, J. 1989. *Blood Ties: Life and Violence in Rural Mexico*. Tucson: University of Arizona Press.

Grove, R. 1995. *Green Imperialism: Colonial Expansion, Tropical Island Edens, and the Origins of Environmentalism, 1600–1860*. Cambridge: Cambridge University Press.

Guinier, Lani. 1994. *The Tyranny of the Majority: Fundamental Fairness in Representative Democracy*. New York: Free Press.

Gupta, A. 1998. *Postcolonial Developments: Agriculture in the Making of Modern India.* Durham, NC: Duke University Press.

Gupta, A., and J. Ferguson. 1997. *Culture, Power, Place: Explorations in Critical Anthropology.* Durham, NC: Duke University Press.

Haber, P. 1996. "Identity and Political Process: Recent Trends in the Study of Latin American Social Movements." *Latin American Research Review* 31:171–187.

Haenn, N. 1999. "The Power of Environmental Knowledge: Ethnoecology and Environmental Conflicts in Mexican Conservation." *Human Ecology* 27:477–490.

——. 2000. *"Biodiversity Is Diversity in Use": Community-Based Conservation in the Calakmul Biosphere Reserve.* Arlington, VA: The Nature Conservancy.

——. 2002. "Nature Regimes in Southern Mexico: A History of Power and Environment." *Ethnology* 41 (1): 1—26.

——. 2003. "Risking Environmental Justice: Culture, Conservation, and Governance at Calakmul, Mexico." In *Social Justice in Latin America*, ed. T. Wickham-Crawley and S. Eckstein, 81–102. New York: Routledge Press.

——. Forthcoming. "The Changing and Enduring Ejido: A State and Regional Examination of Mexico's Land Tenure Counterreforms." *Land Use Policy.*

Hart, J. M. 1987. *Revolutionary Mexico: The Coming and Process of the Mexican Revolution.* Berkeley: University of California Press.

Harvey, N. 1998. *The Chiapas Rebellion: The Struggle for Land and Democracy.* Durham, NC: Duke University Press.

Hemmati, M. 2002. *Multi-Stakeholder Processes for Governance and Sustainability: Beyond Deadlock and Conflict.* London: Earthscan.

Hernández López, J. 2000. "Astillero." *La Jornada*, May 18, Internet edition, México, D.F.

Hewitt de Alcántara, C., ed. 1992. *Economic Restructuring and Rural Subsistence in Mexico: Maize and the Crisis of the 1980s.* Geneva: United Nations Research Institute for Social Development.

Holland, D., et al. 1998. *Identity and Agency in Cultural Worlds.* Cambridge, MA: Harvard University Press.

Hostettler, U. 1996. *Milpa Agriculture and Economic Diversification: Socioeconomic Change in a Maya Peasant Society of Central Quintana Roo, 1900–1990s.* Ph.D. thesis, University of Berne.

INEGI (Instituto Nacional de Estadística, Geografía e Informática). 1993. *Chiapas Hablantes de Lengua Indígena: Perfil Sociodemográfico.* Aguascalientes, Ags: INEGI.

——. 2001a. *Tabulados Básicos: XII Censo General de Población y Vivienda 2000.* Aguascalientes, Ags: INEGI.

——. 2001b. *Cuaderno Estadístico Municipal: Edición 2000.* Aguascalientes, Ags.: INEGI.

Jackson, M. 1998. *Minima Ethnographica: Intersubjectivity and the Anthropological Project.* Chicago: University of Chicago Press.

de Janvry, A., G. Gordillo, and E. Sadoulet. 1994. "NAFTA and Mexico's Corn Producers." Working paper, Dept. of Agricultural and Resource Economics, University of California, Berkeley.

———. 1997. *Mexico's Second Agrarian Reform: Household and Community Responses*. La Jolla, CA: Center for U.S.–Mexican Studies.

Johnson, B. 1999. "Conservation, Subsistence, and Class at the Birth of Superior National Forest." *Environmental History* 4 (1): 80–99.

Jones, G. D. 1989. *Maya Resistance to Spanish Rule: Time and History on a Colonial Frontier*. Albuquerque: University of New Mexico Press.

———. 1999. *The Conquest of the Last Maya Kingdom*. Stanford, CA: Stanford University Press.

Jones, G. 2000. "Between a Rock and a Hard Place: Institutional Reform and the Performance of Land Privatization in Peri-Urban Mexico." In *Current Land Policy in Latin America: Regulating Land Tenure under Neoliberalism*, ed. A. Zoomers and G. van der Haar, 201–6. Amsterdam: Royal Tropical Institute.

La Jornada. 1997. "BM: entorpece la violencia criminal la lucha contra la pobreza en AL." March 3, Internet edition. México, D.F.

Joseph, G., and D. Nugent. 1994. "Popular Culture and State Formation in Revolutionary Mexico." In *Everyday Forms of State Formation: Revolution and the Negotiation of Rule in Modern Mexico*, ed. G. Joseph and D. Nugent, 3–23. Durham, NC: Duke University Press.

Keys, E. 1998. "Historical Parallels to Sustainable Development Discourse: A Review Essay." *Revista Geográfica* 124:79–85.

———. 2002. *From Mouth to Market: the Adoption of Chili Cultivation and Its Land Cover Effects in Calakmul, Mexico*. Ph.D. diss., Clark University, Worcester, MA.

Kingsolver, B. 2002. *Small Wonder: Essays*. New York: HarperCollins.

Klepeis, P., and C. Vance. 2003. "Neoliberal Policy and Deforestation in Southeastern Mexico: An Assessment of the PROCAMPO Program." *Economic Geography* 79 (3): 221–240.

Klor de Alva, J. 1995. "The Postcolonization of the (Latin) American Experience: A Reconsideration of 'Colonialism,' 'Postcolonialism,' and 'Mestizaje.'" In *After Colonialism: Imperial Histories and Postcolonial Displacements*, ed. G. Prakash, 241–275. Princeton: Princeton University Press.

Knight, A. 1986. *The Mexican Revolution*. Lincoln: University of Nebraska Press.

———. 1998. "The United States and Mexican Peasantry, circa 1880–1940." In *Rural Revolt in Mexico: U.S. Intervention and the Domain of Subaltern Politics*, ed. D. Nugent, 25–63. Durham, NC: Duke University Press.

Konrad, H. 1991. "Capitalism on the Tropical-Forest Frontier: Quintana Roo, 1880s to 1930." In *Land, Labor, and Capital in Modern Yucatán: Essays in Regional History and Political Economy*, ed. J. Brannon and G. Joseph, 143–171. Tuscaloosa: University of Alabama Press.

Kottak, C., and A. Costa. 1993. "Ecological Awareness, Environmentalist Action, and International Conservation Strategy." *Human Organization* 52 (4): 335–341.

Lambert, D. P. 1996. "Crop Diversity and Fallow Management in a Tropical Deciduous Forest Shifting Cultivation System." *Human Ecology* 24:427–453.

Latour, B. 1987. *Science in Action: How to Follow Scientists and Engineers Through Society.* Cambridge, MA: Harvard University Press.

Leon Pinelo, A. 1958 (1639). *Relación sobre la pacificación de las provincias del Manché I Lacandon.* Madrid: Gráficas Minerva.

Lewis, H. 1989. "Ecological and Technical Knowledge of Fire: Aborigines versus Park Rangers in Northern Australia." *American Anthropologist* 91 (4): 940–961.

Leyva Solano, X. 2001. "Regional, Communal, and Organizational Transformations in Las Cañadas." *Latin American Perspectives* 28:20–44.

Leyva Solano, X., and G. Ascencio Franco. 1996. *Lacandonia al filo del agua.* México, D.F.: Centro de Investigaciones y Estudios Superiores en Antropología Social.

Li, T., ed. 1999. *Transforming the Indonesian Uplands: Marginality, Power and Production.* Amsterdam: Harwood Academic Publishers.

Liebow, E. 2002 (1993). "Inside the Decison-Making Process: Ethnography and Environmental Risk Management." In *The Applied Anthropology Reader,* ed. J. H. McDonald, 299–310. Boston: Allyn and Bacon.

Lomnitz-Adler, C. 1992. *Exits from the Labyrinth: Culture and Ideology in the Mexican National Space.* Berkeley: University California Press.

Lutz, C., and J. Collins. 1993. *Reading National Geographic.* Chicago: University of Chicago Press.

Mallon, F. 1995. *Peasant and Nation: The Making of Postcolonial Mexico and Peru.* Berkeley: University of California Press.

Margolius, R., and N. Salafsky. 1998. *Measures of Success: Designing, Managing, and Monitoring Conservation and Development Projects.* Washington, DC: Island Press.

Martínez Alomía, G. 1991. "Causas de la decadencia de Campeche." In *Campeche: Textos de su historia,* vol. 2, ed. A. Negrín Muñoz, 203–257. México, D.F.: Instituto de Investigaciones Dr. José María Luis Mora.

Mattiace, S. 2003. *With Two Eyes: Peasant Activism and Indian Autonomy in Chiapas, Mexico.* Albuquerque: University of New Mexico Press.

McCarthy, T. 2002. "Let Them Run Wild." *Time: Latin American Edition* 160 (9): 44–49.

Mendes, C. 1989. *Fight for the Forest: Chico Mendes in his Own Words.* London: Latin America Bureau.

Milton, K. 1996. *Environmentalism and Cultural Theory: Exploring the Role of Anthropology in Environmental Discourse.* New York: Routledge Press.

Miranda, F. 1958. "Rasgos fisiográficos." In *Los recursos naturales del sureste y su aprovechamiento,* ed. E. Beltrán, 159–173. México, D.F.: Instituto Mexicano de Recursos Naturales Renovables, A.C.

Mohanty, C. 2002. "'Under Western Eyes' Revisited: Feminist Solidarity Through Anticapitalist Struggles." *Signs: Journal of Women in Culture and Society* 28 (2): 499–535.

Muratorio, B. 1991. *The Life and Times of Grandfather Alonso: Culture and History in the Upper Amazon*. New Brunswick, NJ: Rutgers University Press.

Murphy, J. 1998. "Ways of Working in the Forest: Mediating Sustainable Development in Calakmul." Paper presented at 97th Annual Meeting of American Anthropological Association, Philadelphia, PA.

Myllyntaus, T., M. Hares, and J. Kunnas. 2002. "Sustainability in Danger? Slash-and-Burn Cultivation in Nineteenth-Century Finland and Twentieth-Century Southeast Asia." *Environmental History* 7:267–302.

Nader, L. 1990. *Harmony Ideology: Justice and Control in a Zapotec Mountain Village*. Stanford, CA: Stanford University Press.

National Public Radio. 1999. "Bob Thompson Discusses Why He Gave $128 Million to His Employees from the Sale of His Business." *All Things Considered*, August 2.

Netting, R. 1993. *Smallholders, Householders: Farm Families and the Ecology of Intensive, Sustainable Agriculture*. Stanford, CA: Stanford University Press.

Neumann, R. 1998. *Imposing Wilderness: Struggles Over Livelihood and Nature Preservation in Africa*. Berkeley: University of California Press.

Nigh, R. 2002. "Maya Medicine in the Biological Gaze: Bioprospecting Research as Herbal Fetishism." *Current Anthropology* 43 (3): 451–477.

Nugent, D. 1993. *Spent Cartridges of the Revolution: An Anthropological History of Namiquipa*. Chicago: University of Chicago Press.

Oates, J. 1999. *Myth and Reality in the Rain Forest: How Conservation Strategies Are Failing in West Africa*. Berkeley: University of California Press.

O'Brien, K. L. 1998. *Sacrificing the Forest: Environmental and Social Struggles in Chiapas*. Boulder, CO: Westview Press.

O'Faolain, N. 1998. *Are You Somebody? The Accidental Memoir of a Dublin Woman*. New York: Holt.

O'Neill, K. 1996. "The International Politics of National Parks." *Human Ecology* 24 (4): 521–539.

Ostrom, E. 1990. *Governing the Commons: The Evolution of Institutions for Collective Action*. Cambridge: Cambridge University Press.

Otero, G. 1999. *Farewell to the Peasantry? Political Class Formation in Rural Mexico*. Boulder, CO: Westview Press.

Parnell, P. 1988. *Escalating Disputes: Social Participation and Change in the Oaxacan Highlands*. Tucson: University of Arizona Press.

Parra Mora, L., and J. Hernández Díaz. 1994. *Violencia y cambio social en la región Triqui*. Oaxaca, México: Universidad Autónoma "Benito Juárez" de Oaxaca.

Paulson, S., L. Gezon, and M. Watts. 2003. "Locating the Political in Political Ecology: An Introduction." *Human Organization* 62 (3): 205–217.

Peet, R., and M. Watts 1996. *Liberation Ecologies: Environment, Development, Social Movements*. New York: Routledge Press.

Peine, J. D., J. C. Randolph, and J. J. Presswood Jr. 1995. "Evaluating the Effectiveness of Air Quality Management within the Class I Area of Great Smoky Mountains National Park." *Environmental Management* 19 (4): 515–526.

Peluso, N. 1992. *Rich Forests, Poor People: Resource Control and Resistance in Java.* Berkeley: University of California Press.

Peluso, N., and M. Watts, eds. 2001. *Violent Environments.* Ithaca, NY: Cornell University Press.

Pérez, M., and V. Cardoso. 2002. "Para apoyar el campo, establecen 'blindaje agroalimentario' y una política de subsidios." *La Jornada,* Internet edition, México, D.F.

Pigg, S. 1992. "Inventing Social Categories Through Place: Social Representations and Development in Nepal." *Comparative Studies in Society and History* 34 (3): 491–453.

Pimbert, M., and J. Pretty. 1995. *Parks, People and Professionals: Putting "Participation" into Protected Area Management.* Geneva: United Nations Research Institute for Social Development.

Pino Castillo, E. 1998. *Migrar a la espesura.* Campeche: Gobierno del Estado de Campeche.

Pohlenz, J. 1989. "Antropología, etnicidad e identidad nacional en la frontera sur de México." In *El Redescubrimiento de la frontera sur,* ed. J. Hernández Palacios and J. Manuel Sandoval, 17–24. México, D.F.: Universidad Autónoma de Zacatecas, Universidad Autónoma Metropolitana.

Ponce Jiménez, M. 1990. *Montaña chiclera Campeche: vida cotidiana y trabajo (1900–1950).* México, D.F.: Centro de Investigaciones y Estudios Superiores en Antropología Social.

Posada García, M. 1996. "Sin castigo, 90 percent de delitos denunciados en el país, afirma De la Barreda." *La Jornada,* Internet edition, México, D.F.

Posey, D. 2002. *Kayapó Ethnoecology and Culture.* New York: Routledge Press.

Primack, R., D. Bray, H. Galletti, and I Ponciano, eds. 1998. *Timber, Tourists, and Temples: Conservation and Development in the Maya Forest of Belize, Guatemala, and Mexico.* Washington, DC: Island Press.

Procuraduría Agraria 1993. *Nueva Legislación Agraria: Artículo 27 constitucional, Ley Agraria, y Reglamento de la Ley Agraria en Materia de Certificación de Derechos Ejidales y Titulación de Solares, Segunda edición.* México, D.F.: Procuraduría Agraria.

Quintana Roo: Album Monográfico. 1995 (1936?). Mérida, Yucatán.: Multicolor, S.A. de C.V.

Rappaport, R. 1984 (1967). *Pigs for the Ancestors: Ritual in the Ecology of a New Guinea People.* New Haven: Yale University Press.

Reed, N. 1964. *The Caste War of Yucatan.* Stanford, CA: Stanford University Press.

Reyes Osorio, R., R. Stavenhagen, S. Eckstein, J. Ballesteros. 1974. *Estructura agraria y desarrollo agrícola en México.* México, D.F.: Fondo de Cultura Económica.

Robles Ramos, R. 1958. "Geología y geohidrología." In *Los recursos naturales del sureste y su aprovechamiento,* ed. E. Beltrán, 53–92. México, D.F.: Instituto Mexicano de Recursos Naturales Renovables, A.C.

Rocheleau, D., B. Thomas-Slayter, and E. Wangari, eds. 1996. *Feminist Political Ecology: Global Issues and Local Experiences.* New York: Routledge Press.

Rockett, I. 1998. "Injury and Violence: A Public Health Perspective." *Population Bulletin* 53:1–40.

Roseberry, W. 1996. "Hegemony, Power, and Languages of Contention." In *The Politics of Difference: Ethnic Premises in a World of Power*, ed. E. Wilmsen and P. McAllister, 71–84. Chicago: University of Chicago Press.

Rubin, J. 1997. *Decentering the Regime: Ethnicity, Radicalism, and Democracy in Juchitán, Mexico*. Durham, NC: Duke University Press.

Rus, J., R. A. Hernández Castillo, and S. Mattiace, eds. 2003. *Mayan Lives, Mayan Utopias: The Indigenous Peoples of Chiapas and the Zapatista Rebellion*. Lanham, MD: Rowman & Littlefield.

Sabloff, P. 1981. *Caciquismo in Post-Revolutionary Mexican Ejido-Grant Communities*. Research Paper Series No. 7, Latin American Institute. Albuquerque: University of New Mexico.

Sandstrom, A. 1991. *Corn Is Our Blood: Culture and Ethnic Identity in a Contemporary Aztec Indian Village*. Norman: University of Oklahoma Press.

Schmink, M., and C. Wood. 1987. "The 'Political Ecology' of Amazonia." In *Lands at Risk in the Third World: Local Level Perspectives*, ed. P. Little and M. Horowitz, 38–57. Boulder, CO: Westview Press.

Schoenbrun, D. 1998. *A Green Place, A Good Place: Agrarian Change, Gender, and Social Identity in the Great Lakes Region to the 15th Century*. Portsmouth, NH: Heinemann.

Schwartz, N. 1990. *Forest Society: A Social History of Petén, Guatemala*. Philadelphia: University of Pennsylvania Press.

———. 1999. "An Anthropological View of Guatemala's Petén." In *Thirteen Ways of Looking at a Tropical Forest*, ed. J. D. Nations, 14–19. Washington, DC: Conservation International.

Schwartzman, S., A. Moreira, and D. Nepstad. 2000. "Rethinking Tropical Forest Conservation: Perils in Parks." *Conservation Biology* 14 (5): 1351–1357.

Scott, J. 1998. *Seeing Like a State: How Certain Schemes to Improve the Human Condition Have Failed*. New Haven: Yale University Press.

Shiva, V. 1988. *Staying Alive: Women, Ecology, and Development in India*. London: Zed Books.

Shore, B. 1996. *Culture in Mind: Cognition, Culture, and the Problem of Meaning*. Oxford: Oxford University Press.

Sierra, C. J. 1991. "La Colonización: Proyectos y Realizaciones." In *Campeche: Textos de su historia*, vol. 1, ed. A. Negrín Muñoz, 303–314. México, D.F.: Instituto de Investigaciones Dr. José María Luis Mora.

Simonian, L. 1996. *Defending the Land of the Jaguar: A History of Conservation in Mexico*. Austin: University Texas Press.

Sluyter, A. 2002. *Colonialism and Landscape: Postcolonial Theory and Applications*. Lanham, MD: Rowman and Littlefield.

Snook, L. 1998. "Sustaining Harvests of Mahogany (*Swietenia macrophylla* King) from Mexico's Yucatan Forests: Past, Present, and Future." In *Timber, Tourists, and*

Temples: Conservation and Development in the Maya Forest of Belize, Guatemala, and Mexico, ed. R. Primack, D. Bray, H. Galletti, and I. Ponciano, 61–80. Washington, DC: Island Press.

Soederberg, S. 2001. "From Neoliberalism to Social Liberalism: Situating the National Solidarity Program within Mexico's Passive Revolutions." *Latin American Perspectives* 28:104–123.

Sponsel, L., R. Bailey, and T. Headland. 1996. "Anthropological Persepctives on the Causes, Consequences, and Solutions of Deforestation." In *Tropical Deforestation: The Human Dimension*, ed. L. Sponsel, T. Headland, and R. Bailey, 3–52. New York: Columbia University Press.

Stedman-Edwards, P. 2000. "Socioeconomic Root Causes of Biodiversity Loss: The Case of Calakmul, Mexico." In *The Root Causes of Biodiversity Loss*, ed. A. Wood, P. Stedman-Edwards, and J. Mang, 231–254. Sterling, VA: Earthscan and World Wildlife Fund.

Stephen, L. 1999. "Indigenous Rights and Self-Determination in Mexico: Introduction." *Cultural Survival Quarterly*. 23 (1): 23–26.

Stonich, S. 1993. *"I am Destroying the Land!": The Political Ecology of Poverty and Environmental Destruction in Honduras*. Boulder, CO: Westview Press.

Sullivan, P. 1989. *Unfinished Conversations: Mayas and Foreigners Between Two Wars*. Berkeley: University of California Press.

Taussig, M. 1987. *Shamanism, Colonialism, and the Wild Man: A Study in Terror and Healing*. Chicago: University of Chicago Press.

Terán, S., and C. Rasmussen. 1994. *La Agricultura de los Mayas Prehispánicos y Actuales en el Noreste de Yucatán*. Mérida: Universidad Autónoma de Yucatán.

Terborgh, J. 1999. *Requiem for Nature*. Washington, DC: Island Press.

Toledo, V. 2000. "Montes Azules: Imposible conservar sin desarrollo y viceversa." *La Jornada*, Internet edition, México, D.F.

Tsing, A. 1993. *In the Realm of the Diamond Queen: Marginality in an Out-of-the-Way Place*. Princeton: Princeton University Press.

——. 1999. "Becoming a Tribal Elder, and Other Green Development Fantasies." In *Transforming the Indonesian Uplands: Marginality, Power, and Production*, ed. T. Li, 159–202. Amsterdam: Harwood Academic Publishers.

Turner II, B. L., J. Geoghen, and D. Foster, eds. 2003. *Integrated Land Change Science and Tropical Deforestation in Southern Yucatán: Final Frontiers*. Oxford: Clarendon Press.

de Vos, J. 1996 (1988). *Oro Verde: La conquista de la selva Lacandona por los madereros tabasqueños, 1822–1949*. Mexico, D.F.: Fondo de Cultura Económica.

de Vries, P. 2002. "Vanishing Mediators: Enjoyment as a Political Factor in Western Mexico." *American Ethnologist* 29 (4): 901–927.

Twinam, A. 1999. *Public Lives, Private Secrets: Gender, Honor, Sexuality, and Illegitimacy in Colonial Spanish America*. Stanford, CA: Stanford University Press.

Umlas, E. 1998. "Environmental Networking in Mexico: The Comité Nacional para la Defensa de los Chimalapas." *Latin American Research Review* 33 (3): 161–189.

United Nations. 2002. *Report of the World Summit on Sustainable Development: Johan-nesburg, South Africa, 26 August–4 September 2002*. New York: United Nations.

USMAB (United States Man and Biosphere Program). 1990. *Bibliography on the Inter-national Network of Biosphere Reserves*. Washington, DC: U.S. Department of State.

Vargas-Cetina, Gabriela 2002. *De lo Privado a lo Público. Organizaciones en Chiapas*. México, D.F.: Centro de Investigaciones y Estudios Superiores en Antropología Social/Miguel Angel Porrúa.

Vaughan, M. K. 1999. "Cultural Approaches to Peasant Politics in the Mexican Revolu-tion." *Hispanic American Historical Review* 79:269–305.

Vayda, A., and B. Walters. 1999. "Against Political Ecology." *Human Ecology* 27:167–179.

Warman, A. 1980. *"We Come to Object": The Peasants of Morelos and the National State*. Baltimore: The Johns Hopkins University Press.

Warren, K. 1998. *Indigenous Movements and Their Critics: Pan-Maya Activism in Guate-mala*. Princeton: Princeton University Press.

WCED (World Commission on Environment and Development). 1987. *Our Common Future*. Oxford: Oxford University Press.

Wells, M., S. Guggenheim, A. Khan, W. Wardojo, and P. Jepson. 1999. *Investing in Biodiversity: A Review of Indonesia's Conservation and Development Projects*. Washington, DC: The World Bank.

West, P. 2000. *The Practices, Ideologies, and Consequences of Conservation and Develop-ment in Papua New Guinea*. Ph.D. diss., Rutgers University, New Brunswick, NJ.

West, P., and S. Brechin. 1991. *Resident Peoples and National Parks: Social Dilemmas and Strategies in International Conservation*. Tucson: University of Arizona Press.

Western, D., and M. Wright, eds. 1994. *Natural Connections: Perspectives in Community-Based Conservation*. Washington, DC: Island Press.

Wexler, M., and D. Bray. 1996. "Reforming Forests: From Community to Corporate Forestry in Mexico." In *Reforming Mexico's Agrarian Reform*, ed. L. Randall, 235–246. Armonk, NY: M. E. Sharpe.

Whatmore, S., and L. Thorne. 1997. "Nourishing Networks: Alternative Geographies in Food." In *Globalising Food: Agrarian Questions and Global Restructuring*, ed. D. Goodman and M. Watts, 287–303. New York: Routledge Press.

Whigham, D., J. Lynch, and M. Dickenson. 1998. "Dynamics and Ecology of Natural and Managed Forests in Quintana Roo, Mexico." In *Timber, Tourists, and Tem-ples: Conservation and Development in the Maya Forest of Belize, Guatemala, and Mexico*, ed. R. Primack, D.Bray, H. Galletti, and I. Ponciano, 267–282. Wash-ington, DC: Island Press.

White, P. S. 1995. "Conserving Biodiversity: Lessons from the Smokys." *Forum for Applied Research and Public-Policy* 19 (2): 116–120.

Whitmore, T. C. 1990. *An Introduction to Tropical Rain Forests*. Oxford: Clarendon Press.

Wilbanks, T. 1994. " 'Sustainable Development' in Geographic Perspective." *Annals of the Association of American Geographers* 84 (4): 541–556.

Wilk, R. 1991. *Household Ecology: Economic Change and Domestic Life among the Kekchi Maya in Belize*. Tucson: University of Arizona Press.

———. 2002. "Consumption, Human Needs, and Global Environmental Change." *Global Environmental Change* 12:5–13.

Wilmsen, E. N. 1989. *Land Filled with Flies: A Political Economy of the Kalahari*. Chicago: University of Chicago Press.

Wilshusen, P., S. Brechin, C. Fortwangler, and P. West. 2002. "Reinventing a Square Wheel: Critique of a Resurgent 'Protection Paradigm' in International Biodiversity Conservation." *Society and Natural Resources* 15 (1): 17–40.

Wyckoff-Baird, B., A. Kaus, C. Christen, and M. Keck. 2000. *Shifting the Power: Decentralization and Biodiversity Conservation*. Washington, DC: Biodiversity Support Program.

Young, R. J. C. 2001. *Postcolonialism: An Historical Introduction*. Oxford: Blackwell Publishers.

Zabin, C. 1998. "Free Markets and Forests: Community-Based Forestry in the Era of Neoliberal Reform." In *The Transformation of Rural Mexico: Reforming the Ejido Sector*, ed. W. Cornelius and D. Myhre, 401–425. La Jolla, CA: Center for U.S.–Mexican Studies.

Index

About the Author

Nora Haenn is an assistant professor at Arizona State University. Her interests in the ingenuity of campesinos in southern Mexico have led her to various topical concerns. Her previous publications have contrasted farmers' and foresters' categorizations of forests and addressed frontier migratory flows, among other issues. This is her first book.